Creative Ideas for Children's Worship

Creative Ideas for Children's Worship

Based on the Sunday Gospels, Year B

Sarah Lenton

Theological consultant:
Andrew Davison

CANTERBURY
PRESS
Norwich

© Text and cartoons Sarah Lenton 2012

First published in 2012 by the Canterbury Press Norwich
Editorial office
13–17 Long Lane,
London, EC1A 9PN, UK

Canterbury Press is an imprint of Hymns Ancient and Modern Ltd
(a registered charity)
13A Hellesdon Park Road, Norwich,
Norfolk, NR6 5DR, UK

www.canterburypress.co.uk

British Library Cataloguing in Publication data

A catalogue record for this book is available
from the British Library

978 1 84825 1120

Typeset by Regent Typesetting, London
Printed and bound in Great Britain by
CPI Group (UK) Ltd, Croydon, CR0 4YY

This book is dedicated to
the memory of my father,
Henry Trevor Lenton

Contents

THE SESSIONS

Where two descriptions are given, the first is the name of the Sunday in the Church of England and the second is the name in the Roman Catholic Church. Very occasionally the readings are different for the two Churches. In that case two different scripts are provided and marked accordingly.

Acknowledgements

This book is the result of seventeen years of ecumenical work in the London parishes of Our Lady of Lourdes, Acton (Catholic), and St Michael and All Angels, Bedford Park (Anglican). Both churches were unstintingly generous in their provision of space, time and resources, and to everyone involved, priests, congregations and children, I offer heartfelt thanks.

The children's church in Acton owes its existence to the enlightened leadership of Bishop Pat Lynch (then the parish priest) and his lay administrator Ellie McKeown.

Ellie, working on the 'vocation by compulsion' principle, roped in a large and varied group to look after the children, and in the fullness of time her net caught me. The immediate cause of my recruitment was Nicholas Rodger, one of the founder members of the group, who brought his fine scholarship – and scarcely less remarkable dramatic skills – to an already talented team. Among them I am particularly grateful to Sr Miriam McNulty, Janusz Jankowski, Peter Robertson, Margaret Fry, Joan Hughes and Susan Cunningham. To Deacon Tito Pereira, whose devotion to the gospel was the dynamo that powered our team meetings, and whose ideas I have shamelessly plundered, I owe more than a mere acknowledgement can express.

In Bedford Park, Fr Kevin Morris has been equally generous in his encouragement and support. The press gang is as active at St Michael's as it is at Our Lady's, and among our 'volunteers' I am extremely grateful to Wendy Callister, Bernadette Halford, Nicola Chater and Pamela Bickley, all of whom have led the team with a commitment that went way beyond the call of duty.

To my family, who have endured eighteen years of disrupted Sunday mornings, my brothers Christopher and Andrew, whose features I default to whenever I draw the Apostles, and my sister Jane for giving the dialogue some sort of street credibility, I offer as always my love and thanks.

Fr Andrew Davison's meticulous reading of the text, as theological consultant, has ensured the scripts are faithful to the teaching of the Church (any errors that have crept in since his scrutiny are my own). I am deeply grateful to him and to Christine Smith and Mary Matthews of the Canterbury Press, paragons of encouragement and patience, David Beresford for doing the photo shoots, Rosemund Green for the set of bird photos for Script 9, Anne Tennant, a friend in need when the unedited scripts threatened to overwhelm me and, last of all, Margaret Stonborough, who insisted that I responded to Nicholas's call in the first place, and has found it involved her in more prop making and keyboard bashing than she can ever have anticipated.

Introduction

Children

Children are part of the Church. Everyone knows that, and most churches do their best to make them feel at home. Even so, there are times, particularly at the beginning of the Eucharist, when it seems kind to offer the kids an alternative to a full set of Bible readings and the sermon.

Enter Children's Church! Or Sunday School, Children's Liturgy, Children's Club, it doesn't matter what you call it.

The idea is that the children are shepherded out of church to a hall – or somewhere suitably out of earshot – where they hear the Gospel and worship Almighty God in their own way, and at their own pace. They reappear at Communion time to rejoin their families at the altar, ready with a presentation to share their discoveries with the rest of the congregation.

Such a group presupposes adult leaders, and if you're one of them – and don't have time to think up children's activities week after week – this book is for you.

Scripts for Children's Church

Our purpose is to provide material that will help children acquire a familiarity with the life of Christ and the events of the church year, in a way that is vivid and memorable. Better still, they'll enjoy it. The material does not require a great deal of preparation, nor a degree in theology – in fact you and the children will probably learn the faith together.

This book provides a session for every Sunday of the liturgical year B,* in the form

---

* The readings for the Eucharist are arranged in three cycles, A, B and C, and run from the beginning of the liturgical year (Advent Sunday) to its end (Christ the King). Sets of scripts will be published in time for year C (2012), followed by a book for the festivals that come up every year, such as harvest festival and all the major saints' days.

of an easy-to-use script. Each one is headed up by the theme of the day, a list of the toys, props and pictures you'll need, the prayers that open and close each session, the Gospel reading and (most importantly) your 'lines': the sort of things you'll say to the kids, their (probable) response, and the games and activities that will reinforce the Gospel message. Given a modicum of preparation (see below), all you'll have to do on Sunday is set up the hall, print off the script, and the children's session should practically run itself.

Pictures

The book is full of pictures and each session comes with its own set of images: these can be found on the CD-Rom attached to the back cover.

Children's Church and the Eucharist

The main act of worship on a Sunday is the Eucharist. The service is composed of two sections: the Liturgy of the Word, and the Liturgy of the Sacrament. The Liturgy of the Word is, naturally, centred on the Bible: it reaches its climax with the Gospel

reading and is concluded by the sermon that follows. The Liturgy of the Sacrament is centred round the altar as bread and wine are consecrated and we receive the Body and Blood of Christ.

These sessions provide a child-friendly Liturgy of the Word that parallels the adult version going on in church, and allows the children to return to church in plenty of time for the Liturgy of the Sacrament. As a result they follow the structure of the Eucharist closely.

The normal pattern in parishes where I have worked is: the children are sent out by the priest, with their own Gospel Book, at the beginning of the service. They reassemble in the church hall and join in a simplified version of the prayers of penitence and the Opening Prayer. Then they turn their attention to the Gospel – which is where the fun begins.

The Gospel passages are so rich that we've found the most effective way to teach them is to concentrate on one leading idea. Pentecost, for example, could be about the Holy Spirit coming in tongues of fire, or giving the disciples the gift of language, but we've gone for His appearance as a 'mighty rushing wind'.

The children may not realize immediately that blowing peas across the floor with straws has anything to do with this, but everything in the Pentecost script (games, story and meditation) is about air, and they'll have got the idea by the end of the session.

Growing in the Christian Faith

A major advantage of these scripts is that the children hear exactly the same Gospel as the rest of the church, so their contribution at the end of the service will tie in with something the adults have already encountered. Added to which, living with these scripts, Sunday by Sunday, means that children and leaders experience a whole Christian year together and discover that church is more interesting (and a great deal more energetic) than they'd realized.

Setting up a Children's Church Team

Recruitment

Recruitment to a Children's Church team is usually done via a press gang. All the same, an assurance that the load will be spread evenly over the year usually calms people down – that, and a guarantee that all a leader has to do is follow a script: everything else will be provided.

Leaders

The liturgies in this book assume that a 'leader' is someone who feels OK about getting up in front of children and presenting a script, but there's plenty of scope for more nervous types who may prefer to help from the side. It's good to have a variety of 'voices' presenting the session, so two leaders are the basic minimum to make it effective, four leaders mean you can give people Sundays off, and twelve leaders are practically ideal.

Team Meetings

You will find it helpful to meet at least once a term. There will be rotas and practical matters to discuss of course, but the core of these meetings should be a read through of the sessions coming up. Each script comes with its Gospel reading, notes on understanding the passage, and suggestions for activities and devotions. Talking this through will help you get on top of the material and indicate what toys and props you'll need to gather. This is also the moment to modify the scripts to suit local circumstances.

Child Protection/Safeguarding

Churches have clear rules about child protection, find out what they are and follow them. If you have any uncertainties about the national requirements, consult the websites of the Catholic Diocese of Westminster (Safeguarding Advisory Service) – www.rcdow.org.uk – or, for the Anglican version – www.london.anglican.org (Child Protection) – or consult the published guidelines, *Protecting All God's Children* (Church House Publishing). The national website – www.direct.gov.uk – also advises on keeping children safe. All three sites give ample information. It is now mandatory for all volunteers to have a CRB check; it is also important to note that (at least) two adults must always be present with the children in your care. Larger parishes may have a children's advocate who will help advise you and sort out the paperwork. It's good practice to keep a register of all the sessions – it helps you find out who the kids are.

The School Year

Children's Church usually only operates in school terms, as there can be a sharp decline in numbers in the holidays. However, we've provided a session for every Sunday in the year – just in case the church is heaving with children after all.

Young Children

As a rule of thumb liturgy works best with children who have started school and are used to basic school rules, like sitting quietly on the floor, putting up their hands before they speak and playing games in an organized way. You don't have time to

instil this into a riotous toddler. If parents want to bring small children along, ask them to remain to look after them. Sending little ones in under the care of a sibling doesn't usually work.

Teenagers

You'll find that some of the older children don't want to move on, partly because they like you and partly because they feel children's liturgy is more fun than adult church. Obviously you'll know your own kids and how to deal with this. Teenagers can be very helpful as auxiliary helpers, as long as they are *never* allowed to stand along the back wall! See below . . .

Cool Dudes

Cool dudes who hang around at the back are the death of liturgy. From about the age of eleven onwards, kids have a tendency to drift to the back wall, lean up against it, and watch the proceedings with their mates. With all the sympathy in the world for teenage angst, you can't let this happen. If you do, you'll get a hall divided between enthusiastic little kids, cool

dudes, and a middle group who want to copy the big ones. You have to sort this. Liturgy is about participation; big kids are fine if they want to join in, otherwise – back to the service in church.

Discipline

Children's Church is not school. Nobody has to come but, as kids have to be *somewhere* in the church complex, they're either with you – and behaving – or back in church. The irritating thing about sending children back to church is you have to accompany them there, or call their parents out to collect them. Fortunately the resulting interview between parent and child usually ensures it never happens again.

Some subversive types might think it great fun to shout out silly answers but you can usually block this by applying a 'hands up' only rule. Gameboys and iPods are a total bore. We killed an outbreak of texting once by saying, 'Hands up who's got a mobile?' Up shot the hands. 'OK, bring them down the front and leave them on the table.' (Of course this only works once.)

Parents

Some parents process out with their children to settle them, or look after the little ones. 'Spare' parents should be encouraged to return to the main service.

Helpers

They can be parents, big kids, Confirmation candidates, or nervous adults thinking about committing to Children's Church at a future date: they are unbelievably useful. Be realistic about what they can actually do.

Runners

You need to know when to bring the children back into church and it's useful to have some well-disposed people in church ready to nip round and tell you when the Offertory (or whatever your agreed cue is) is about to start. Teenagers can be very helpful here – especially if they're able to tell you the news via a mobile.

Clergy

As the children's and adults' liturgies should form an organic whole, make sure your priest knows what's going on, particularly when it comes to the presentation. Some priests prefer to be the one who asks the children what they've been doing, others are happy to let the team get on with it. Either way, check there's time for a presentation at the end – if there isn't, don't rehearse it. There's nothing worse than a pew full of disappointed kids.

Setting Up

The most basic requirement is a separate room. Obviously you have to take what is given, but it is surprising how quickly you can adapt any space to your needs.

Rooms/Halls

If you are given a room, clear away as much furniture as you can and make an empty space at one end. If you're given the church hall, mark off one bit as the holy area – the place from which you'll be leading prayers and reading the Gospel. Limits are important in church halls as the mere sight of acres of floorboards makes children want to rush around.

Furniture

Try to appropriate a cupboard or filing cabinet to store your props. You'll need a lectern or a little table on which to place the Gospel Book (see below under *Gospel*). Another table at the front is also very useful: you can drape it in the liturgical colour of the day, and use it to focus attention on the icon, candle, toy, or whatever you are going to use in the liturgy.

Chairs, oddly enough, are not a great idea. They inhibit the children from acting together, and they usually can't resist the temptation to swing their legs and kick the chair in front. Cut the chairs down to a couple for the leaders and visiting grown-ups.

The Floor

Nothing really beats getting the kids to sit on the floor. On mats, if your church has them, but the floorboards if need be. Children are used to sitting on the floor for assembly at school. In small spaces it means you can accommodate more children and bring them nearer the front to see what's going on. If you're up to it, sitting on the floor yourself among the children works very well – especially if you're telling them a story.

Props

Every liturgy comes with a list of the props you'll need; the most frequent are listed below. It looks formidable, but most churches have a fair amount of equipment and a few visits to the toy shop should supply the rest.

Ordinary Equipment

- Either a flip-chart, an easel, or a whiteboard, or a place you can stick up sheets of blank A1 paper.
- Blu-Tack or something similar.
- Large coloured marker pens for the leaders (get bullet point nibs, rather than chisel, they are easier to draw with) or white board markers.
- Matches – but use tapers to actually light the candles; they look nicer and are easier to handle.
- Candle snuffers.
- The use of a photocopier or computer printer.

Useful Extras

- Any costumes: all-purpose Shepherd, King or Angel. Burglars are handy as DIY villains – a mask and any stripy top will do.
- Crowns, even paper ones from a cracker, are invaluable.
- Any helmets: Policeman, Roman Soldier, Knight.
- Flower canes, all sizes.
- Large dice – made by covering square (or near square) cardboard boxes in stout white paper and marking gigantic dots on the sides. Some party shops sell blow-up dice, which are superb for group games.
- Some large, nice-looking rocks, picked up on the beach, at least one large shiny one.
- Toy animals – particularly sheep.
- Crook or old-fashioned wooden walking stick.

- At least one football.
- Toy shop props: plastic swords, crowns, doctor's sets, handcuffs and those useful plastic scythes and pitchforks you can get at Hallowe'en.
- Torches.
- Treasure – plastic pearls, any tacky jewellery, preferably in a 'Jewel Box'.
- Gold-covered chocolate money.
- If you find a confectioner selling chocolate fish at Easter, buy a few – they'll come in handy later on.

Art Extras

- Colouring pens and pencils in working order.
- Ordinary white paper.
- Child-friendly scissors.
- Adult scissors.
- Gold and silver paper.
- Thin card.
- Glue.
- Masking tape.

Holy Props

- A Gospel Book: use one of the recognized translations of the complete Bible rather than a 'children's Bible'. The latter may not have the complete Gospel and much of it will be paraphrased. We recommend the New Revised Standard Version of the Bible (the NRSV), the New Jerusalem Bible (study edition) or, for good simple language, the Christian Community Bible (Catholic pastoral edition).
- The use of a lectionary – that's the list of readings for the church year. Your priest should have one.
- A crucifix.
- Pieces of cloth to hang over the table in the liturgical colours – green, red, purple, white (and gold if you come across some lamé). Synthetic material doesn't crease as badly as the good stuff.
- Candles in portable candlesticks.
- Small handbells.

- A stout candle that can stand securely on its own.
- And, if your church uses them:
  - A holy water stoup and sprinkler.
  - A spare thurible, charcoal and incense (though check the latter won't set the fire alarm off).

Holy Extras

- Icons, posters or postcards of holy pictures, small statues of the saints (plastic is fine!). Try to have at least one image of the patron saint of your church. The National Gallery has an excellent range of posters and postcards on holy subjects by some of the greatest painters in the world. Their website is www.nationalgallery.org.uk. Alternatively you can use images from Wikimedia Commons and the Web Gallery of Art for slide presentation, or simply displayed on your laptop screen, absolutely free. Their website is www.wga.hu/. You'll find references to the pictures they offer in some of the sessions.
- CDs with kids' hymns, Taizé chants and quiet mood music are very useful.
- Sweet-smelling oils – you can get cheap flasks of myrrh and frankincense at cathedral gift shops but aromatherapy oils from chemists are good substitutes.
- Any holy toys, like a Noah's Ark or a crib set.
- Artefacts from the Jewish faith are also very helpful especially for Scripts 23, 50 and 61. An educational supplier, TTS, sells a starter pack with a Torah scroll, Seder plate for the Passover and a Menorah candle stand at a very reasonable price. Their website is www.tts-shopping.com.

Images in Church

Look round your church. Even the plainest building can yield a surprising number of pictures. They can be anywhere: in the windows, carved on the memorials, embroidered on the vestments and painted on the banners. Everything is worth noticing – flames, lambs, keys, clusters of grapes – as well as the more obvious pictures and statues of saints.

DIY Props

'Our Father' cards are a good standby for those moments when you've got five minutes to fill in. You make them by putting the Lord's Prayer, phrase by phrase, on various sheets of A4 paper, laminating them – and shuffling.

The idea is that the children go for a land speed record in reassembling the prayer and then, when they've quietened down, pray it. It works for any prayer or creed you wish the children to learn. (You may want to make some 'Hail Mary' cards for Script 23.)

High Tech Helps

- All forms of projection: scoop up any offers of unwanted projectors (provided they work). See if you can borrow the church's overhead projector, slide projector, or (in very lucky parishes) a digital projector. The latter only works with a laptop.
- A portable music player.
- Keyboard.
- Extension leads.
- Gaffer tape or masking tape to stick over leads and ensure the kids don't trip up.
- A roving mike, for the presentation back in church, is a great asset.

How to Use this Book

Once you've got your team, a hall and some children – you'll need a liturgy.

Simply find out what Sunday Gospel you should be preparing for, and look it up in the contents list. The Sundays are listed in chronological order, so once you've found your first, all should be plain sailing.

However, church being what it is, there are a couple of complications. Given the variable date of Easter, we have to allow for some extra Sundays before Easter (in case it's late) or some extra Sundays after Easter (in case it's early). There is also a tiny amount of variation between the Catholic and Anglican Gospels in Year B. The clergy will know exactly what Sunday it is, just ask them, or your parish office. If in doubt, get the Bible reference from your priest, look it up in the Index of Biblical References, and you'll find the right script.

Other Christian churches also follow the lectionary we've based this book on, so the material will be useful for them as well.

Photocopying

After you've established what Gospel you're going to do, gather the toys and props during the week, and photocopy the script for any leader without a book. You might also like to photocopy the sections of the Kyries (the 'Lord have mercy' prayers) on three separate strips of paper for individual children to read out.

If there are pictures involved, find the set suggested on the CD-Rom and print them up as large as possible. All the pictures that make a 'scene' are provided separately, so you can copy them on to A4 (or A3 if you've got the resources) and combine them on an A1 sheet of paper.

Getting Ready

- Set up the hall on the day, with all the objects and scripts you'll need to hand.
- Read the script through and agree with the other leader on who says what.
- Alert the children's music group (if you have one) to the hymns on offer.
- Some scripts call for help from a couple of children, find your volunteers and run through their contribution (it's always very easy).
- That's it, you're ready to go.

Following the Scripts

The scripts follow a simple format. Each section is headed up in bold and, as long as there are no lines for you to speak in the section, the font looks normal.

Like this:

SET UP

- A list of props, extra people, etc.
- A crook (a walking stick will do).
- Toy sheep, etc.

If a section contains remarks by you, your lines stay in normal font, but any instructions now appear in italics, like this:

Put the toy sheep on the floor, and grasp the crook

Leader	OK, now there are a couple of things you need to know about sheep.

Any question you ask the children comes with the expected answer in bold font, enclosed in round brackets.

Leader	Today we're thinking about sheep – and the people who look after them.
	Anyone know what they were called?
	(**Shepherds**)

The only other font change happens when you pray. Prayers said by one person come in normal font, prayers said by everyone are in bold.

Lord have mercy
Lord have mercy
Christ have mercy
Christ have mercy

God's Capital H

You'll notice that God's personal pronoun (He, Him or His) always has a capital H. In the pilot sessions for this book we found this a helpful way of remembering just who we were talking about (especially when doing the liturgy at speed).

A Typical Script, Section by Section

SENDING OUT

The first thing you need to do is organize your exit from the church. Ask if you can place the children's Gospel Book on the altar and gather your troupe together. At a given moment (usually after the entrance hymn) the celebrant hands the Gospel Book to one of the children (chosen in advance) and sends them out. The whole team processes out, following the Gospel as it is held aloft.

You'll probably find that you pick up stragglers and shy kids as you leave church.

WELCOME

Once you're all in the hall, welcome the children. Keep it brief and go straight into:

THE SIGN OF THE CROSS

If this is not a usual devotion in your church, you may find it helpful to run through the Sign like this:

1   ✠ **In the Name of the Father,** – *on 'Father' you touch your head, that's the Father in Heaven*
2   **and of the Son** – *bring your hand down – the Son came down to earth*
3   **and of the Holy Spirit.** – *touch your heart, the Spirit lives in our hearts*
4   **Amen** – *finish the Shape of the Cross by touching your right side*

A little cross ✠ in the text flags up the times it is usual to make the Sign of the Cross.

Making the Sign of the Cross can have an extraordinarily quietening effect on children. However, if they *are* slightly chatty at the beginning, do the old trick of going silent yourself until they get unnerved and stop talking. Reinforce this by saying things like, 'Thank you Charlie' to any phenomenally well behaved child.

One leader I knew surprised everybody one Sunday by asking the children to make the Sign of the Cross very quietly (he had a hangover). The kids looked sideways at one another. 'How do you do a *noisy* sign of the cross?' you could see they were thinking – even so, a breathless hush ensued.

THE KYRIE

Preface the Kyrie with a brief, 'Let's look back at the week – is there anything we wish we hadn't done? Anything we'd like to say sorry for?' Keep it light.

If you've got three children prepared to read the three petitions of the Kyrie, have them at the front, give them a hand if necessary, and join the children in the response:

Lord have mercy
Christ have mercy
Lord have mercy

It's extremely important that all grown-ups in the room take part in the prayers and follow the proceedings as seriously as the children. Gossiping mums at the back should be politely banned.

PRAYER FOR FORGIVENESS

This is the 'layman's absolution' and can be said by a leader, or repeated by everyone. If the children don't know it, you may ask them to repeat it after you, line by line.

OPENING PRAYER

The moment when the theme of the day starts to appear.

BEFORE THE GOSPEL

A huge change of gear takes place as you prepare for the Gospel reading. The idea is that the children should be able to follow the Gospel when they hear it and to achieve this the scripts try everything: games, mini-dramas, startling demonstrations (like how stupid it is to build a wall out of jelly). Anything to get them going.

It's here that you begin to interact with the children. Ask them questions, the simpler the better. Children love putting their hand up (some toddlers do it automatically but all you get from them is a sweet smile).

As soon as the Gospel Book has been set up, move into:

THE GOSPEL PROCESSION

Obviously the Sunday Gospel is the dynamo of the whole session. Everything – songs, prayers and games – derives from it and, when it's read, it either sets up the message for the day, or clinches it. Either way Jesus calls the shots.

To make this apparent to the children it's helpful to read the Gospel with some ceremony.

Depending on how your space is shaped, you can place the Gospel Book on its own special lectern, or table, at the back of the hall and process it to the front, or you can place it down the front and process it into the middle of the children. Or you can just move it from a small table at the front to a lectern beside it. The point is, it should be moved.*

You can't replicate the solemn reading of the Gospel in church (unless you have a deacon or priest present) so don't top and tail it with the customary acclamations. You can, however, set it apart. Hold the Gospel Book up as it's processed – Jesus is present in His Word, just as He will be present later on in the Bread and Wine of the Eucharist. Flank it with candles – you'll have no lack of volunteers – and invest in some hand bells. Dinging the bells as the Gospel is processed is a marvellous job for very small kids.

If you're blessed with a music group you might like to sing some 'Alleluias' as the Gospel is processed.

There is no Gospel Procession in Advent or Lent. This is not something we've taken over from church – actually Gospel processions happen all year round – but

---

* The Eastern Orthodox invented the Gospel procession to dramatize Jesus' wanderings through Galilee: they directed that the Gospel, and its reader, should process from the altar, 'wander' through the church and land up in the midst of the people.

it's a helpful way of marking these seasons with the children. You'll see the rationale for this change when you do the sessions.

THE GOSPEL

Normally you read the Gospel straight; however, keep an eye on the script because in some cases we give you a paraphrase to read out instead. All our paraphrases contain at least one sentence (usually many more) of a recognized translation of the Bible. The children must hear the genuine Word of God.

If you are reading straight from the Bible, think of ways of making it accessible: make the dialogue sound real, cut verses not dealt with in the session, change *denari* into pounds or *tunics* into shirts. Having said that, it is often appropriate to offer the kids an old-fashioned phrase as part of their cultural heritage. Many of them know already one shouldn't hide one's light 'under a bushel', or that the Rich Fool said to himself that he could 'eat, drink and be merry'. Take a view: stylistic gear changes are part of the modern Christian package.

AFTER THE GOSPEL

You wrap the Gospel up: sometimes in a pithy sentence or two, more often in an extended activity. This might be a game, or a devotion, or some music. The activity always includes a rehearsal for a presentation back in church (if you're doing one).

DIY ART

Colouring pictures is not a major feature of this book. When it happens it appears as a group activity, and is usually timed – so the children produce art work at speed (this seems to motivate the less arty). However, some of the pictures on the CD-Rom are in black and white, to give the kids who like to colour in a chance to show their skill.

There are many occasions when the children can make their presentation as well as perform it, particularly if the presentation involves pictures. There's no reason, except time, why they should hold up versions of the pictures on the CD-Rom. The congregation is going to be much more interested in stuff the children have produced themselves.

GAMES

All the board games can be played either by a group of children crowded round the board, or a large group, split into teams, who play via a representative. In the latter case, most members of the team get a chance to roll the enormous Children's Church dice.

Energetic games which normally require rushing around have been offered in two versions. One for spaces in which children *can* run around, and another for more restricted venues.

Jesus appears to have been deeply uninterested in people who came first, so make sure you cheer the losers.

MUSIC

Hymns, traditional and modern, are a wonderful way to finish the session, but they depend on somebody having the musical confidence to lead them. If you can't rustle up a piano or guitar player, you can download karaoke style music for many popular hymns via the internet, and there are CDs available with children's songs on. Any member of the team who works in a local church school is invaluable here as they'll know what songs the kids sing in assembly.

If you are intending to sing, think about the words: writing them up on a flip-chart is quicker than children fiddling round with hymn books. (On the other hand, if you've got the time, some kids find it thrilling to look up 'number 143'.)

REHEARSING THE PRESENTATION

The congregation deserve to hear what the children have been up to. Choose good readers and run the presentation through with the kids. It's almost bound to be fun, try to get it slick and well timed as well.

PRAYER

You won't be able to have an extended session on prayer every Sunday, but get the children used to the idea of a prayer circle. Put a large candle in the middle (the sort that can stand on its own base) as a focus of attention. Or pass round one of the many objects suggested in the scripts.

Give the children alternatives to verbal prayer, sprinkle them with water, bless them with incense. Let them wave their arms about to the movements of an interactive hymn, or reflect on the power of the Holy Spirit by feeling a fan blowing in their faces. Explore the Catholic tradition: most children like bells, icons, holy bookmarks and statues, and they are usually up for making some of these objects themselves. (Like the Free Trade Rosary, made by knotting a decade of the rosary in a bit of string.) Give the children a chance to pray privately.

Quiet music in the background is a help, but keep the sessions fairly short. There is a moment beyond which even the most pious child can't concentrate.

Every now and then these sessions will provoke a distressing revelation. A child might be anxious about a sick relative, or show an awareness of a family grief they only dimly understand, like a miscarriage. In the immediate situation, give the child time to talk (or add the stories for kids in distress from Year A, p. 309) afterwards, have a private word with the parents.

THE FINAL PRAYER

Make sure you gather for a formal prayer before you go back to church: a brief 'Glory Be . . .' is fine.

COMING BACK TO CHURCH

When you come back depends on your priest and the number of children who receive Holy Communion. Some parishes like the children to help with the Offertory procession, others prefer them back at the moment when the people are coming to the altar.

Depending on numbers, you may want the children to rejoin their parents or (if this is too disruptive) reserve a couple of pews for them down the front. Their presentation happens either at the Offertory or, more usually, after Communion.

Do your best to promote a 'guaranteed success' atmosphere in the church – and congratulate the kids yourself.

EXTRAS

Mass/Holy Communion/Eucharist

Anglicans and Catholics use different names for this great sacrament – this book uses all three.

Gender

The sessions acknowledge that Jesus and the Apostles were male, the Virgin Mary and many of Jesus' disciples female, and that Angels, though technically neuter, often appear as 'a young man in white'. However, though the pronouns are gender specific, there's no reason for the kids to be. You'll find that most girls are happy to play St Peter or the good Samaritan, boys don't mind being angels, and everyone enjoys being sheep, lepers and so on. Do your best to cast the children even handedly.

Health and Safety

Obviously anybody leading an organized activity for children needs to be aware of Health and Safety. All these scripts have been test run three times with no problems, but venues differ (as do children). Look at each script beforehand to work out potential flash points (the Race to the Tomb, for example) and follow the Health and Safety protocols of your own church.

Saints' Days

Sometimes a major saint's day falls on a Sunday – or your priest decides to celebrate All Saints' Day on the nearest Sunday to 1 November. The last script in the book (Script 65) is a 'filler' session, which can be adapted to cover practically any saint in the calendar.

Frequently Used Prayers

The Sign of the Cross

✠ In the Name of the Father,
and of the Son
and of the Holy Spirit.
Amen

The Prayer for Forgiveness

May God our Father
Have mercy upon us
✠ Forgive us our sins
And bring us to eternal life.
Amen

The Lord's Prayer

Our Father, who art in Heaven,
hallowed be thy Name,
thy Kingdom come,
thy will be done,
on Earth as it is in Heaven.
Give us this day our daily bread.
And forgive us our trespasses,
as we forgive those who trespass
against us.
And lead us not into temptation,
but deliver us from evil.
For thine is the Kingdom,
the power and the glory,
for ever and ever.
Amen

Modern Version of the Lord's Prayer

Our Father in Heaven,
hallowed be your name,
your Kingdom come,
your will be done,
on Earth as in Heaven.
Give us today our daily bread.
Forgive us our sins
as we forgive those who sin
against us.
Lead us not into temptation
but deliver us from evil.
For the Kingdom, the power,
and the glory are yours
now and for ever.
Amen

Glory Be

Glory be to the Father, and to the Son, and to the Holy Spirit:
as it was in the beginning, is now, and ever shall be, world without end,
Amen

Hail Mary

Hail Mary full of grace,
the Lord is with thee.
Blessed art thou among women
and blessed is the fruit of thy womb, Jesus.
Holy Mary, Mother of God,
pray for us sinners now
and at the hour of our death.
Amen

Script 1   'Get Ready!'

Advent Sunday

St Mark 13.32–37

THEME

Advent is an exciting time. Christmas is coming, and today's Gospel sounds adventurous. Who was the guy who went off on his travels? And why do his servants have to be so on the ball? This session introduces the children to the idea that Christians have to be alert and up for anything.

SET UP

- The liturgical colour is Purple.
- Flag up the change of colour in church by wearing some purple – tie, scarf, socks, anything.
- No bells are used in preparation for the Gospel, and there is no separate Gospel Procession – just place the Gospel on the table or lectern at the front.
- Pictures from the CD-Rom.
- A stuffed animal, preferably a toy lion or (failing that) a teddy.
- Check with the priest that it's OK to run down the aisle when you go back to church.
- Optional Advent Wreath.

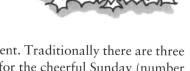

(An Advent Wreath helps define the Sundays in Advent. Traditionally there are three Purple candles (for Sundays 1, 2 and 4) a Pink one for the cheerful Sunday (number 3) and sometimes a White candle in the middle for Christmas Day.)

WELCOME *the children and lead them in* **The Sign of the Cross** ✠ **(p. xxxvi).**

Leader   Right this Sunday I want us to be on our toes, ready for anything. Does anyone know what position a runner gets into at the start of a race?

They probably do, show them the classic stance

OK, we all look as if we're at the start of a race.
Christians look a bit like that in church – you change one leg . . .

Get the kids to copy you as you move your back leg

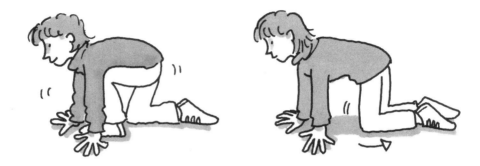

And bring your hands up. *(Put your hands together for prayer)*
Now *we* are at the start of something – our service.
Let's say the Kyrie together.

The Kyrie and Opening Prayer are short this morning as the children are probably kneeling on bare boards.

THE KYRIE   Lord have mercy
                  Lord have mercy

                  Christ have mercy
                  Christ have mercy

                  Lord have mercy
                  Lord have mercy

Ask the children to repeat **The Prayer for Forgiveness** *after you* (**p. xxxvi**).

OPENING
PRAYER
God our Father
Thank you for bringing us together.
Help us to be very wide awake this morning
And ready for anything. **Amen**

INTRODUCING ADVENT

Run through the change to Advent Purple in church

Leader   Anyone notice the colour in church today?

Give them a hint 'What colour's my tie?' (**Purple**)

Yes, the church is in purple.
Fr *Name* is dressed in purple, I've got purple socks on – it's Purple time.
This particular Purple time is called Advent.

Introduce the Advent Wreath if you've got one

OPTIONAL ADVENT WREATH

Run through the colours on the Advent Wreath and help a child light a Purple candle, for the first Sunday of Advent.

BEFORE THE GOSPEL

Leader   Advent means 'coming'.
We're getting ready for somebody to come.
Can you guess who? (**Jesus**)
Jesus is coming. We'll see Him in the Crib at Christmas, looking like a tiny baby.
But actually Advent isn't just about Jesus coming at Christmas, it's also about His *Second* Coming. The one that hasn't happened yet – at the End of the World.
That's a bit worrying – when do you think the End of the World may happen? Tomorrow? (**No**)

Go with the flow, most kids are quite confident the End of the World is not going to affect them. If they want to speculate on the timescale, throw it open. The small ones normally think that ten years is far enough away, the older ones – after some hasty arithmetic – usually suggest a hundred. Make sure somebody suggests thousands of years hence

Well, any of us may be right, because we don't know.
Fortunately, when it does happen, Jesus will be right there in the middle of it, so we'll be fine.

Actually, the early Christians were so looking forward to seeing Jesus again that they wanted the End of the World to come right now.

Their favourite prayer was 'Come, Lord Jesus!'

They were the sort of people who would have really enjoyed today's Gospel. Let's hear it.

Remind the children that we don't have bells or processions in Purple time. Read the Gospel, putting up the pictures from the CD-Rom as you go

THE GOSPEL *St Mark 13.32–37*

Adapt verse 32 to read

Jesus said, 'Nobody knows when I shall come again, neither the angels in Heaven . . .' *etc.*

AFTER THE GOSPEL

A Leader goes through the pictures

Leader   So Jesus said that His Second Coming was like the master of a house going off on a journey.

He left his servants behind, and told them to do something.

What was it? (**Watch out, be ready**)

Yup, you can see one servant at the door, looking down the road.

Can you see any other watchful servants?

Anyone nodded off?

Encourage the little kids to point out the various characters

Jesus told this story to explain His Second Coming. He's like the master who's gone off on a journey, and He's left His servants – that's us Christians – behind. But we're not to nod off, we must be awake, looking out for Him, because He might turn up anytime.

So Christians have to be ready.

We can be ready in lots of ways.

By being the sort of people Jesus will be happy to find when He comes back: kind people, prayerful people, *alert* people.

Alert means being ready for anything.

OK, let's go down the end of the room and practise being alert.

GAMES

If you've got a big enough hall you can do the running game suggested below. If your room is too small, you can turn the game (Ready, Steady, Go!) into Ready, Steady, Jump! or Ready, Steady, Sit! and so on.

Ready, Steady, Go!

Leader	Can you remember how runners get ready for a race? *(Line the kids up)*
	OK when I say 'go', run down to the other end of the room.
	Anyone who moves before 'go' is out. *(Be merciful the first time round)*
	Ready – *(pause)* – steady – *(pause)* – GO!

Down the other end

Let's get this right because being alert means you don't rush around. You listen up, ready for anything.

Run the race a couple more times. Congratulate the children and then play the next, and much quieter, game

OK we've sorted being alert, now let's see how good we are at being watchful.

Lion Cub

Select a person to be the lion. (Start off with a Leader.)
The lion sits with its back to the children, who are sitting at least ten feet away.
Place the stuffed animal (its cub) behind the lion and get the kids to sneak up, one by one, to steal it. If the lion hears somebody it roars and the thief, if caught standing, has to go back to sit with the others. If the thief has managed to sit before the roar, they can carry on.
Anyone who manages to steal the cub is the lion next time round.
(Since some kids take the precaution of roaring practically continuously, make sure other leaders or teenagers take a turn, on the understanding they let the cub-napper win.)

REHEARSAL

Practise your presentation for when you go back into church (see below).

FINAL PRAYER

Get the children settled for prayer. Ask them to kneel as if starting a race and, when you say 'Pray!', kneel properly for prayer

> OK, ready, steady – pray!

> Lord Jesus,
> This Advent help us to be alert and watchful
> Come Lord Jesus,
> Come at Christmas
> Come at the end of time
> Come into our hearts. **Amen**

BACK IN CHURCH

Make sure the main aisle of the church is free of buggies and walking sticks
Line the children up at the back of church; a Leader goes to the front

Leader   This morning we discovered that Jesus wants His Church to be ready and alert this Advent.

To the children

Are you ready? *(The children adopt the starting-a-race position)*
Right, ready, steady – go!

The children run down the aisle and turn to face the congregation

So children, what message have we got for the church this morning?

Kids   **Get ready!**

Script 2   'Repent!'

Advent 2

St Mark 1.1–8

THEME

St John the Baptist appears in the desert. The session introduces the children to this vivid saint and we learn what 'repent' means.

John's famous diet of locusts and wild honey has been slightly adapted. The word used in St Mark's Gospel is 'akris', which is Greek for either locust, cricket or grasshopper. We've gone for grasshoppers – they're easier to make.

SET UP

- The liturgical colour is Purple.
- Rucksack.
- Bottle of water.
- Blanket – the rougher the better.
- Jar of honey.
- Bible.
- Some grasshoppers – either make a few out of clothes pegs, or fold some paper ones, see instructions on the CD-Rom. (At the time of writing, natty solar-powered grasshoppers were being sold on the Internet for about £3.)
- Prime another Leader or helpful teenager to be John the Baptist, and a small child to be a wild beast – no lines are involved, the script provides all their cues.
- Tuck the jar of honey and the grasshoppers out of sight, down the front.
- Optional Advent Wreath (p. 1): the first Purple candle should be lit before the session begins.

WELCOME *the children and lead them in* **The Sign of the Cross** ✠ **(p. xxxvi).**

Ask the children if they noticed the colour in church – highlight anything in the hall that's purple. Bring forward any kids who are wearing purple (however minimally)

Leader   We're in Purple time. It's called Advent.
                  Purple is a dark serious colour. Christians think it's a good idea to be serious sometimes, especially when they think about the things they've done wrong. Fortunately, we know that we only have to say sorry for God to forgive us.
                  Let's say sorry now.

THE KYRIE   Lord Jesus, we're sorry for the times we've forgotten you,
                  Lord have mercy
                  Lord have mercy

                  Lord Jesus, we're sorry for the times we've been unkind,
                  Christ have mercy
                  Christ have mercy

                  Lord Jesus, thank you for never forgetting us,
                  Lord have mercy
                  Lord have mercy

Ask the children to repeat **The Prayer for Forgiveness** *after you* (**p. xxxvi**).

OPTIONAL ADVENT WREATH

Help a child to light the second candle on the Advent Wreath – another purple one.

OPENING   God our Father,
PRAYER   Thank you for bringing us here this morning
                  Thank you for Advent
                  (Thank you for our Advent Wreath)
                  Help as we listen, learn, and play this morning,
                  Through Jesus our Lord. **Amen**

BEFORE THE GOSPEL

St John Goes to the Desert

Leader   Right, this is the second Sunday of Advent, and we're going to hear about a rather odd saint.
                  His name was John.

'John' comes forward with the rucksack

> John realized when he was fairly young that God wanted him to be a prophet.
> So one day he took a rucksack and packed up.
> He put in a Bible and a bottle of water. *(He does so)*
> And went off to pray to God in the desert.
> Bye John! *(John tramps off and sits on the side)*
> John's gone to the desert. Do you think he's taken enough with him? *(The children will almost certainly say no, see if they can tell you what John ought to have packed – food, sun screen, sun specs, more clothes)*
> Well, let's see what happens . . .
> John got to the desert . . . *(John tramps back and looks round)*
> He knew this was the place where God wanted him to be, so he trusted that God would send him some food.
> And, sure enough, he found some wild honey. *(John finds the jar of honey)*
> *(Ad lib)* Well, yes it is in a jar, but it was the best we could do . . .
> And some nice yummy . . . *(John pounces on a grasshopper)* grasshoppers . . . *(John apparently eats the grasshopper)*
> Then, as nights are cold in the desert, John managed to catch a wild beast . . . *(Child, covered in the blanket, enters. John pounces again)* skinned it *(John removes the blanket, exit Child)* and made a nice jacket out of it. *(John wraps it round himself)*
> Then John read his Bible . . . *(John sits down quietly and does so)* said his prayers, and stayed alone in the desert, very close to God.
> After a while he realized God wanted him to give a message to the people of Israel. So John packed up. *(He does so)*
> *(Ad lib)* Don't forget the grasshoppers . . .
> And moved off to the River Jordan. *(Exit John, watch him tramp off)*
> There he goes, off to tell the people of Israel God's message.
> Let's find out what it was in the Gospel.

There's no Gospel Procession in Advent.

THE GOSPEL *St Mark 1.1–8*

You might prefer to start at verse 4 and change 'locusts' to 'grasshoppers'.

AFTER THE GOSPEL

Leader	So, what was John's message? *(See what the children come up with)* He had two actually.

Leader   So, what was John's message? *(See what the children come up with)*
He had two actually.
One was that God was about to send somebody to Israel who was much greater than John. Can you guess who that was? (**Jesus**)
It was Jesus. John was sent by God to prepare the way for Jesus.
And he did that with his second message.
That was 'repent!'
Does anyone know what repent means? *(Some children will know it means being sorry for your sins)*
Yup, it means being sorry for the things you've done wrong. But it's being sorry in a very special way.
I'll give you a demonstration.
Supposing *Name* gets something wrong – like forgetting where the door is. Watch this.
Name! Can you go through the door?

Another Leader Easy!

And he or she walks confidently off to a blank wall. Just as they get there, shout

Leader   Stop! *(And then)*
Repent!
Other Leader *(Stopping, but still looking at the wall)* What was that?
Leader   Repent – turn round!
Other Leader Oh, turn round, right. *(And they do)*
Leader   You see, repent means 'turn round'. If you're doing something wrong, stop what you're doing, turn round and start again.
Let's see if *Name* can find that door . . .

Run the same exercise a couple more times with the other Leader about to crash into all sorts of obstacles. The kids have to shout '**Stop!**' *and* '**Repent!**' *to extricate them. Eventually they turn round the right way and get through the door*

Other Leader There you are, I said it would be easy . . .

ACTIVITY

If you've got the materials you could get the children to make their own personal grasshoppers. Otherwise, use the grasshoppers you've already made to practise your presentation (see below)

REHEARSAL

Practise your presentation for when you go back into church (see below)

FINAL **PRAYER**	God our Father, You sent St John the Baptist to prepare the way for your Son, Help us to hear John's message and repent of our sins. **Amen**

Finish with a **Glory be . . . (p. xxxvii)**.

BACK IN CHURCH

Leader

Today we've been in the desert with John the Baptist and we've come back with . . . *(the children hold up the grasshoppers)*
some grasshoppers.
Grasshoppers are very good at jumping – watch this.

The kids spring up in the air, holding their grasshopper above them

That helped us understand John's message.
He told everyone to 'repent'.
Watch this.
OK grasshoppers, 'jump'! *(They do)*
Now 'repent'! *(The children jump again, turning round as they do so)*
Repent means 'Turn round'.
If you're going down the wrong path, 'repent'! *(The children turn with another jump)* And go down the right one.

(CD2.1)

Script 3   'Rejoice!'

Advent 3

John 1.19–28

THEME

Advent 3 is *Gaudete* Sunday, the moment when Advent lightens up. Gaudete means 'rejoice' and is the first word of the Entrance Antiphon (the verse that starts the service in some churches). All the readings urge us to cheer up – except the Gospel which, oddly enough, is about a confrontation between John the Baptist and some men from Jerusalem who have come down to investigate him. However, John isn't intimidated. He sticks to the message God has given him, and continues to proclaim that Jesus Christ is on His way.

Traditionally the vestments for Gaudete are rose-coloured but, as not everyone has a rose set, the priests may still be in purple. However, that needn't stop the Children's Church from being liturgically correct! See if you can find something pink to wear.

SET UP

- The liturgical colour is Pink.
- This session requires a bit of advance preparation:
  - Letter (in envelope) from St Paul – text on **pp. 13–14** below.
  - Postbag of letters (in envelopes) to the Children's Church – see the texts on CD-Rom.
  - Four empty cardboard boxes (from the local supermarket) labelled: '*Sacramento*', '*Los Angeles*', '*San Francisco*' and '*Santa Barbara*' (labels are on the CD-Rom).
- Someone prepared to stand outside the hall and deliver letters on cue (see below).
- Waste paper basket.
- Pony Express 'letters' from the CD-Rom. Photocopy several copies of these. There should be about four letters for each child.
- Optional Advent Wreath: two Purple candles should be lit before the session begins.

WELCOME *the children and lead them in* **The Sign of the Cross** ✠ (**p. xxxvi**).

THE KYRIE	Lord Jesus, you came to tell us how much God loves us,
	Lord have mercy
	Lord have mercy

Lord Jesus, you came to help us say sorry,
Christ have mercy
Christ have mercy

Lord Jesus, you came to bring us God's forgiveness,
Lord have mercy
Lord have mercy

Ask the children to repeat the **Prayer for Forgiveness** *after you* (**p. xxxvi**).

PINK SUNDAY

Remind the children about Advent

We've been in Purple for nearly three weeks now, but today we lighten up.
The right colour for today is . . . ?
Let's see if you can guess.

Bring forward some kids dressed in pink; show them your pink tie . . .

Yup, it's Pink.
Purple seasons always have one Pink Sunday in them, to cheer us up.

OPTIONAL ADVENT WREATH

Leader   OK, given it's Pink Sunday, which candle shall we light? (**Pink!**)

Help a child to light the Pink candle

OPENING	God our Father,
PRAYER	Fill us with joy today,
	The birthday of your Son Jesus is getting closer and closer,
	Help us to celebrate that day with love and happiness. **Amen**

BEFORE THE GOSPEL

Letters

Ad lib the start of a session, only to be interrupted. Knock on door

Leader	Good heavens who's that? Come in! *(Enter a messenger)*
Messenger	Special delivery for the Children's Church. *(Hands over a letter)*

Leader	*(Examine the letter; get a child to open it and another to read it)*
Kid	*(reads)* Dear Christians,
	Be happy at all times.
	Hold on to everything that is good.
	God has called you and He will never let you down.
	God bless you,
	PAUL.
Leader	That's a very nice letter. It makes me feel quite cheerful.

Place it carefully in front of you

Knock on door Another knock! Who is it now? *(Enter a postman with a bag of letters)*
Goodness is all that for us?
I'll need some help.

Pull out the top letter. You'll have to spike the envelopes somehow – perhaps with colour- coded 'stamps' – so you know which letters are cheerful and which contain bad news. The first letter should be the one from a teacher about doubling up homework. Ask a child to open it and read it out

Leader	Blimey, what do you think of that?
	What a ghastly letter – let's put it over there . . .

Go through all the letters. The little ones can open some of the envelopes even if they can't read, try to make sure they get happy letters. You know the children, so dish out the letters as you see fit. (You may have already altered the text of the ones on the CD-Rom or thought up some appropriate ones yourself.) By the end you should have a pile of good news and a pile of bad. Hold up the 'good' letters

Leader	Well, what do we think of these letters?
	These seem OK, full of good news.
	But what about these? *(Pick up the bad news)*
	They're awful.
	Let's chuck them.

Bring forward a waste paper basket and get a child to throw them in

This is Pink Sunday, I'm not in the mood for bad news.
What's the Gospel today?

Another Leader *(Picking the Gospel up and flicking through)*

Well, it seems to be about good news.

Leader	Great, let's hear it.

There's no Gospel Procession in Advent

THE GOSPEL *John 1.19–28*

Optional Paraphrase

While John the Baptist was baptizing people in the River Jordan, some men from Jerusalem came down to investigate him.
'Who are you?' they asked. 'Are you the Saviour God is going to send?'
'No', said John.
'Are you Elijah back from the dead?'
'No,' said John.
'Are you one of the prophets?'
'No,' said John.
'Listen,' said one of the men, 'we've got to take an answer back to Jerusalem – WHO ARE YOU?!'
'I am a Voice,' said John, 'calling out in the desert "Get ready, the Lord is coming!"'
The men from Jerusalem were not impressed. 'So you're not the Saviour, you're not Elijah, you're not one of the prophets – how dare you stand here baptizing people?'
But John didn't let them scare him. He looked them straight in the eye and said, 'I'm here to baptize people and, let me tell you, the Saviour has come. He's standing here in the crowd. Nobody knows Him yet – but He's much more important than me. I'm not fit to do up His sandals.'

AFTER THE GOSPEL

Put up picture **CD3.1** *from the CD-Rom and remind the children who John the Baptist was. They might remember him from last Sunday*

Leader	I love that story. John had some good news to tell and he wasn't going to let any tough guys from Jerusalem stop him. What was John's news?

Take all answers and establish it was that Jesus was coming – in fact He'd arrived

I wonder how good we'd be at telling the good news? Let's find out.

GAMES

The Pony Express

Run the Pony Express game.
Four boxes are placed at one end of the room. They are labelled: 'Sacramento' **(CD3.2)**, *'Los Angeles'* **(CD3.3)**, *'San Francisco'* **(CD3.4)** *and 'Santa Barbara'* **(CD3.5)**.
Gather all the kids down the other end of the room.
Divide the children into teams. (They don't have to be equal numbers as the smaller teams will simply run more laps.)

Deal out the Pony Express letters facedown into piles for each team. Any leftover letters are not used, so each team has the same number of cards.

On 'Go', the first child from each team picks up the top card and delivers it to the correct destination. He or she returns to tag the next child who does the same. The first team to deliver all their messages wins.

(You may decide to place a referee by each box, to make sure the letters are going in the right one.)

Stampede

If your group is fairly small you can finish by dishing out three or four letters to each child and run everyone at once in a 'stampede' to find the fastest Pony Express rider in the room.

REHEARSAL

Finish by choosing four Pony Express riders to deliver a letter sent to each of the towns for your presentation in the church. Practise your presentation for when you are back in church (see below).

FINAL PRAYER	We'll end by remembering what a happy Sunday this is. John the Baptist told us that the Saviour was coming. In fact He'd already arrived, so the response for our last prayer is:

The Lord is near
The Lord is near

Rejoice in the Lord always,
The Lord is near

God has sent me to bring good news to the poor,
The Lord is near

Be strong, fear not, God is coming to save us,
The Lord is near.

Lord God,
We thank you for the message of John the Baptist,
Grant that we will greet your Saviour with joy when He comes on Christmas Day. **Amen**

BACK IN CHURCH

Bring the children down to the front

Leader	Today we were very impressed with the way John the Baptist stuck to proclaiming the good news, even when he was being investigated by the guys from Jerusalem. We decided to spread the good news ourselves and today we've got four Pony Express riders who've galloped all this way to tell us . . .
Rider 1	Rejoice, the Lord is near!
Rider 2	God has sent us to bring the good news.
Rider 3	Jesus is coming!
Rider 4	Jesus is already here!
Leader	In fact, this whole Sunday could be summed up in one word . . .
All the children	**Rejoice!**

Script 4　Hail Mary

Advent 4

St Luke 1.26b–35, 38

THEME

The last Advent Gospel tells the story of the Annunciation. This session concentrates on the courtesy of Gabriel's greeting (we use the traditional 'Hail!') and the courtesy of God Himself. He asks the Virgin Mary to bear His Son, and it's quite clear she has a real choice.

This provides a springboard for that very biblical prayer, the Hail Mary.

SET UP

- The liturgical colour is Purple.
- Pictures from the CD-Rom.
- Beanbag or large soft ball.
- Crib figures and crib, minus Baby Jesus. (A small toy-shop crib is fine.)
- Warn your clergy that they'll get a formal Latin greeting in the presentation.
- Optional Advent Wreath – for once, leave all the candles unlit.

WELCOME *the children and lead them in* **The Sign of the Cross** ✠ **(p. xxxvi).**

Leader	Well, this is the last Sunday of Advent.
	That must mean it's nearly . . . ? (**Christmas!**)
	When is it? *(Let them tell you)*
	Are you ready? What have you been doing?

See what they come up with: making cards, buying presents, singing carols

	Fantastic, Christmas is coming. Let's be ready for it by leaving behind all the silly and wrong things we did last week.
THE KYRIE	Lord Jesus, you came to tell us how much God loves us,
	Lord have mercy
	Lord have mercy

Lord Jesus, you came to help us say sorry,
Christ have mercy
Christ have mercy

Lord Jesus, you came to bring us God's forgiveness,
Lord have mercy
Lord have mercy

Ask the children to repeat **The Prayer for Forgiveness** *after you* (**p. xxxvi**).

OPTIONAL ADVENT WREATH

Leader   Which Sunday in Advent is this? (**Four**)
                Four! Well, we'll need four children to light these candles . . .

This is the countdown: have four children lined up and ask everyone to count each candle as it gets lit

Everybody   1 . . . 2 . . . 3 . . . 4!
Leader   We're nearly there!

OPENING   God our Father,
PRAYER   Every year you make us happy at Christmas time,
                Grant that on Christmas morning we will come to church
                To greet your Son with love and joy. **Amen**

BEFORE THE GOSPEL

Courtesy

Leader   Christmas is full of greetings. We've just prayed that we hope to
                greet Jesus on Christmas morning, we do that by coming to church.
                If I greet a friend on Christmas day, what do I say? Watch me –

Go up to a child or another Leader and shake them by the hand, saying

                Merry Christmas!
                On ordinary days I greet friends differently.

Shake an adult by the hand

                Good morning!

Greet a child   Hiya!

                Why do we shake hands?

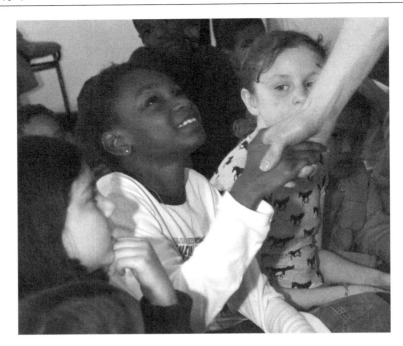

Kids normally say because it's polite. If they want to know why we use this particular gesture, you could say that the traditional idea is that it's to show you aren't holding a weapon

It's polite. The old-fashioned word for politeness is 'courtesy'.
We do a lot of odd things to be courteous.
Sometimes we don't shake hands, sometimes we kiss each other –
like this . . . *(Do a formal kiss with a Leader, cheek to cheek × 2)*
The French greet each other like that, but they do it three times.

Show them And the French who live in Paris do it *four* times.
(Ad lib) I think that's enough . . .
The Chinese and Japanese don't kiss or shake hands. Do you know
what they do? Can you show me? (**Bow**)
Supposing you were introduced to the Queen, what would you do?

Ask the children to show you. (**Bow or curtsey**)

Courtesy is a way of getting on with each other. If two people meet
and are polite it shows they respect each other.
All human beings have a go at courtesy. Back in Roman times they
did it like this . . . *(Walk up to another grown-up, raise your hand
and say:* Ave *Name!)*

They respond in similar fashion

> 'Ave' is Latin for 'Hail': I'll do that again in English.

Raise your hand and say to the other Leader: Hail *Name!*

He or she raises their hand and says 'Hail Name!' back

Leader   Can you do that? *(Greet a child or two)* Hail *Name!*

Then greet all of them, raise your hand

> Hail Children! *(With any luck they'll respond)*
> Thank you, that was very courteous.
> Now I don't know what language they speak in Heaven, but whenever angels come down to Earth they always greet people in the Roman way.
> We're going to hear about an angel in today's Gospel, listen out for his greeting.

THE GOSPEL *St Luke 1.26–35, 38*

There is no Gospel Procession in Advent.
Make sure that, whatever translation you are using, Gabriel says, 'Hail Mary!'

AFTER THE GOSPEL

Run through the Gospel, putting up the pictures as you get the answers

Leader   What was the Angel's name? **(Gabriel) CD4.1**
Whom was he sent to? **(Mary) CD4.2**
How did he greet her? **(Hail Mary!) CD4.3**
So the angel was courteous. **(Yes)**
And now the big question, what was his message?

(Take all answers, but establish that God was going to send Mary a baby)

> Let's think about that. Mary wasn't married yet, and the baby she was being asked to look after wasn't Joseph's. It was God's own Son.
> That was a huge job.
> And what God wanted to know was, would she do it?
> Do you think Mary could have said 'No'?

(Take all answers)

> Actually she could have said 'No'.
> God is just as courteous as His creatures.

He doesn't force people to do anything. Mary could easily have said 'No'.

So once Gabriel told her about the baby God was going to send, you must imagine everyone in Heaven holding their breath as they waited for her reply.

CD4.4   What did she say? (**Yes, I am God's servant. Let it happen as you say**) That was a wonderful answer.

If Mary hadn't said 'Yes', Jesus would never have been born.

The Church has thanked God for Mary ever since – and it's done that by using the same greeting Gabriel used when he turned up in her house in Nazareth.

Let's thank God for Mary as well.

Hail Mary . . . (see p. xxxvii)

ACTIVITY

The children will need a break. Brisk them up by getting them to greet each other with a beanbag or soft ball.

Get them and the adults in a circle. An adult starts the game by throwing the beanbag at another adult and saying, 'Hi, I'm Name, who are you?' He or she answers, 'Hi, I'm Name', and throws it to somebody else. Once you've established everyone's name, switch to the Roman version.

For this you say 'Hail Name!' and throw it on. Try to get the game going faster and faster. Be on hand to help the little ones.

REHEARSAL

Practise your presentation for when you go back into church (see below).

FINAL PRAYER

Set up a crib set, with the children's help. Go through the various characters – Mary, Joseph, donkey, ox, shepherds, angels – whatever you've got

Leader   There's one person missing, who's that? (**Jesus**)

When will He come? (**At Christmas**)

Yes, they're all waiting for Christmas: Mary, Joseph, the shepherds – even the donkey – and so are we.

Let's look at the Crib as we pray,

God our Father,
Be with us as we wait for Christmas.
Help us to be as obedient as Mary,
As faithful as Joseph,
As watchful as the shepherds,
And as joyful as the angels. **Amen**

BACK IN CHURCH

Leader   Today we have been learning how courteous God and the angels
              are.
              The children are going to show *Name of your priest* how the angels
              greet us.

Children   **Hail *Name*!**

*Hopefully you'll get a response: add a couple of other clergy, servers or any adults in
range*

Leader   Then we discovered how courteous God was.
              He *asked* Mary if she would bear His Son.
              Fortunately she said 'Yes'
              And we would like to greet her now.

Children   **Hail Mary,**
              Full of grace,
              The Lord is with you,
              Blessed art thou among women.

They can carry on if the priest wants them to, otherwise finish here with an **Amen**

(CD4.1)

(CD4.2)

Specimen cartoons for this script

Script 5   Away in a Garage

Christmas 1 (Church of England)

St Luke 2.15–21

THEME

The shepherds come to the Stable. Today's session offers a new take on this very well-known story. It ends with the naming of Jesus, so do your best not to mention His name until you get to the end of the script.

SET UP

- The liturgical colour is White or Gold.
- Pictures from the CD-Rom, stick them up on a large sheet of paper as you tell the story. The pictures are in black and white for the children to colour in.
- Glue.
- Scissors.
- Blank white paper for the children to draw on.
- Colouring pens.

WELCOME *the children and lead them in* **The Sign of the Cross** ✠ **(p. xxxvi).**

THE KYRIE	Lord Jesus, you came to bring us back to God, Lord have mercy **Lord have mercy**
	Lord Jesus, you came to heal us from our sins, Christ have mercy **Christ have mercy**
	Lord Jesus, you came to tell us how much God loves us, Lord have mercy **Lord have mercy**
OPENING PRAYER	This morning we're going to say the verse of a carol together, it's one you know very well. As you say it, I want you to think about the Christmas story.

It starts 'Away in a manger'.

Away in a manger, no crib for a bed,
The little Lord Jesus laid down His sweet head.
The stars in the bright sky looked down where He lay,
The little Lord Jesus asleep in the hay.

God our Father,
As we celebrate the birth of your Son, help us to think about the
Christmas story and understand it a little better,
Through Jesus Christ our Lord. **Amen**

BEFORE THE GOSPEL

Leader **CD5.1**	OK, today I'm going to tell you a story: Just before Christmas a young man called Joe got an official letter: He had to go and fill in some forms in *Name*.

Insert the name of the next town to yours

CD5.2	Well, Joe didn't have a car, but he and his wife managed to get his motorbike going, and off they went. When they got to *Name*, they found all the hotels were full and they couldn't think where they were going to spend the night. But
CD5.3	fortunately a mate of Joe's said he could doss down in his garage. And that night Joe's wife, Mary, had a baby. There wasn't a cot in the garage, but Joe found – what do you think he found? What could he use as a cot?

The children will spot the 'old box'

CD5.4	So Joe pulled out an old box, stuffed it full of newspaper, and they laid the baby in that.
CD 5.5, 5.6	Then Joe and Mary stood by the box, so the baby could see them. All three of them felt very happy. Has anyone heard a story like this before? (**Yes!**) OK – who's Joe? (**Joseph**) And did he and Mary really sleep in a garage? (**No, in a stable**) And what about that packing case? (**No, it was a manger**) What is a manger? (*Sometimes they know – it's an animal feeding* *trough*) You mean Joseph and Mary put a new baby in a feeding trough? That's weird. Actually the Christmas story *is* weird. Let's hear the next bit.

THE GOSPEL PROCESSION *(see p. xixx)*

THE GOSPEL *St Luke 2.15–21*

AFTER THE GOSPEL

Leader	So who came to visit the new baby? (**Shepherds**)
	That's odd too – imagine a bunch of shepherds turning up to visit you in hospital just after you were born.
	Can you imagine what your Mum would say?
	'What are you doing here?'
	'Oh, it's OK, an angel told us to come.'
	She'd think they were nuts.
	So if we go back to Joe and his garage, how are we going to get this bit of the story in?
	Why do you think the angels sang to the shepherds?

A rhetorical question: probably because the shepherds were the only people awake – they were keeping watch over their sheep

> So whom would the angels find awake nowadays? Who works at night?

Policemen, mini-cab drivers, office cleaners – anybody the children come up with

> OK, let's draw them.

ACTIVITY

Ask the children to draw some equivalents of the shepherds, and the gifts they might bring (in one session a kid drew a mini-cab driver offering Jesus his sandwich).
Add equivalents to the animals in the stable – the children usually come up with urban foxes, cats, mice and a friendly rat.
Angels don't change – ask for a couple of traditional angels in the sky.
Stick everything on to the main picture.

BEFORE THE FINAL PRAYER

Look at the picture together

Leader	Do you remember me saying that the Christmas story is weird?
	It really is, you know – the trouble is we know it so well, we need to re-tell it sometimes, to wake us up a bit.
	Look at our picture:
	When God arrived on earth as a tiny baby, He was born to poor people.

He didn't have a cot or a proper room to stay in. He was surrounded by animals and visited by strangers.

But that was fine, God loved the world so much, He didn't mind where He landed up.

And one thing in the story never changes: the baby's name.

Mary and Joseph – called Him . . .? (**Jesus**)

Let's pray to Jesus right now.

FINAL PRAYER

This is taken from the 'Litany to the Holy Name of Jesus'

Repeat the response after me: **'Hear us and bless us'**

Jesus, Son of God
Hear us and bless us

Jesus, Son of Mary
Hear us and bless us

Jesus, friend of children
Hear us and bless us

Jesus, joy of the angels
Hear us and bless us

Jesus, good Shepherd
Hear us and bless us

Lord Jesus,
you lived with Mary and Joseph in an earthly home
Bless our families and homes, so that we may live in peace with you and one another,
We ask this for your Name's sake. **Amen**

BACK IN CHURCH

Bring in the picture

Leader   Today we drew a picture of what it might look like if Christmas had happened last week.
We decided that Mary and Joseph would have probably ended up in a garage, they would have laid the Baby in a packing case, and the angels would have sung to some bus drivers *(or whoever you have chosen)* who'd have come to visit Him.

We're going to put our version of the story at the back of the church – and you'll see lots of changes.

But one bit of the story never changes, and that is that Mary and Joseph called the Baby –

Children   **Jesus!**

(CD5.1)

(CD5.2)

(CD5.4)

Specimen cartoons for this script

Script 6 Simeon Finds the Messiah

Christmas 1, the Holy Family (Roman Catholic)

St Luke 2.22–32

THEME

This Gospel is heard again at Candlemas (the feast that commemorates the Presentation of Christ in the Temple) which is held on, or near, 2 February.

This session concentrates on the patience of Simeon as he waits for God's salvation, and his amazing flash of insight when he sees the six-week-old Jesus, and realizes the Messiah has arrived.

SET UP

- The liturgical colour is White or Gold.
- Any sort of timer or alarm clock that you can set to go off in two minutes.
- Pictures from the CD-Rom.
- Plastic cups.
- Toy soldiers, knights, Playmobil characters, plus a Shepherd, King and Baby Jesus from a crib set: they should each be small enough to be hidden under the plastic cups.
- An A1 sheet of paper on which you have drawn a numbered grid and set the toys, under their cups, on a table before you start.
- Put the Infant Jesus under the cup at the far end.
- Make a die, out of a large cardboard box, with only ones, twos and threes on it. (This means that a fair number of toys will be revealed when you play the game.)
- A tray – for the presentation back in church.

WELCOME *the children and lead them in* **The Sign of the Cross** ✠ *(p. xxxvi)*.

THE KYRIE	Lord Jesus, you came to bring us back to God,
	Lord have mercy
	Lord have mercy

Lord Jesus, you came to heal us from our sins,
Christ have mercy
Christ have mercy

Lord Jesus, you came to tell us how much God loves us,
Lord have mercy
Lord have mercy

Ask the children to repeat **The Prayer for Forgiveness** *after you* (**p. xxxvi**).

OPENING	God our Father,
PRAYER	Mary and Joseph brought Baby Jesus to the Temple
	Thank you for bringing us to church this morning.
	Help us to know that Jesus is here as well,
	Help us to pray to Him
	And hear Him. **Amen**

BEFORE THE GOSPEL

Queues

Leader	I think we'll start by talking about queues. Anyone here been in a queue?
	Hands up if you've stood in a bus queue.

Register the show of hands

Or the queue for the check-out?
Or got stuck in a queue on the motorway?
I wonder how good we are at waiting. Let's see . . .

Ask the kids to stand up

I've got a timer here; we won't sit down until it goes off.

Set it for two minutes (ad lib as the time passes)

This is ghastly isn't it?

About 30 seconds before the time is up, one of the other Leaders says

I can't stand waiting any more! *(and sits down)*

Leader   Oh dear, I can see *Name* doesn't like waiting. But I think we'll stick
                          it out . . .

Off goes the timer – everyone sits

Leader   Fantastic, you all did really well. (Well, nearly all of you . . .)
                          Mind you, it was only two minutes.
                          I've got a story here of a man in the Bible who had to wait all his life
                          for something to happen.
                          We're going to hear about him now.

One Leader narrates the story, the other puts up the pictures

The Story of Simeon

CD6.1   Once there was a little boy called Simeon. He lived in Jerusalem and
                          his father used to read the Bible to him every night.
                          There was one bit of the Bible Simeon really liked, that was God's
                          promise that one day He would send somebody to save the world
                          from evil.
                          Nobody knew what the Saviour's name would be, so He was always
CD6.2   called the Messiah.
CD6.3   His Dad told Simeon, 'Messiah means somebody who's been
                          anointed. That's one of the ways God blesses us.'
                          Simeon felt the Messiah couldn't come soon enough, and he began
CD6.4   to watch out for Him.
                          As he got older, he realized that he probably wasn't going to bump
                          into the Messiah in the street, but he spent a lot of time praying to
                          God about Him.
                          And one day God answered him and said, 'Simeon, I promise you
                          will not die before you have seen my Messiah.'
                          Simeon thanked God – and settled down to wait a bit longer.
CD6.5   He got older
CD6.6   and older
CD6.7   and older,
                          in fact he got so old that he sometimes wondered if the Messiah was
                          going to arrive at all. But he hung on.
                          And one day God said to him, 'Simeon, I want you to go to my
                          Temple – this minute!'
                          Well, Simeon was very old by now, but he practically ran to the
CD6.8   Temple and when he got there, he found . . .
                          We'll find out what he found in the Gospel.

THE GOSPEL PROCESSION

THE GOSPEL *St Luke 2.22–32*

Optional Paraphrase

When Jesus was six weeks old, Mary and Joseph took Him to the Temple to present Him to the Lord. They also took a pair of doves with them, as a sacrifice.

At that time there was a man living in Jerusalem whose name was Simeon. He was a good faithful man and was waiting for the day when God would save the people of Israel. God had revealed to him that he would not see death until he had set eyes on the Messiah, and that very day, prompted by the Holy Spirit, he came to the Temple just as Mary and Joseph arrived with Jesus. Simeon went up to them, took the Child in his arms, and blessed God saying:

'Lord, now let your servant depart in peace. You have kept your promise to me and I have seen, with my own eyes, how you intend to save your people. You have sent a light which will lighten the whole world and bring glory to your people Israel.'

AFTER THE GOSPEL

Leader   So Simeon eventually saw the Messiah.
Who was it? (**Jesus**)
I think that was brilliant of Simeon.
He'd waited for the Messiah all that time, he didn't have a clue what the Messiah would look like – but as soon as he saw Baby Jesus, he knew at once who He was.
He'd found the Messiah.
I wonder how good we would be at finding the Messiah?

GAME

Bring forward the table, very carefully! Establish where the start and finish is and let the children throw the die in turn (or in two teams if there are too many to play this individually).

Choose which end of the room the die is going to bounce in – as you protect the table. A throw of three means the child moves on three spaces and turns up the cup on that square to reveal the toy – and so on.

Do a bit of patter as each toy is revealed.

Leader   Hmm, Bob the Builder – do you think he's the Messiah? (**No!**)
Ah, a King – what about him for the Messiah?

This could go either way. If someone says 'yes' respond with

'Yup, well, lots of people thought He'd come as a King.'

Naturally the child who gets to the end first and reveals the actual Messiah – Jesus – has won

> Well done, you've found the Messiah!

Leader   Hands up everyone who thought we'd find a Baby Jesus under one of these cups. *(Most hands should go up)*
Brilliant. Let's tell the church what we've discovered.

REHEARSAL

Practise your presentation for when you go back into church (see below).

FINAL PRAYER

Finish with the **Hail Mary . . . (see p. xxxvii)**, *or*

> God our Father,
> We thank you for sending us your Son, the Messiah.
> Holy Simeon,
> **Pray for us.**
> Holy Mary,
> **Pray for us.**
> Holy Joseph,
> **Pray for us. Amen**

OPTIONAL CAROL

If you want to end on a quiet note, gather the children into a prayer circle and show them the Christ Child (either the little one you've just used, or a larger one from a crib set). Comment on His smallness and ask them to pass Him round carefully as they sing 'Away in a manger'.

BACK IN CHURCH

Put about four toys (including the Christ Child) under their cups, place on a tray and bring them back into church. All the toys should be relatively serious – a soldier, a king and a shepherd. Have a child behind each cup, ready to reveal the toy

Leader   Today we heard how Simeon recognixed Jesus as the Messiah.
We wondered if we could do the same.
What's under that cup, *Name*?

Child pulls off the cup and holds up the toy

> A knight . . .
> Could that be the Messiah?

No? Let's see what else we've got –

Go through the other toys, ending of course with Baby Jesus

A little Baby!

Turn to all the children

So which of these is the Messiah?

Kids   **Baby Jesus!**

Hold the Christ Child up

Leader   Simeon and the children completely agree
about this: Jesus is God's Messiah.

(CD6.1)

(CD6.3)

Specimen cartoons for this script   (CD6.8)

Script 7   Coming Home

Christmas 2 (Roman Catholic)

St John 1.9–14

THEME

The Gospel comes from the first chapter of St John. It is part of the great poem that opens St John's Gospel, but it's not an easy text for children. This session uses the story of Odysseus as a way into the verse: 'He came to His own home, and His own people received Him not.'

SET UP

- The liturgical colour is White or Gold.
- Print up one set of pictures from the CD-Rom, to use while telling the story.
- Print up the same set on a smaller scale, so they fit on to one side of A4, for the children to fill in the speech bubbles and colour in.
- An icon, picture or small plastic statue of Jesus: a crucifix is fine.
- A Bible.
- A large unconsecrated wafer.

WELCOME *the children and lead them in* **The Sign of the Cross** ✠ (**p. xxxvi**).

THE KYRIE   Lord Jesus, you came to bring us back to God,
Lord have mercy
Lord have mercy

Lord Jesus, you came to heal us from our sins,
Christ have mercy
Christ have mercy

Lord Jesus, you came to tell us how much God loves us,
Lord have mercy
Lord have mercy

Ask the children to repeat **The Prayer for Forgiveness** *after you* (**p. xxxvi**).

| OPENING PRAYER | Lord Jesus,
When you were born
Nobody seemed to notice,
Just Mary and Joseph and some shepherds.
Help us to notice you
And recognize you
In church,
In the Bible,
In other people. **Amen** |

BEFORE THE GOSPEL

Story Time

Two Leaders present this story, one reads, the other puts up the pictures and adds the captions to the speech bubbles (The captions are on the CD-Rom)
The narrator should either sit on the floor with the children, or pull up a chair. Either way, gather them round you

Leader **CD7.1**	OK, today I'm going to tell you a story – it's about a man who lived a long time ago and looked like this. He was a Greek and his name was Odysseus. He was the king of the island of Ithaca, where he lived with his wife
CD7.2	Penelope, his son Telemachus, and his dog Argos. But one day Odysseus was called away to fight the Trojans. So he
CD7.3	left Ithaca and sailed to Troy with all the other Greek kings. Has anyone heard of the Trojan War?

See what happens, they might have done it in school, or seen the film Troy

	Well, the Trojan War lasted ten whole years and, the moment it was over, Odysseus jumped in his ship and headed for home. But he never seemed to get there. First he landed on the island of the god of the winds, Aeolus.
CD7.4	The god gave him a bag of winds, to make his ship go faster. But Odysseus' sailors (thinking it was a bag of gold) snuck up to it one night, opened it and let all the winds out at once.
CD7.5	The ship immediately whizzed off in the wrong direction – and Odysseus had to start all over again. As he journeyed back he kept hitting dangerous islands.
CD7.6	There was Circe's island, where she turned all his sailors into pigs. (Odysseus managed to turn them back.)

CD7.7	And Cyclops' island,
	where the giant one-eyed Cyclops captured the whole crew and began to eat them one by one.
	Fortunately Odysseus rescued them before too many had gone.
CD7.8	Then there was the sea god, Poseidon.
	Odysseus had blinded Cyclops when he'd freed his men but, unfortunately, Cyclops was Poseidon's son.
	The sea god was furious and sent winds, waves – everything he could think of – to stop Odysseus getting home.
CD7.9	It took Odysseus ten years to get back to Ithaca and, when he landed, he'd been away twenty whole years.
	It was a terrible homecoming.
	Nobody recognized him: not his wife, nor his son, nor any of his people.
	Only Argos the dog realized who he was.
	He was a very old dog by now, but, as Odysseus passed him,
CD7.10	he had just enough strength to drop his ears and wag his tail.
	Then he died.
	Poor Odysseus, what a way to come home. Of course it all ended up fine, with Odysseus and Penelope and Telemachus living happily
CD7.11	ever after, but Odysseus never forgot coming home to his own island, his own kingdom, and being treated as a stranger.

Sum up	
Leader	Now that story is a legend – it all happened a long time ago and nobody knows whether Odysseus was a real person or not.
	We're going on to hear the Gospel, which of course is *not* a legend: Jesus is a real person and the people who wrote the Gospels knew Him and His friends. Yet in a curious way, the Gospel this morning reminds me of the story of Odysseus. Listen carefully and see if you can work out why.

THE GOSPEL PROCESSION

THE GOSPEL *St John 1.9–14*

Preface the Gospel with:

> In this Gospel, St John describes the moment when Jesus arrived on Earth.

Optional Paraphrase

> The true light,
> that shines on everyone,
> came into this world,
> The world that He had made –
> and no one knew Him.
> He came to His own people,
> and they did not welcome Him.
>
> Yet a few people recognized Him
> and to them He gave the power to be children of God.
>
> God became a human being
> and lived here with us.
> And we saw His glory,
> the glory of the only Son of the Father,
> full of grace and truth.

AFTER THE GOSPEL

Leader   Can you guess why I'm reminded of Odysseus in that Gospel?

See what they come up with, by the end establish it's because:

> Jesus came to His kingdom, to the world He'd made – and nobody knew who He was.
> Well, a few people did – Mary and Joseph, of course, and later some friends, like St John. But not very many.
> When St John wrote about Jesus coming to Earth later on, he felt it was terrible that nobody recognized Him, but Jesus Himself just got on with it.
> He loves people whether they know who He is or not.

ACTIVITY

Colour in the Odysseus pictures – give the children a set with the speech bubbles blank so they can add their own captions. (Some captions are provided on the CD-Rom, but you can encourage the children to put in their own captions.)

BEFORE THE FINAL PRAYER

Gather the children into a circle, have the image of Jesus, the Bible and the unconsecrated wafer to hand

Leader	Christmas is all about the time when Jesus came down to Earth.
	But of course He doesn't live on Earth now.
	Where does Jesus live? (**Heaven**)
	Quite right. Even so, Jesus can still be found on Earth – and now it's up to us to recognize Him.
	We can see pictures of Jesus in church.

Show the children the image of Christ that you've brought

We can hear Jesus in the Bible.

Open the Bible and read out a verse of a Gospel (St Mark 10.14 or any of the Beatitudes in St Matthew 5 would be fine)

Best of all, we can touch Jesus in the bread at Mass.

Pass the unconsecrated wafer round the circle

Now, at the moment, this is *just* bread but, after the priest has held it and prayed Jesus' words over it, our Lord enters the bread. It still looks and feels like bread, but now it has become His Body for us.

REHEARSAL

Practise your presentation for when you go back into church (see below).

FINAL	Lord Jesus,
PRAYER	We thank you for still visiting your people
	Help us to recognize you
	In church,
	In the Bible,
	In the Holy Bread at the altar. **Amen**

BACK IN CHURCH

Select three children to bring in the image of Christ, the Bible and the unconsecrated wafer. A grown-up reads the script, it needs good timing – and of course he or she has to reassure the congregation that the children are holding up an unconsecrated wafer

Leader	Today we heard how, when Jesus first came to Earth, nobody recognized Him.
	But we realized that we could recognize Jesus . . .

Child 1 holds up the image

> in the pictures of Him in church.
> We could hear Him . . .

Child 2 holds up the Bible

> in His Holy Gospel.
> And we could touch Him . . .

Child 3 holds up the wafer

> in the Holy Sacrament.
> Of course, this piece of bread is unconsecrated, but it's good to
> know Jesus can come among us in something as ordinary as this
> bread.

(CD7.1)

(CD7.2)

(CD7.5)

(CD7.7)

Specimen cartoons for this script

Script 8　Epiphany

St Matthew 2.1–12

THEME

Today is about presents, the presents given to the Christ Child – and the one He gave to us: Himself.

SET UP

- The liturgical colour is White or Gold.
- Either a crib set – but keep the Kings back – or a large picture of the Nativity: a Christmas card is fine, but make sure it contains no Kings. Have a card that *does* have the Kings on it.
- Small sock with a lump of coal in its toe (a piece of charcoal from the censer or a barbecue works well: if you're really stuck, char a wine cork).
- Letter from Father Christmas on the CD-Rom: put it in an envelope and address it to the leader who'll read it out.
- The Kings' gifts – wrapped up – consisting of:
  - Grains or oil of myrrh (if you live near a cathedral shop) or any sweet-smelling oil in a bottle.
  - Some incense grains.
  - A bag of gold coins, either chocolate coins, or the 'Pirate coins' you can get from party shops.
- Photocopy the Present Sheet from the CD-Rom.
- Pencils for the children.

WELCOME *the children and lead them in* **The Sign of the Cross ✠ (p. xxxvi).**

THE KYRIE　　Lord Jesus, you came to bring us back to God,
　　　　　　　　Lord have mercy
　　　　　　　　Lord have mercy

　　　　　　　　Lord Jesus, you came to heal us from our sins,
　　　　　　　　Christ have mercy
　　　　　　　　Christ have mercy

Lord Jesus, you came to tell us how much God loves us,
Lord have mercy
Lord have mercy

Ask the children to repeat **The Prayer for Forgiveness** *after you* (**p. xxxvi**).

BEFORE THE OPENING PRAYER

Look at the crib set together

Leader   Today is the last day of Christmas.
Soon we'll have to put away our crib and pack up our cards and decorations.
Let's look at them for the last time.

Go through the various characters in the Nativity scene, including the animals

Mary, Joseph, Jesus, the shepherds – wait a moment, there are some people missing.
Who haven't we got? (**The Kings, the Wise Men**)

Add the Kings, or swap to a picture that shows them

That's better.
The Kings turned up a little later than the others
and this Sunday we remember their visit to Baby Jesus.

Ask the children to kneel

OPENING   Lord Jesus,
PRAYER   Today, three Kings knelt before you,
We kneel before you as well.

Today, the Three Kings worshipped you,
And we have come to church to worship you.

Today you gave the Three Kings your blessing,
Grant us your blessing this morning. **Amen**

BEFORE THE GOSPEL

Presents

With the sock, letter and Kings' gifts

Leader   Well, as this is the last day of Christmas, I think it would be nice to look back over the holiday.
Let's think back to Christmas morning.
Anyone here get a stocking? Put your hand up –

React to the forest of hands

> Actually, so did I. Here it is. *(Hold it up)*
> It's very small, isn't it?
> Now in my family we're always told that Father Christmas only leaves presents for good children, bad ones get a lump of coal.
> And this Christmas, when I opened my stocking I found . . .

Pull out the coal – and encourage the other Leaders to respond with a panto 'Ah!' otherwise some tender-hearted child may feel sorry for you

> And I got a letter. *(Read letter out loud)*
> It was all very sad.
> Did that happen to any of you? (**No!**)
> *(React)* No???!!
> You mean every single one of you was good last year???
> Well I'm dashed!
> Of course Christmas is a time for presents.
> I got presents (eventually).
> You got presents.
> And Baby Jesus got presents.
> Here they are. *(Show the children the wrapped gifts)*
> Let's hear about them in the Gospel.

THE GOSPEL PROCESSION

THE GOSPEL *St Matthew 2.1–12*

AFTER THE GOSPEL

Leader   *Go through the Gospel together*
             Who brought Jesus presents? (**The Three Kings/Wise Men**)
             And what did they bring? (**Gold, Frankincense and Myrrh**)
             We've got them here . . .

Ask some kids to help you open the presents

Identify them – if you've got grains of Frankincense or Myrrh, let the children finger them

> They're just like dried glue – they're made from tree gum.

If the spices are in oil, let the children sniff the scent, or drop a spot on their open palms
Place the gifts in front of the Crib or the Nativity picture, saying as you go . . .

The Kings brought Jesus some Gold,
to show He was a King.
And some Myrrh.
Myrrh was used to anoint the dead. This gift shows that Jesus was a
real human being, He was going to die, just like us.
And Frankincense.
Frankincense can be put in an incense burner. It gives off a super
smell, and lots of smoke, and we use it sometimes when we worship
God.
Frankincense shows us that Jesus is God.
The Kings' presents were amazing – very expensive and full of
meaning.

ACTIVITY

Leader   Christmas is a time for presents.
CD8.1   I've got a picture here of all the people who gave Jesus Christmas
                  presents. Can you work out what presents they gave?

*This sheet can either be photocopied separately for the kids to fill in themselves, or as
one big picture for you to work on as a group*
*The 'answers' are also supplied, but it's more interesting to see what the children
come up with*
*When you get to the penultimate picture (a child bringing its present to Jesus) you
may need to stop for a discussion:*

                  What can we give Jesus?

The very last picture is Jesus' present to us (Himself)

FINAL PRAYER

Gather the children round the three gifts

                  Today we remember the Kings' gifts.
                  The first gift was Gold,
                  Repeat after me 'Blessed be Jesus, King of the Universe'
                  Blessed be Jesus, King of the Universe.

                  The second gift was Myrrh,
                  Blessed be Jesus, the Son of Man
                  Blessed be Jesus, the Son of Man.

The third gift was Frankincense,
Blessed be Jesus, True God of True God
Blessed be Jesus, True God of True God. Amen

OPTIONAL SONG

'Bethlehem of noblest cities' *works well, but the children are more likely to know* 'We three Kings'.

BACK IN CHURCH

Go back, with four children bearing the three gifts and either the Infant Jesus from a crib set, or a picture of Him as a baby
Some churches refer to the little crib set Jesus as a 'bambino', the Italian for 'child'

Leader   Today we heard about the Three Kings and the presents they brought to Jesus.

A child holds up the Gold

They brought Him Gold, to show He was a King.

A child holds up the Myrrh

And Myrrh, to show He was a Man.

A child holds up the Frankincense

And Frankincense, to show that He was God.
Jesus gave the Kings a present as well . . .

A child holds up an image of Baby Jesus

Himself.

(CD8.1)

Script 9 The Baptism of Jesus

Epiphany 1, Ordinary Time 1

St Mark 1.9 –11

THEME

This session focuses on the Holy Spirit hovering over Jesus in the form of a dove.

SET UP

- The liturgical colour is White or Gold.
- Bird-watching kit: anorak, binoculars, pocket guide to birds if you've got one. (If you happen to have a real bird-watcher among you, encourage him or her to come in with their kit, telescopes, portable hides, sludge-coloured clothes – anything!)
- Pictures from the CD-Rom.
- A picture of Piero della Francesca's 'Baptism of Christ' (you can buy reproductions of it from the National Gallery in London, or show it on your laptop via the Web Gallery of Art: http://www.wga.hu).

WELCOME *the children and lead them in* **The Sign of the Cross** ✠ **(p. xxxvi).**

THE KYRIE   God our Father,
                   You always hear those who say they are sorry,
                   Lord have mercy
                   Lord have mercy

                   Lord Jesus,
                   We are sorry for the times we have forgotten you,
                   Christ have mercy
                   Christ have mercy

                   God, the Holy Spirit,
                   Be with us in the coming week, as we try not to sin again,
                   Lord have mercy
                   Lord have mercy

Ask the children to repeat **The Prayer for Forgiveness** *after you* (**p. xxxvi**).

OPENING	God our Father,
PRAYER	Today you called Jesus 'your beloved Son'.
	We know you love us too,
	Help us, in the week ahead, to act as your beloved children,
	We ask this in the Name of Jesus,
	Who lives and reigns with you and the Holy Spirit for ever. **Amen**

BEFORE THE GOSPEL

Hobbies

Leader	Does anyone know what a hobby is?
	(**It's an activity – something you're interested in and take trouble over.**)
	Anyone here got a hobby? *(Go with the flow)*

Identify any grown-up, or kid, who you know has got a hobby – car engines, ballet, football, pop music

There are some weird hobbies around, I know someone who . . .

Add any weird hobby you know about – I use the person I knew who went round photographing all the London bus stops

The nice thing about hobbies is that they usually need kit.
I've got a pile of kit here . . .

Start going through the bird-watching paraphernalia and putting it on

Can anyone guess what my hobby is?

Give some hints if the children don't get it

What can I see through my binoculars?
Hmm, well, it's covered in feathers, sitting on a nest – yup definitely a bird.
Now what sort?

Look it up in your bird book – or, more excitingly, on your iPhone

You're right – I'm a bird-watcher.

Birds

If you've got a bird-watcher present (a kid may be one) do a short interview

>Where do you watch birds?
>Do you have to be really quiet?
>Have you got binoculars?
>What's the best bird you've ever seen?

Depending on your location, and the number of kids present, you may be able to set up a brief moment with the binoculars: with any luck they'll at least spot a pigeon

>It's nice to spot birds and work out what they are.
>I wonder how many birds we know?

Put up the pictures of birds from the CD-Rom **(CD9.1–9.11)** *and see how you do (all the photos are labelled)*

>Everyone likes birds – and there are lots of stories about them.
>Let's look at a few.

Put up pictures of some biblical birds and talk them through
the Spirit of God, hovering over the waters of creation like a bird, in Genesis 1 **(CD9.12)**
the dove Noah sent off from the Ark **(CD9.13)**
the raven feeding Elijah in the wilderness **(CD9.14)**
the sparrow Jesus talked about in St Matthew 10.29 **(CD9.15)**

>OK, a bird flies into the Gospel today – listen carefully and see if you can spot it.

THE GOSPEL PROCESSION

THE GOSPEL *St Mark 1.9–11*

AFTER THE GOSPEL

Leader   Did anyone notice the bird? (**It was a dove**)
>Was it a real dove?

Take any answer – then go back to the Bible

>'And the Spirit, like a dove, descended on Him.'
>Well, it wasn't an ordinary dove – it was God the Holy Spirit in the form of a dove.

The Holy Spirit

Leader	God the Holy Spirit is very mysterious.

He's like the air around us, extremely important – but invisible.

Every now and then people think they see Him – in a flame, or a puff of wind, or as a bird.

I wonder why He appeared as a dove when Jesus got baptized?

It's probably something to do with the Bible.

Look through the story pictures again

He didn't turn up with bread – so He wasn't a raven.

He didn't fall off a roof, so He wasn't a sparrow.

Turn to the Creation and Noah pictures

It's these two pictures that interest me.

They've both got water in them. This one has a bird hovering over the water – and this one has a bird with an olive branch.

When people thought of this story *(the Genesis picture)* they thought of the Spirit of God hovering over the new world.

And when they saw this one *(the Noah picture)* they thought of the dove bringing back the olive branch to show that God had made peace with the world.

So at Jesus' Baptism, the Holy Spirit appeared as a dove, hovering over water and bringing God's peace.

Show the children the Piero della Francesca picture – tell them who painted it.

Where's the Holy Spirit in this picture?

The kids can't fail to spot the dove

And which one is Jesus? *(That's easy too)*

OK, so we've got God the Spirit, God the Son . . .

but hey, where's God the Father?

He's in the story too.

Anyone remember when? *(See if they remember the Voice)*

Go to the Gospel

'And a Voice came from Heaven, saying "You are my Son . . . "'

Why didn't Piero put that in? (**You can't paint a Voice**)

No, but you can hear a Voice.

Look really carefully at the people in the front of the picture.

Only one of them seems to have any ears – who is it? (**Jesus**)

Yup, and they're very big ones.

Piero, the painter, is telling us that Jesus *heard* His Father's voice.

The whole Trinity is in that picture – God the Father, being heard by God the Son, with God the Spirit hovering above.

ACTIVITY

Create a Baptism of Jesus picture together.
Talk through the bits of the story you will need: Jesus, John the Baptist baptizing Him, the River Jordan, the dove, and God the Father in some form or another (some kids represent Him with golden rays, others put in a speech balloon).
Split up the jobs: some kids draw, others colour in, others paste it up on a large piece of paper.
If you have lots of children to employ, ask them to do people from the crowd, lining up to be baptized, or provide some palm trees for the banks of the river.
An easily assembled black and white version is provided on the CD-Rom **(CD9.16–CD9.19)** *if you're running out of time.*

REHEARSAL

Practise your presentation for when you go back into church (see below).

BEFORE THE FINAL PRAYER

Either gather round your picture, or look at the Piero picture again

Leader   Jesus got baptized, just like us.
               And, when He was baptized, the Holy Trinity was present.
               Baptism is all about the Holy Trinity.
               When we were baptized, the priest poured water on us and baptized us he said . . .

Touch the picture lightly as you mention the persons of the Trinity

               'I baptize you in the Name of the Father, and of the Son, and of the Holy Spirit.'

MUSIC

The hymn 'I believe in God the Father . . .' works well here.
You could say the words together as a prayer, in which case ask the children to recite after you:

               I believe in God the Father,
               I believe in God the Son,
               I believe in God the Spirit,
               God the Three and God the One. Amen

FINAL PRAYER

Finish with a **Glory be . . . (p. xxxvii)**.

BACK IN CHURCH

Take in your picture and either ask the priest to go through it with you, or present it using the following script

Leader	Today we heard about the Baptism of Christ, and we noticed that all the Persons of the Holy Trinity were present.
Child 1	Jesus was there – that's God the Son.
Child 2	A dove hovered over Jesus – that's God the Spirit.
Child 3	And Jesus heard a Voice from Heaven – that was God the Father.
Leader	And we remembered that we were baptized . . .
All the children	**In the Name of the Father, and of the Son, and of the Holy Spirit.**

(CD9.8)

(CD9.6)

(CD9.10)

Specimen pictures for this script

Script 10   Ladders

Epiphany 2 (Church of England)

St John 1.43–51

THEME

This Sunday's Gospel records the conversation between Jesus and Nathaniel. This follower of Jesus only appears in St John's Gospel, though he might be the disciple called Bartholomew in the other Gospels. Nathaniel knows Philip, one of Jesus' first disciples and, since he's not impressed by his friend's description of Jesus, he decides to go and see for himself.

Jesus seems to be amused by Nathaniel's wary behaviour, and compliments him on being a 'true Israelite'. In the conversation that follows, Our Lord reveals that the normal traffic between Heaven and Earth is about to be restored.

The story of Jacob's Ladder is a useful springboard for understanding this idea.

SET UP

- The liturgical colour is White or Gold (for Epiphany) but your church may have already reverted to Green – check with your priest.
- Bible.
- Marker pen.
- Materials to make a toy ladder (see the CD-Rom).
- Two notices to hang on the ladder: 'Out of Order' and 'Normal Service is Resumed'.
- Pictures from the CD-Rom: print up **CD10.4**, the ladder, as large as you can, and print several copies of **CD10.5**, the angels.
- Paper and pencils for the children.

WELCOME *the children and lead them in* **The Sign of the Cross** ✠ **(p. xxxvi).**

THE KYRIE   Lord Jesus, you came to bring us back to God,
Lord have mercy
Lord have mercy

Lord Jesus, you came to heal us from our sins,
Christ have mercy
Christ have mercy

Lord Jesus, you came to tell us how much God loves us,
Lord have mercy
Lord have mercy.

Ask the children to repeat **The Prayer for Forgiveness** *after you* (**p. xxxvi**).

OPENING **PRAYER**	Lord Jesus, You came to save us Grant that we will follow in your footsteps here below, So that, once our life is over, We will ascend to your home in Heaven, And live with you for ever. **Amen**

BEFORE THE GOSPEL

Lifts and Ladders

How you start this session will depend on where you live. If there are children who live in tower blocks in your group, you can go straight in and talk about their lift systems. If you are a village or suburban community, you may need to refer to lifts in shopping centres, car parks or underground stations. However you get on to the subject, ask the children . . .

Leader   Have you ever been in a lift?
                What's the longest lift you've ever been in?
                Anyone been up to the fourth floor?
                The fifth?

See how far they'll go

                Supposing you see this notice on the lift doors?

Put up the 'Out of Order' notice

                What happens then? (**You have to walk up**)
                Well, at least there are staircases around.
                But supposing this happened?
                (Draw a set of stairs)

And stick the 'Out of Order' notice on that

                What would you do?

Take all answers, but establish that you'd never get up at all. If some bright child comes up with the fire brigade, or a helicopter, take it one step further – draw a fireman's ladder, or add the helicopter wire, and stick the notice on that

Actually when lifts, or stairs, go out of order, they normally get fixed pretty quickly.

But this morning we're going to hear about a very odd ladder that seems to have got out of order for a very long time.

It turns up at the very beginning of the Bible . . .

Rifle through the Bible and show the kids when you find it (Genesis 28)

and it's called Jacob's ladder.

Jacob's Ladder

Get into story-teller mode. Sit on the floor (if you can) or get a chair and sit with the children. Another Leader puts up the pictures

Leader	A very long time ago, a man called Jacob was on the run.
CD10.1	He'd cheated his brother Esau and, because Esau was much bigger and stronger than him, he decided to clear off and live somewhere else for a while.
	So off he went, running all the way, until he felt that Esau was a long way behind and he could stop. It was already night, and Jacob
CD10.2	looked round for somewhere to sleep.
	It didn't look promising. He seemed to have hit a bit of country with no houses, no huts, nothing – just rocks. So he found a nice smooth

CD10.3   stone, tucked that under his head for a pillow, and went to sleep.
And that night, Jacob had a dream. He saw a ladder, planted on the
CD10.4   ground, with its top reaching to Heaven.
CD10.5   And, as he looked closer, he saw the angels of God climbing it – up
and down.

Ask the children to help you stick the angels on

Then Jacob dreamt he turned round – and saw God, standing beside
him. God said, 'Jacob, I am the God of your Father and Grandfather.
I shall keep you safe in all your journeys, and bring you back to the
land on which you are lying. This land will be yours and I shall bless
you and all your descendants.'
Jacob woke up – but there was nothing there: just rocks, and sky
and silence.
'Truly,' he said, 'God was in this place, and I never knew it. How
awesome is this place! It is nothing other than the gate of Heaven!'
CD10.6   And he took his stone, and piled a cairn up on top of it.
And he poured oil on the cairn, and named the place Bethel.* And
from that moment on, Jacob became a slightly nicer person, and
served God as best he could for the rest of his life.

Sum up

Leader   I think that's a very cheerful story. I like the way God appears to
somebody who's got things wrong and still blesses him.
And, though it's only a dream, I love the idea of there being a ladder
between Earth and Heaven. Look at it – *refer to the picture* – there
are God's angels going up and down, visiting us, going back to see
God, and coming down again to see how we're getting on.
It sounds a great idea. But, unfortunately, something seems to have
happened to that ladder. *(Put up the 'Out of Order' sign)*
Something went wrong, and it became less easy for the angels to visit
us, or for human beings to feel there was a direct line to God.
That's one of the reasons Jesus came to Earth.
In the Gospel today, Jesus makes a new friend, Nathaniel, and as
they talk, the story of Jacob's ladder comes up in their conversation.
See if you can spot it.

THE GOSPEL PROCESSION

---

* Bethel means 'The House of God'.

THE GOSPEL *St John 1.43–51*

Optional Paraphrase

Jesus called Philip to be His disciple and Philip rushed off to tell his friend Nathaniel. He found him sitting under a fig tree. 'We have found the Messiah!' he said, 'the Saviour God promised to send us. He is Jesus the son of Joseph from Nazareth.'
Nathaniel came from the nearby town of Cana and he didn't think much of Nazareth, 'Oh yes?' he said, 'Can anything good come out of Nazareth?'
Philip answered, 'Come and see.'
When Jesus saw Nathaniel coming towards him He said, 'Ah, here comes a true Israelite!'
'How do you know me?' asked Nathaniel.
Jesus answered, 'Before Philip talked to you, I saw you, sitting under a fig tree.'
'Rabbi!' said Nathaniel, 'You really are the Messiah!'
Jesus said, 'Do you believe me just because I said "I saw you under a fig tree"? You are going to see greater things than that. You will see the angels of God, ascending and descending over the Son of Man.'

AFTER THE GOSPEL

Go through the conversation, clearing up any difficult words. 'Saviour' is probably the easiest way of explaining 'Messiah', 'Rabbi' means 'teacher', and the 'Son of Man' is one of the ways Jesus referred to Himself

Leader   Nathaniel was very impressed that Jesus knew he'd been sitting under a fig tree when Philip ran up. But Jesus said he'd see greater things than that.
Can you remember what? (**He'd see the angels of God ascending and descending over Jesus Himself**)
So Jacob's ladder *(take down the 'Out of Order' notice)* has been sorted *(Put up the 'Normal Service is Resumed' notice)*
Once Jesus had done His work, the angels were able to come and go again, and the direct link between Earth and Heaven was repaired. And it wasn't just to be angels going up and down, human beings could go up and down as well.

ACTIVITY

Ask the children to draw pictures of themselves and stick them on the ladder. Or (if you have limited space and time) stick on the representative set of kids from the CD-Rom (**CD10.7**). *Add the children's names to the pictures.*

REHEARSAL

For the presentation, a little home-made ladder (template on the CD-Rom) looks very effective but, if you haven't got the time, the ladder picture (CD10.4) *you've been using for the story works just as well.*

Practise your presentation for when you go back into church (see below).

FINAL PRAYER

Gather the children round whichever ladder you decide to use

> So there's a ladder to Heaven. One we can climb up.
> How do we get on it? *(Rhetorical question)*
> We come to church!
> The first rung of that ladder is our church.
> Let's thank God for repairing the way to Heaven.

> Almighty God,
> You saw that the ladder between Heaven and Earth had been broken
> And you sent your Son Jesus to repair it.
> Help us to get on the first rung and, at the end of our lives,
> Find our way to the top,
> Where you live with Jesus and the Holy Spirit, for ever. **Amen**

MUSIC

There's a carol in the Oxford Book of Carols, *number 58, called 'Jacob's Ladder'. It's got a good swinging tune, an easy chorus, and ought to be better known!* (CD10.8)

BACK IN CHURCH

One child comes in with the ladder, another pair bring in the notices

Leader	Today we listened to the story of Jacob's ladder –
Child 1	*Holds up the ladder*
Leader	And we realized that the ladder that joined Earth and Heaven had somehow got broken . . .
Child 2	*Puts on the 'Out of Order' notice*
Leader	But then we read the Gospel and discovered that Jesus said Nathaniel would see the angels of God ascending and descending to Earth once again –
Child 3	*Puts on the 'Normal Service is resumed' notice*
Leader	Jesus came to repair that ladder.

Also on the CD as CD10.8a and CD10.8b

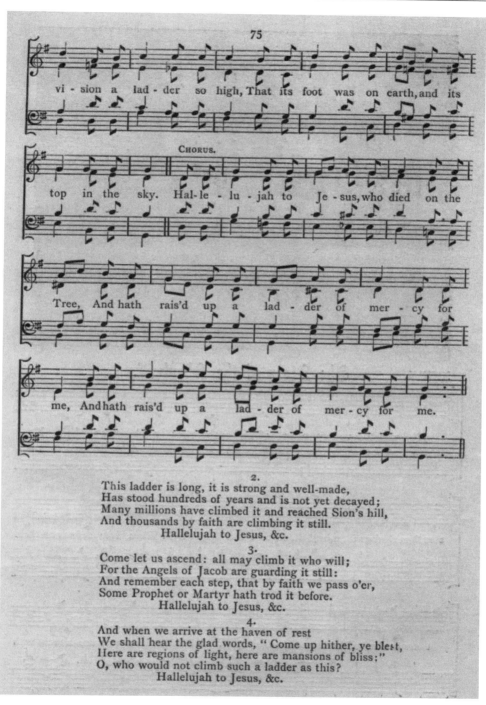

75

vi - sion a lad - der so high, That its foot was on earth, and its

CHORUS.

top in the sky. Hal - le - lu - jah to Je - sus, who died on the

Tree, And hath rais'd up a lad - der of mer - cy for

me, And hath rais'd up a lad - der of mer - cy for me.

2.
This ladder is long, it is strong and well-made,
Has stood hundreds of years and is not yet decayed;
Many millions have climbed it and reached Sion's hill,
And thousands by faith are climbing it still.
Hallelujah to Jesus, &c.

3.
Come let us ascend: all may climb it who will;
For the Angels of Jacob are guarding it still:
And remember each step, that by faith we pass o'er,
Some Prophet or Martyr hath trod it before.
Hallelujah to Jesus, &c.

4.
And when we arrive at the haven of rest
We shall hear the glad words, " Come up hither, ye blest,
Here are regions of light, here are mansions of bliss;"
O, who would not climb such a ladder as this?
Hallelujah to Jesus, &c.

(CD10.8b)

Script 11   Following Jesus Home

Ordinary Time 2 (Roman Catholic)

St John 1.35–42

THEME

Christmas is over and everybody has gone back to work. The church is in Ordinary Time (flagged up by the green vestments) school has started up and, in the Gospel today, we hear about Jesus starting His ministry.

Jesus starts from scratch. He hasn't got any disciples, but John the Baptist hails Him as the 'Lamb of God', and St Andrew runs off to follow Him.

We'll be focusing on St Andrew, because he's a brilliant example for us, not only does he follow Jesus – he brings other people along too.

SET UP

- The liturgical colour is Green.
- Pictures from the CD-Rom.
- Print up the *Follow Jesus Home* board game from the CD-Rom. Print up a pile of disciple pictures for the children to collect as they go round the board, and print up as many 'counters' as you have children playing.
- A huge die for the board game. Tapping 'inflatable dice' into Google will bring up an excellent selection, but it's just as easy to make one out of a cardboard box covered with sturdy white paper. Make the dots with a large black marker pen.

WELCOME *the children and lead them in* **The Sign of the Cross** ✠ (**p. xxxvi**).

Ask everyone to think through last week – if the children have just gone back to school, bring that in

Leader	How did the first week go?
	Did anything go wrong?
	Anything we wish we hadn't done?
	Let's put that right, right now . . .

THE KYRIE	Lord Jesus, we are sorry for the times we forgot you, Lord have mercy **Lord have mercy**
	Lord Jesus, we are sorry for the times we were unkind, Christ have mercy **Christ have mercy**
	Lord Jesus, we thank you for always listening to us, and forgiving us, Lord have mercy **Lord have mercy.**

Ask the children to repeat **The Prayer for Forgiveness** *after you* (**p. xxxvi**).

OPENING PRAYER	God our Father, We thank you for bringing us here this morning. We thank you for the holidays, And we thank you for term time. Help us, wherever we are, At school, at home, or in church, To follow your Son, Jesus Christ. **Amen**

BEFORE THE GOSPEL

Leader	Ever since Christmas we've been thinking about the start of Jesus' life.

Use pictures from the CD-Rom to run through Jesus' life so far

CD11.1	We've seen Him as a baby
CD11.2	And as a toddler.
CD11.3	We hear about Him getting lost
CD11.4	And then Jesus grows up and gets baptized.

Put this picture at the end of the row and fill up the gaps with the three pictures below

CD11.5	But, we never hear about Him going to school
CD11.6	Or playing
CD11.7	Or being a teenager. The Gospel jumps over all that and catches up with Him when He's about 30.
CD11.8	Up to then, we think Jesus did an ordinary job as a carpenter. But when he was about 30, He decided it was time to start His proper job – the one God had sent Him to do. We're going to hear how it all started in the Gospel.

THE GOSPEL PROCESSION

THE GOSPEL *St John 1.35–42*

AFTER THE GOSPEL

Talk about the story briefly

Leader	I think that's a rather odd story – did you notice what Jesus did? (**Nothing, He just walked past . . .**)

This is the only Gospel in which Jesus just turns up in the background.
He doesn't say a thing.
That's because He's just beginning.
He hasn't got any disciples, but people still notice Him.
John the Baptist calls Jesus the 'Lamb of God' and two of John's disciples run after Him.
We know the name of one of them. Did you hear who it was? (**Andrew**)
Yup, Andrew followed Jesus home – then he dashed off to find his brother Simon Peter and took *him* along as well. I think Andrew had the right idea.
We're going to play the *Follow Jesus Home* game to see how he did it.

GAME

Depending on numbers, stick up the board game (**CD11.9**) *for two teams to compete, or gather the children round a table for them to play individually.*
If it's a team game, get a child from each team to thrown the enormous die – change the child for each throw.
The game involves the children moving a couple of little disciples round the board (**CD11.10**), *going backwards or forwards, according to the fall of the die, and winning extra disciples as they go* (**CD11.11**). *The winners are the first to get to Jesus' home, bringing at least two extra disciples with them. (Any unfortunate child who gets 'Home' without two disciples starts again at square 14.)*
At the end, congratulate the winners, cheer the losers – and indicate that as long as you end up in Jesus' home it doesn't matter how long it takes.

REHEARSAL

Practise your presentation for when you go back into church (see below).

FINAL PRAYER
St Andrew was Jesus' first disciple, which is a pretty good thing to be. I think it would be a good idea to ask St Andrew to pray for us:

Holy Andrew, friend of Jesus,
Pray for us

Holy Andrew, first of the disciples,
Pray for us

Holy Andrew, brother of Peter,
Pray for us

Holy Andrew, patron saint of Scotland,
Pray for us

Holy Andrew,
pray for us that we,
like you and your brother Peter,
may follow Jesus all our lives
and find our way to His home in Heaven. **Amen**

BACK IN CHURCH

Range the children in a line down the front of the church: ask them to straighten their left arm from the shoulder, clench their fist and touch the next person's shoulder, so there's at least an arm's length between them. Once they've done that, they stand with their arms by their sides

Leader
In the Gospel today we heard how St Andrew followed Jesus home.

Stand behind the child at the end of the line

Andrew *(tap the kid lightly on the shoulder)* ran off at once and got his brother Peter *('Andrew' takes the next child's hand)*, who then brought him to Jesus.

(Go behind the next kid) And Peter found another disciple and brought him/her to Jesus. *('Peter' takes the next child's hand)*
(Go behind the next kid) And *Name (use the child's actual name)* found *Name* and brought him/her to Jesus.

Same business along the whole line. Join the line at the very end

And eventually *Name* looked round for another disciple and brought me!

The last kid holds your hand. Everybody holds up their linked hands

That's how the Good News was passed on – and we think it's a really good way to bring people to Jesus.

(CD11.9)

Specimen cartoon for this script

Script 12   The Wedding at Cana

Epiphany 3 (Church of England)

St John 2.1–11

This Sunday is one on which the Anglican and Roman Catholic lectionaries divide. Church of England groups should follow this Script 12, while Roman Catholics should go to Script 13, *Getting Wet*. (Anglicans will find that they'll have a chance of doing Script 13 when they get to the Third Sunday before Advent – right at the end of the Church's year!)

THEME

Jesus' first miracle seems to me a wonderful example of the virtue of Temperance. All that wine, produced at exactly the right time. This session introduces the children to the idea that virtue is a matter of balance.

SET UP

- The liturgical colour is White or Gold, though some churches may already have changed to Green. Check with your priest.
- Pictures from the CD-Rom.
- A length of duct or gaffer tape, about 3 inches wide and at least 10 feet long, or some beanbags (see below).
- Glass or transparent cup in a plastic holder, to conceal the spot of red food colouring (or Ribena) on the bottom. (If you can't find a plastic holder, hold the glass by its base with the napkin round it when you pick it up.)
- Large clear glass jug of water.
- A waiter's napkin.

WELCOME *the children and lead them in* **The Sign of the Cross** ✠ (**p. xxxvi**).

THE KYRIE   God our Father, you always forgive those who admit they've done
wrong,
Lord have mercy
Lord have mercy

Lord Jesus, we are sorry for the times we have been unkind,
Christ have mercy
Christ have mercy

God the Holy Spirit, help us to listen to you in the coming week,
Lord have mercy
Lord have mercy.

Ask the children to repeat **The Prayer for Forgiveness** *after you* (**p. xxxvi**).

OPENING   God our Father,
PRAYER   You created all things,
Sun and Moon, Earth and Sky.
You created us, and gave us things to eat and drink.
Help us to thank you for all your gifts
And learn to use them properly,
Through Jesus Christ your Son. **Amen**

BEFORE THE GOSPEL

Balancing Acts

Leader   *Put up picture*
CD12.1   Can anyone tell me what this girl is doing? (**Walking on a tightrope**)
Have you ever seen anyone do this?
What's it like?

*Establish it's usually done high above people's heads. It's scary to watch and difficult
to do*

What would be a good way to learn to be a tightrope walker?

Take all answers

I think you might start like this.

Make a line with the tape along the hall floor

That's the rope – and now you learn to balance.
Let's have a go.

GAMES

Tightrope game

Line up the kids and get them to walk down the tape.
Watch them carefully, a part of their foot should always be on it.
Get the little ones to negotiate it first – then make it more difficult: the kids walk faster,
then they run, then they hop, then they walk backwards, then they carry something on
their head – like a beanbag or a plastic cup.
Keep up the pace, anyone whose foot comes off the tape goes to the back of the line.

Penguin Alternative

If your hall floor won't take a tape, bring in some beanbags, put the children in teams,
and get them either to hop a specified distance with a beanbag on one foot, or shuffle
across like a penguin, keeping the beanbag on both feet.
Anyone who drops their bag is out.

After the Games

Leader	Yup, well I can see you are all brilliant at balancing. Anytime one of you wants a job, the circus will snap you up.
	But there's other sorts of balancing too.
CD12.2	Look at this chap.
	This is a Christian, trying to be brave.

Wobble picture 2 one way as you add picture 3

CD12.3	He's trying to make sure he doesn't wobble into being a coward . . .

Wobble it the other way as you add picture 4

CD12.4	Or wobble the other way by rushing into danger.
	Being good *(get picture 2 straight again)* means wobbling on a tightrope, until you get your balance.
CD12.5	Jesus was very good at it.
	Let's think about food and drink for a moment.
	If you eat and drink too much, people think you are greedy.
	But if you're funny about food, and don't share it, or only eat broccoli, people think you are mean.
	Jesus was fine about food. He knew there was a time to fast.

CD12.6 *Wobble Jesus one way*

	Do you remember how He fasted for 40 days in the desert . . . ?
CD12.7	And a time to feast *(wobble Jesus the other way)*
	Let's hear about that in the Gospel.

THE GOSPEL PROCESSION

THE GOSPEL *St John 2.1–11*

Read the Gospel freely. It's a very good story, have the spiked glass ready plus a large jug of water: pour the water in (from an immense height) at verse 8: 'He said to them, "Now pour it out . . ."' *Add the line,* 'The water had become wine.'
If you make sure the 'servant' doing the pouring flourishes the napkin over his arm, the children are so fascinated by the napkin they don't inspect the glass.

AFTER THE GOSPEL

Leader	That's one of the great stories: Jesus saved the wedding feast at Cana by turning water into wine.
	Jesus thought it was absolutely OK to have loads to eat and drink –
CD12.7	at the right moment.
	It's all a matter of balance.
	And, just like a tightrope walker, it's something we have to practise.
	Fortunately, God is always ready to help.
	We'll ask for His help now.

REHEARSAL

Practise your presentation for when you go back into church (see below).

FINAL PRAYER	God our Father, You sent your Son into the world To teach us how we should live. Help us not to be mean, or greedy, But follow Jesus By being careful and generous With the things you give us, For His Name's sake. **Amen**

BACK IN CHURCH

The children start off down the back of the church, one of the Leaders goes to the front

Leader   Today we learnt how important balance was.

The kids come down the aisle, their hands outstretched as if on a tightrope
They form up at the front of the church in a line

We realized that we could fast . . .

The kids (arms still outstretched) lean one way

Or feast . . . *(They lean the other way)*
But, if we follow Jesus' example, we can fast *and* feast – and keep our balance. *(The kids straighten up)*
Christians are well-balanced people.

(CD12.1)

Specimen cartoon for this script

Script 13 Getting Wet . . .

Ordinary Time 3 (Roman Catholic)
3 before Advent (Church of England) – see Script 12

St Mark 1.16–20

THEME

This session picks up the first disciples' sudden plunge into the Sea of Galilee as they follow Jesus' call. Being a Christian often involves you getting wet.

SET UP

- The liturgical colour is White (Anglican) or Green (Roman Catholic). Check with your priest before you set up.
- Something to scatter holy water with. An aspergillum (if your church has one) or a bunch of leafy stems (like some sprigs of rosemary), bound together at one end.
- Some holy water in a bowl.
- Print up the 'Splosh!' picture from the CD-Rom four times.

WELCOME *the children and lead them in* **The Sign of the Cross** ✠ **(p. xxxvi).**

Leader	Let's think about the last week.
	Anything we wished we hadn't done?
	Anything we forgot?
	We'll put that right now –
THE KYRIE	Lord Jesus, we are sorry for the times we forgot you,
	Lord have mercy
	Lord have mercy
	Lord Jesus, we are sorry for the times we were unkind,
	Christ have mercy
	Christ have mercy

Lord Jesus, we thank you for always listening to us, and forgiving
us,
Lord have mercy
Lord have mercy

Ask the children to repeat **The Prayer for Forgiveness** *after you* (**p. xxxvi**).

BEFORE THE OPENING PRAYER

Leader   Every Sunday we ask God to forgive us, and of course He loves us so
much that He does immediately.
But sometimes it's good to *feel* forgiven.
One of the ways we can feel God's forgiveness is by having holy
water splashed on us.
It reminds us that God washes away our sins.

*Produce the aspergillum/bunch of twigs to show the children how we pray with holy
water*
A leader splashes you with water and says

Leader 2   'May God wash away your sins.'
Leader 1   (*Cross yourself and say*) 'Amen'.
Can you manage that?

*It's impossible to splash kids without a fair amount of squeaking, but try and get
them to say* **'Amen'** *even if they're grinning from ear to ear. Don't forget any grown-
ups present*

OPENING PRAYER

Leader   May God wash away all our sins:
Everyone   ✠ **Amen.**

BEFORE THE GOSPEL

Leader   OK, everyone nice and wet?
Go on, I didn't splash you that much . . .
Can you think of another time in church when somebody gets wet?

Mime the action of scooping water over a baby if they hesitate

(**Baptism**)
Being holy and being wet often go together.
Let's hear that in the Gospel.

THE GOSPEL PROCESSION

THE GOSPEL *St Mark 1.16–20*

Put up Splosh! pictures as you go

As Jesus was walking by the Sea of Galilee, He saw two brothers, Simon Peter, and his brother Andrew, casting a net into the sea, because they were fishermen.

Jesus said to them, 'Come after me, and I will make you fishers of men.'

And at once they left their nets and followed Him.

CD13.1   Andrew first *(Splosh!)*

CD13.1 (copy)   Then Simon Peter *(Splosh!)*

Jesus walked on a little further and saw two other brothers, James, the son of Zebedee, and his brother John. They were in a boat, mending their nets. Jesus called to them as well – and immediately . . .

CD13.1 (copy)   James first *(Splosh!)* . . .

CD13.1 (copy)   And then John *(Splosh!)*

left their boat and followed Him.

AFTER THE GOSPEL

Leader   So we've got some very wet new disciples – can you remember who they were? (**Andrew, Simon Peter, James and John**)

And Jesus told them that they'd no longer be catching fish – but people.

Well, we're very like those fishermen.

Jesus has asked us to follow Him.

We were sploshed with water at our Baptism and He wants us to bring other people into His Church – to catch them for Him. I wonder how good we'd be?

Let's find out.

ACTIVITY

Chain Tag

Leader   I'm going to ask *Name* (Leader 2) to be St Peter.

And the rest of you are the rest of the world – spread out.

The children scatter round the room

To make this game even more exciting, chalk or tape a boundary round the room: any child who steps over the perimeter is 'out'. Naturally you can only do this on the sort of floor that can take it

Right Peter, there's the world. It's your job to catch people for Jesus – good luck!

He or she catches a child and they join hands

Fantastic, one whole new disciple – can you catch some more?

Off they go, all the people who are caught join hands and rush round trying to catch everyone else. They can only catch people if the chain is intact. The last person caught becomes St Peter in the next game

Alternative

If you have limited space, the Fishing Game from Script 9 in the first book in this series (Year A) *would be a popular alternative.*

FINAL PRAYER

Bring the children into a circle

How many people did we catch? *(Tot them up)* Brilliant.
Did you notice something?
We could only catch people if we were all holding hands.
I think Jesus would have liked that game.
He wanted His friends to stick together.
It's why we try to get on with each other in church.
Let's hold hands now as we pray the Family Prayer of the Church.

Our Father . . . (see p. xxxvi).

BACK IN CHURCH

Line the children up at the front

Leader   Today we heard how Jesus asked Andrew and Peter and James and
John to catch people for Him.
We thought we would have a go.
So *Name* caught *Name*.

The first kid in the line holds hands with the second kid

And *Name* caught *Name*.

The second kid holds hands with the third
Using this formula, go along the whole line, until all the children are holding hands

And we ended up with a whole room full of new disciples – all
holding hands.
We thought Jesus would like that.

Script 14   Demons

Epiphany 4, Ordinary Time 4

St Mark 1.22–23, 25, 26–27

THEME

Jesus deals with a demon in today's Gospel. It's a difficult theme to tackle because we neither want to frighten children with bogies, nor water down the Gospel. Fortunately, Jesus came to rid us from these nightmares.

SET UP

- The liturgical colour is White (Anglican) or Green (Roman Catholic). Check with your priest before you set up.
- Pictures from the CD-Rom.
- A leader prepared to be a maniac (see below).
- A picture/icon/statuette of Jesus – the Sacred Heart statue for example, or Jesus the Good Shepherd.
- The Our Father cards (see p. xxiii).

WELCOME *the children and lead them in* **The Sign of the Cross ✠ (p. xxxvi).**

THE KYRIE   Lord Jesus, you came to free us from evil,
Lord have mercy
Lord have mercy

Lord Jesus, you came to save us from our sins,
Christ have mercy
Christ have mercy

Lord Jesus, with you beside us, nothing can frighten us
Lord have mercy
Lord have mercy

Ask the children to repeat **The Prayer for Forgiveness** *after you* (**p. xxxvi**).

OPENING
PRAYER

From Psalm 46

Repeat the response after me: **God is our help**
God is our help

God is our refuge and our strength,
He is always ready to help in time of trouble,
God is our help

So we will never be afraid
Though the mountains tremble and the seas roar,
God is our help

Come and see what the Lord has done,
He makes wars to cease in all the world,
'Be still' He says, 'and know that I am God',
God is our help

BEFORE THE GOSPEL

The Terrible Story of Jim

Leader	OK, I'm going to kick off by telling you a story:
CD14.1	It's about this boy – Jim.
	One day, Jim decided to have a feast.
	So he snuck into the kitchen and got together all his favourite foods.

Put up the following pictures as you go through them

CD14.2	Jam doughnuts
CD14.3	Cream cakes
CD14.4	A tin of peaches and
CD14.5	Fizzy drinks with loads of E numbers.
CD14.6	He put everything in a bowl

Stick all the food pictures on the picture of the bowl

CD14.7	Topped it off with chocolate
	And ate it up.
	Then suddenly, Jim felt awful.
	He couldn't think what the matter was.
CD14.8	He had a tummy ache
CD14.9	He felt dizzy
CD14.10	He went green
	When, luckily for him, the whole lot came back up and he was unbelievably sick.
CD14.11	But goodness, he felt better.

All that horrible stuff had come out of him – and he thought
'I'm never going to put all that rubbish in my tummy ever again.'
And ever after he stuck to ordinary grub.

Demons

Leader   Now, oddly enough, what happened to Jim can happen to a person
who's feeling bad-tempered and unhappy.
It's as though there's something inside them that needs to come out.
When Jesus was alive, people called the things inside us that make us
nasty and miserable 'demons'.
I don't know if they were right about demons, but they were right
about one thing – if there *is* something horrid inside you, it had
better come out at once.
Jesus agreed.
If He ever met a man or woman who felt they had a demon inside
them, He cured them at once.
Let's hear how He did it in the Gospel.

THE GOSPEL PROCESSION

THE GOSPEL *St Mark 1.22–23, 25, 26–27*

Optional Paraphrase

Jesus and His disciples came to the town of Capernaum, and on the Saturday Jesus
went to the synagogue and began to teach.
A man with an evil spirit in him came into the synagogue and began to scream. Jesus
ordered the spirit, 'Be quiet, and come out of that man!'
The evil spirit shook the man hard, gave a loud scream, and came out of him.
The people standing round were amazed and said, 'What's going on? This man can
order evil spirits about –and they obey Him!'
And the news about Jesus spread all round the countryside.

AFTER THE GOSPEL

Leader   Just imagine what that scene was like.
A maniac came in – like this . . .

Ask another Leader to be a maniac (it just needs some arm flapping)

And Jesus calmed him down.

Put out your hand and say 'Be Quiet'. The maniac goes quiet at once

Reading the story now, we don't know whether the man really did have an evil spirit, a demon, inside him or whether he was just mad.
But something was wrong
Something evil was attacking him.
Jesus couldn't bear it and got rid of it.
He can still do that.
For example, you may be angry – how do we act angry?

Get some kids down the front to be angry
See what they come up with and (if they need it) show them some gestures: stamp your feet, shake your fist, cross your arms, hump your shoulders

Right, all be angry together. *(They all do)*
Now Jesus turns up – and touches you.

Touch each kid on the shoulder

The anger disappears – and you calm down.

Each kid goes quiet

The same thing happens if you ever feel unhappy, or frightened, or furious.
Talk to Jesus about it, and He'll help you at once.
When we go back to church we need to tell the grown-ups how quickly Jesus helps us. Let's practise the presentation now.

REHEARSAL

Practise your presentation for when you go back into church (see below).
You may feel that the children need a break. Either get them running round in a game (a simple relay race will do) or put the Our Father cards together at super speed.

MUSIC

The round 'Father, in my life I see . . .' works well here.

FINAL PRAYER

Gather round a picture of Jesus, talk the children through the image. When we see a picture of Jesus we see how much God loves us

Jesus came to comfort the unhappy
To heal the sick
To free the captives
To find the lost
And to gather God's people in His arms.

Our Father . . . (see p. xxxvi).

BACK IN CHURCH

The children stand in a line down the front
Leader 1 stands with four kids in front of him/her

Leader 2   Today we heard how Jesus started His ministry.
                        He came to the unhappy

Child 1 puts hands to face

                        And to the sick.

Child 2 sits down and hunches up

                        He came to the captives

Child 3 puts hands in front – as though they were bound

                        And to the lost,

Child 4 moves slightly away from the others

                        And He healed them all.

Leader 1 lightly touches each of the children (and retrieves Child 4). They all free up

                        In fact, He came to gather all God's people in His arms.

All the kids hold hands, raise them up, and bow

(CD14.8)   (CD14.9)   (CD14.10)   (CD14.11)

Specimen cartoons for this script

Script 15   Jesus' Busy Day

Proper 1, Ordinary Time 5
(Sunday between 3 and 9 February
if earlier then 2 before Lent)

St Mark 1.21, 29–39

THEME

The Gospel this morning follows Jesus as He lives through one busy Saturday.
The most striking feature of St Mark's account is how badgered He is by other
people. It's quite clear that Jesus embraces His ministry. 'That's why I came,' He
says – but no wonder He got up before dawn and retreated to pray alone.
The children re-live Jesus' day by making a cartoon strip. When they've finished
they pause, as He did, to find time to pray.

SET UP

- The liturgical colour is Green.
- DIY comic strip from the CD-Rom. (Take a view as to whether you are going to
  make one huge strip together – or whether the children are going to work on sepa-
  rate squares – and print large or small copies accordingly. Some of the 'Jesus' and
  'crowd' pictures can be duplicated from square to square. It's up to you.)
- White paper.
- Glue, scissors.
- Colouring pens and pencils.
- A prayer candle (see p. xxiii) or an image of Jesus.
- Warn the clergy that you'll be coming in with a masterpiece.
- Optional quiet music: Pachelbel's *Canon*, Handel's *Pastoral Symphony* from the
  Messiah, anything soothing that you can play on a CD player.

WELCOME *the children and lead them in* **The Sign of the Cross** ✠ (**p. xxxvi**).

THE KYRIE   Lord Jesus, you came to call us back to God,
Lord have mercy
Lord have mercy

Lord Jesus, you listened to the sorrowful,
Christ have mercy
Christ have mercy

Lord Jesus, you told sinners how much God loved them,
Lord have mercy
Lord have mercy

Ask the children to repeat **The Prayer for Forgiveness** *after you* (**p. xxxvi**).

**OPENING
PRAYER**   Almighty God,
You sent your Son Jesus into our world
To teach us
And to love us.
Help us this morning to listen to Him in the Holy Gospel,
And learn to follow Him, and love Him,
For His Name's sake. **Amen**

BEFORE THE GOSPEL

Leader   OK we've got a busy morning ahead of us.
It's based on a busy day Jesus spent in Galilee at the very start of His ministry.
That day started early one Saturday morning, it didn't stop until very late at night – and even then Jesus had to get up before dawn the next day, to pray, and carry on with His job.
Let's hear about it in the Gospel.

THE GOSPEL PROCESSION

THE GOSPEL *St Mark 1.21, 29–39*

As you read the Gospel, flag up the number of people who surround Jesus, and the fact that He never stopped.

Optional Paraphrase

Jesus and His disciples came to the town of Capernaum and on the Saturday, Jesus went to the synagogue and began to preach.

There He healed a maniac.

Then He left the synagogue and walked with His friends James and John to the home of Simon and Andrew. When He got there, He found Simon's mother-in-law was sick with a fever, so He healed her, and had some supper.

Then, as the sun began to set, people began to turn up.

Most of them had brought sick relatives with them, and the crowd got bigger and bigger, until eventually the whole town was gathered outside.

Jesus healed many people and eventually got to bed. But, before dawn, He was up and went out of town, to a lonely spot to pray.

Simon and his friends searched for Him and, when they found Him, they said, 'Every-one is looking for you.'

Jesus said, 'We have to move on. We're going to the other villages round here. I must preach to them as well – that is why God sent me.'

So off He went, walking all round Galilee, teaching and healing people.

AFTER THE GOSPEL

Leader   I'd no idea Jesus worked so hard.
                Can you remember all the things He did?
                Let's see if we can put them in order.

ACTIVITY

Sit the children round a large table and spread out the components for the comic strip from the CD-Rom (see below).

The first thing to do is get the sequence right: the captions are in the right order on the CD-Rom, dish them out to the children, so that each child is responsible for making one square of the comic strip **(CD15.1)** *and* **(CD15.2)**.

If any kid comes up with an extra square – like Peter's mother-in-law making supper for example – add it in.

Hand round the cartoons and speech balloons from the CD-Rom for the children to colour in and glue on to their square **(CD15.3–CD15.5)**. *(Of course the strips will look even better if the children draw in their own cartoons.)*

Large groups may have to make two strips, or share out jobs – one child cuts and pastes, the other colours. Small groups have all the fun and anxiety of making two or three squares each.

Place a time limit on this epic and, at the end, admire the result. (Some good extra captions are bound to have been added.)

Shouting for Jesus

Seat the children and think about Jesus' day

Leader   Can you imagine how many people Jesus saw that day?
              And how anxious they were?
              They all wanted Him to heal them.
              They must have pushed and shoved and called out.
              Let's think of some of the things they said.

*The children have just written in the speech balloons so they will probably come up
with some good dialogue. Write up remarks like:*

              Hey Jesus!
              Jesus! Over here!
              Help!
              Cough! cough!
              Oi, what about me?
              Jesus, please help me!
              JESUS!!

*Go through the list, giving one remark to a set of kids and getting them to call them
out one by one*

              Poor Jesus, and the crowd didn't call out one by one like you – they
              shouted all at once.
              Can you do that?

*Cue the children in and then kill the shout (with a finger across the throat). You may
have to practise that to get it crisp*

              No wonder Jesus went away early to a lonely place, to be quiet and
              pray. We all need to do that.
              What shouts do we hear in our ear?
              'You're late!'
              'Come and give me a hand!'
              'What about your homework?'
              'Hurry up!'
              It's right we should do things for people – and even do our homework
              – but just like Jesus, we need space.

FINAL PRAYER

Gather the children round a prayer candle or an image of Jesus
If you've got some music, play it for a minute or two – or sing
Anything quiet – like 'Abba, Abba, Father . . .'

> Lord Jesus,
> One quiet morning
> You knelt in a lonely place
> And prayed to your Father.
> Thank you for this place,
> Where we can be still,
> And pray to you. **Amen**

Leader   Well Jesus knelt and prayed – and then, do you know what He did?
He got up and got on with the job.
I think we'll have to do the same.

BACK IN CHURCH

You will not have time to do anything but go into church with your wonderful cartoon strip

Script 16   Jesus and the Leper

Proper 2, Ordinary Time 6
(Sunday between 10 and 16 February
if earlier than 2 before Lent)

St Mark 1.40–41

THEME

There are so many lepers in the Bible and they are treated so badly that the word 'leper' has come to mean a social outcast. In this session we take the non-PC world of the first century on the chin, and show how Jesus changed everything. Our Lord not only healed lepers, He touched them, and loved them – and made it very clear that His followers were to do the same.

SET UP

- The liturgical colour is Green.
- Touch Bags containing objects the children can feel and identify: a lemon, a bunch of keys, a torch, an egg cup, dried macaroni. Look round your kitchen . . .
- Some pictures of Jesus, anything you or your church possesses, or some images from the Internet. (Keying in Jesus Good Shepherd icon, Duccio *Jesus heals a blind man*, or Giotto *Entry into Jerusalem* and *Washing the disciples' feet*, will bring up some good images.)
- A smooth object, like a polished stone.
- A hand bell.
- Some large self-adhesive coloured spots.
- A kid able to cope with being a leper. (As soon as they realize it means ringing a bell you should have no lack of volunteers.)

WELCOME *the children and lead them in* **The Sign of the Cross** ✠ **(p. xxxvi).**

THE KYRIE   Lord Jesus, you came to call sinners,
Lord have mercy
Lord have mercy

Lord Jesus, you came to heal the sick,
Christ have mercy
Christ have mercy

Lord Jesus, you came to tell us how much God loves us,
Lord have mercy
Lord have mercy

Ask the children to repeat **The Prayer for Forgiveness** *after you* (**p. xxxvi**).

OPENING   Lord Jesus,
PRAYER   When you came to live with us on Earth
There was no one you did not love.
Now you are back in Heaven, you still love us.
Help us to follow your example,
And love one another. **Amen**

BEFORE THE GOSPEL

Hands

Leader   We're going to start today by looking at some pictures of Jesus.
Pull them out   I want you to look particularly at His hands.

Depending on what you've got, ad lib as follows

What is He doing in this picture?

Imitate it: hold your hand up, two fingers and thumb raised

He is blessing us.

Or perhaps He's healing someone, or holding a lamb on His shoulders

Jesus' hands were important. He could do good things with them.
And our hands are important too.
If this room suddenly went dark, how would you walk from here to
here?

Indicate a path

With this chair in the way . . .

Put a chair in the middle of the path

Someone show me . . .
We'll have to pretend it's dark – how about shutting your eyes?

*The child will almost certainly walk across like a sleep walker, arms out. Get one of
the leaders to help her if she needs it*

Oh yes I see, you use your hands to feel your way.
Hands are good at that.
Let's see how much we can discover by just using our hands.

Touch Bags

Set up a session with the Touch Bags: one object per bag. If a kid hesitates, give some very heavy hints. Go for a 100% success rate

Touching things is useful – and it's also rather nice.

Pass round a smooth object like a polished stone

Leader   Feels good, doesn't it?
Sometimes it's nice to be touched.
Dogs like being stroked.
Has anyone here got a teddy bear or a pet?
Do you ever hug them? *(Go with the flow)*
Of course sometimes other people hug you, your Mum or your Dad,
your aunties and uncles – does it make you wriggle?
But you'd feel sorry if they didn't.
Just think how horrible it would be if nobody touched you.
A long time ago, that used to happen to some people.
They were called lepers.

Lepers

Leader   Let's see what used to happen to lepers . . .

Bring the victim forward

Lepers had a horrible skin disease called leprosy.
It made bits of their body look funny.

Get the kid to clench his fists

And covered them with spots.

Put some spots on the child – not too many

People were terrified of getting leprosy and they wouldn't go near
lepers.
All lepers had to have a bell.

Give the kid a bell

And if they came near anybody they had to ring it and shout
'Unclean! Unclean!'

Have the kid do this, react violently, and move away

Blimey, a leper, I don't want to go near him!
You go and sit over there.

If the child is up to it, prompt him to lurch towards the other leaders
They act terrified and get out of his way
Make sure the leper is sitting right across the room by himself before you continue

People kept well away from lepers.
They didn't want to catch their illness and, anyway, they thought lepers were bad. They thought they only had leprosy because God didn't love them.
Do you think they were right? *(Don't comment on the answers)*
Let's see what Jesus thought.

Bring the leper forward

OK leper, you can come over here, but don't touch anybody.

THE GOSPEL PROCESSION

If you ring bells to welcome the Gospel, make sure the leper rings his too

THE GOSPEL *St Mark 1.40–41*

Have the 'leper' stand by you as you read the Gospel

A leper came right up to Jesus.
He knelt in front of Him *(the kid kneels)* and said, 'If you want to, you can make me clean.'
And Jesus, filled with pity, stretched out His hand *(do so, touch the leper on the head)*
and said, 'Of course I want to. Be clean . . .' *(Remove the spots)*
And immediately the leprosy left him and he was made clean.

The child frees up his clenched hands and puts down his/her bell

AFTER THE GOSPEL

Leader   What did Jesus do to the man?
Show me

Have two kids act out Jesus and the leper, get the touch on the head right

The man needed to be healed, but he needed something else:
he needed to know that somebody loved him.
Jesus showed He loved him by touching him.
And His touch showed the man that God loved him too.
Jesus' touch was a blessing.

THE PEACE

Leader   Every Mass, the church asks us to show that we love people by touching them.
Does anyone know when? It's when we all shake hands. (**The Peace**)

Offer a child the Peace

Peace be with you . . . *(Shake hands)*

Ask the children to offer the Peace among themselves: include everyone, including any spare grown-ups or teenagers at the back

REHEARSAL

Practise your presentation for when you go back into church (see below).

MUSIC

'Shalom my friends' *fits well here.*

BEFORE THE FINAL PRAYER

Leader   All next week we'll be using our hands – to pat the dog, to write homework, and play with our friends.
But the best thing we do with our hands is this . . .

Place your hands together

When we put our hands together to pray.

FINAL PRAYER

Hands together **Our Father** . . . (see p. xxxvi).

BACK IN CHURCH

Bring the leper back into church with you and designate a child to play Jesus

Leader   Today we discovered that in Jesus' day people were very unkind to lepers.
They had to ring a bell

The leper does so

And stay away from people.

He does that too

But Jesus stretched out His hands

He does so. The leper kneels and Jesus touches him

And the leper was healed. *(Remove the spots, the ex-leper puts down his bell)*
But, more than that, he knew that Jesus wasn't afraid of him and loved him.

Jesus and the leper stand shoulder to shoulder together. Pick up the redundant bell and look around

Anyone want a bell?

Script 17   The Man Who Came Through the Roof

Proper 3, Ordinary Time 7
(Sunday between 17 and 23 February
if earlier than 2 before Lent)

St Mark 2.1–12

THEME

The man who came through the roof is one of the most appealing stories in St Mark's Gospel. Children are usually delighted to think anyone *can* rip up a roof. (The roof in question was probably made of packed clay resting on beams and branch mats.) There are many things to think about in this passage – Jesus' recognition that the man was more troubled by his sins than his illness, Jesus' ability to forgive sins, the first signs of hostility from the Scribes – but we've chosen to focus on the sick man's faith.

SET UP

- The liturgical colour is Green.
- A sleeping bag, plus a girl or boy prepared to get in it and be carried in by a couple of adults.
- Another leader, with script, to play Jesus.
- Some large kids or grown-ups prepared to play various friends and bystanders. They'll need to see their parts beforehand – they are very easy. (If need be, the Narrator can say all their lines for them.)
- Board game from the CD-Rom. Print up a pile of tokens for the children to gather as they go round the board, and as many counters as there are children playing.
- Large die (see p. xxi).
- *Optional obstacle race.* Anything you can rustle up for an obstacle race – hula hoops, traffic cones, plastic tubs, chairs – anything.

WELCOME *the children and lead them in* **The Sign of the Cross** ✠ (p. xxxvi).

Ask the children to think about last week

Leader	Did we do anything wrong?
	Did things get in a mess?
	Let's get rid of all that by saying the Kyrie.

THE KYRIE	Lord Jesus, you came to find us,
	Lord have mercy
	Lord have mercy
	Lord Jesus, you came to help us say sorry,
	Christ have mercy
	Christ have mercy
	Lord Jesus, you came to tell us how much God loves us,
	Lord have mercy
	Lord have mercy

Ask the children to repeat **The Prayer for Forgiveness** *after you* (**p. xxxvi**).

OPENING	Lord Jesus,
PRAYER	You told us that those who seek will find.
	Help us to look for you,
	And never lose heart,
	Knowing that you are always there to be found
	And that you love us dearly. **Amen**

OBSTACLES

Leader	Today we're going to think about obstacles – things that get in our way.

Take a view as to whether you've got time to run this race and the board game that finishes the session. If you haven't, cut from here to **Before the Gospel** *(below)*

OPTIONAL RACE

Leader	The best way to find out about obstacles is to crash into a few.

Set up an obstacle race with whatever obstacles you have to hand
Chairs are very good. Set them in lines, with hassocks or hymn books on alternate chairs. Children climb over the chairs with nothing on the seat, and crawl under the others
Divide the children into at least two teams, line them up, and set them off one by one. Make sure you have a very obvious finishing line

At the end

Congratulate the winners

Leader   Well, obstacles can be good fun, but they are a dreadful nuisance
              if you're running to catch a bus – or if you're desperate to see
              somebody.

BEFORE THE GOSPEL

Leader   Today we are going to hear about a sick man who ran an obstacle
              course to see Jesus.
              We're going to act the Gospel today.
              You guys are the crowd that clusters round Jesus.
              Make sure you surround Him when I tell you.

*The kid in the sleeping bag and his friends disappear behind the hall door, or
somewhere equally out of sight*

THE GOSPEL PROCESSION

THE GOSPEL *St Mark 2.1–12*

Narrator   Jesus returned to Capernaum

The person playing Jesus walks into the middle of the children

              And so many people collected round His house that there was no
              room left in the house, or round the front door.
              Jesus was surrounded.

Jesus sits down and the children sit round him. The Narrator joins them

              He was still preaching when some people arrived with their friend,
              a paralysed man – but they couldn't get near Jesus.
              They couldn't get through the door, or the window – then they
              looked up at the roof.
              Up they went and the next thing Jesus knew . . .
Jesus   Blessed are the peacemakers,
              Blessed are they that mourn,
              Blessed are . . .

Sound FX from the other side of the door **KNOCK KNOCK KNOCK**

Jesus   What's that noise?
Narrator   Jesus looked up *(Jesus does so)* and discovered they'd made a hole in
              the roof.

(Ad lib) Actually we can't do this bit, we'd get into deep trouble if we made a hole in the roof: you'll just have to imagine it . . .

The door opens and one of the paralytic's friends looks through

Friend 1	Hello Jesus!
Jesus	Hi guys, what are you doing up there?
Friend 2	We've got somebody who wants to see you.
Narrator	And they lowered their paralysed friend through the hole
	He was still in his bed . . .

They carry in the kid in the sleeping bag

And brought him to Jesus.
When Jesus saw their faith . . .

Jesus should grin and get up

	He went straight up to the paralysed man and said:
Jesus	My son, your sins are forgiven.
Narrator	Now some scribes were sitting there and they were irritated when they heard Jesus say this.
Some Scribes	*(Ad lib)* What did he say?
	How can He forgive sins?
	Only God can forgive sins.
Narrator	And Jesus turned to them and said,
Jesus	What's that you're saying?
	Answer me this, what is easier for me to say,
	'Your sins are forgiven' or
	'Pick up your bed and walk'?
Scribes	*(Ad lib)* Well, obviously it's easier for you to pretend you can forgive sins.
	Yeah – you tell him to get up and walk.
	Bet you can't do that . . .
Jesus	Indeed, well to show you that I am the Son of Man, and have power to do both *(turns to the paralytic)*, I order you to get up, pick up your bed and walk.
Narrator	And the paralysed man got up, rolled up his bed, and walked away – in front of them all.

He does just that, taking his cue from the Narrator

Narrator	And everybody was astonished and said,
	'We've never seen anything like this!'

AFTER THE GOSPEL

Leader   So the sick man got through to Jesus.
          But what a lot of obstacles he had to overcome.
          There he was with his legs not working and his bed in the way.
          Well, his friends picked him up and got him to the house
          but then he found lots of people in the way.
          Of course there was the roof – but how was he going to get up there?
          Or take the tiles off?
          He needed loads of things:
          Friends, ropes, a pickaxe – and something else.

Pick up the Gospel and look up the verse 'When Jesus saw their **faith** . . .'

          He needed faith: it was his faith that helped him get over all the
          obstacles. We're going to see how he did it with this game.

ACTIVITY

The board game from the CD-Rom **(CD17.1–CD17.2)**.
Smaller groups can put the game on a table and the children play individually.
Larger groups should have the board printed as large as possible and play as two
teams – try to give every child a chance to throw the die.
The game follows the fortunes of the paralytic and the things he has to acquire along
the way: stretcher, rope, friends, ladder, pickaxe and faith. Nobody can land on the
final square until they've collected a complete set of tokens.

REHEARSAL

Practise your presentation for when you go back into church (see below).

FINAL PRAYER

Leader   OK, so the paralysed man needed all sorts of things to get to Jesus –
          rope, friends, a pickaxe and a stretcher.
          But there was one thing he needed more than anything else.
          What was that? (**Faith**)
          Let's make a profession of faith now.

Ask the children to repeat the following hymn after you. Or, if you've got a musician
handy, sing it

                    I believe in God the Father
                    I believe in God the Son
                    I believe in God the Spirit,

God the Three,
And God the One. Amen

BACK IN CHURCH

Leader Today we heard about the sick man who wanted to see Jesus.
He had a terrible time – there were so many obstacles in the way.

Set up six chairs down the front
A child climbs over each obstacle as it is mentioned

Child 1 He needed a stretcher
Child 2 He needed friends
Child 3 He needed a ladder
Child 4 He needed a pickaxe
Child 5 He needed a rope
Child 6 But most of all, he needed *(The child stands on the last chair)* . . .
Faith!
Everyone He's done it!

A bumpy road to get to Jesus...

(CD17.1)

Script 18   God Camps Among Us
2 before Lent (Church of England)
St John 1.1–3, 14a

THEME

This Sunday's Gospel is the poem that starts St John's Gospel. It's a great passage – but not easy. This session focuses on the phrase 'And the Word was made flesh and dwelt among us'. The literal meaning of the Greek is 'And the Word was made flesh and pitched His tent with us' – a nice concrete idea which gives us a chance to think about tents, camping, and God living among us.

The King James Authorized Version of this passage is worth considering: it's part of the children's cultural heritage and all the words are still in common use.

SET UP

- The liturgical colour is Green.
- Rucksack with a sleeping bag inside – this is used by Leader 2, see below.
- Pictures from the CD-Rom. Print up at least ten copies of **CD18.1**, and a similar number of **CD18.2** (varying the colours). Print one of the **CD18.2** tents as large as you can for the presentation.
- Two tents, either two kids' wigwams, or some sheets over a couple of chairs (experiment if you've got the time – you may need a couple of books to weigh down the sheet, so it doesn't sag in the middle). You'll be putting them up in the course of the session.
- Two Tablets of the law (on the CD-Rom) placed inside a shoe box.
- Make some notices: 'Danger', 'Keep Out!', 'Come In!'

WELCOME *the children and lead them in* **The Sign of the Cross** ✠ (p. xxxvi).

THE KYRIE   Lord Jesus, you came to find us,
Lord have mercy
Lord have mercy

Lord Jesus, you came to help us say sorry,
Christ have mercy
Christ have mercy

Lord Jesus, you came to tell us how much God loves us,
Lord have mercy
Lord have mercy

Ask the children to repeat **The Prayer for Forgiveness** *after you* (**p. xxxvi**).

OPENING   Lord Jesus,
PRAYER   You are the Word of God
                 Help us to hear you in the Gospel this morning. **Amen**

BEFORE THE GOSPEL

Tents

Leader   *Surveying the children*
                 You're looking very bright and cheerful – I bet you all had a good
                 night's sleep.

*It will be just your luck if half of them have actually been on a sleep-over, but go with
the flow*

Tell me, who slept in a bed last night? *(React to the show of hands)*
Gosh, that's impressive.
In a room?
Wow – in a room with a roof?
Well you are a lucky lot.
Now *Name* over there wasn't half so lucky.
Yesterday he went for a walk

Leader 2 picks up his rucksack and tramps off round the room

And when night fell, he pulled out his sleeping bag *(He does)*
And laid it on the ground *(He does this too)*
And just as he was about to get in, down came the rain . . .

Leader 2 does some 'collar turned up on jacket' acting

And he had to find somewhere to shelter.

*A moment for improvisation: Leader 2 looks round and gets under a row of chairs,
or something like that*

What had he forgotten to pack? (**A tent**)
Has anyone ever been in a tent?

See what they come up with – play tents, wigwams in the garden, camping

What sort of people live in tents? (**Campers, Indians, soldiers, Arabs,
scouts and guides**)

OK, let's look at some tents.

CD18.1   *Start sticking up little tent pictures (keep one back)*

Supposing a platoon of soldiers are putting up their tents in enemy country – they're a bit worried that the enemy is near – so they pitch them like this. *(Cluster the tents in a circle)*
And if anyone turned up and wanted to pitch his tent in the middle . . .

Have the rogue tent ready

They'd have to be very sure indeed that he was a friend.

Look at the tent carefully

Hmm, OK, you can go there.

Put it in the circle

The Tent of Meeting

Right, well these are modern tents, but hundreds of years ago, long before the time of Jesus, the Jews lived in tents rather like these . . .

CD18.2

They didn't have a country of their own, so they stuck together, and always pitched their tents close together – except for one. There was always one tent on the outside.

Place the last tent well outside the ring

It was called the 'Tent of Meeting', but no one went near it.
Let's make our own Tent of Meeting – right down the end of the room.

Construct the first tent, as far away as possible

Who do you suppose lived there? *(Rhetorical question)*
If you looked inside – not that you'd dare to – all you would have seen was this:

Produce box   A box with . . .
Open it   . . . two bits of stone inside. And on the stone was written . . .
CD18.3   The Ten Commandments.
Those Commandments had been given by God Himself to the leader of the Jews – Moses.
The Jews put them in a box
Put them back   And they called the box, the Ark. And, when God visited His people, He came to the place where the Ark was resting. In the Tent.

Ask a child to put your Ark in the Tent

> Then they backed off.
> Because God is great and tremendous and fantastic – but He isn't safe.
> Only Moses could go in that Tent.
> The rest of the Jews kept well away, it was too dangerous.

Stick up your 'Danger' and 'Keep Out' notices

> Well, God actually wanted to get nearer His people than that so, when they were ready, He found another way to be among them.
> We'll hear about that in the Gospel.

THE GOSPEL PROCESSION

THE GOSPEL *St John 1.1–3, 14a*

The King James Version
In the beginning was the Word, and the Word was with God, and the Word was God.
The same was in the beginning with God.
All things were made by Him; and without Him was not anything made that was made.
And the Word was made flesh, and dwelt among us.

AFTER THE GOSPEL

Leader	*(Write up)* 'And the Word was made flesh and dwelt among us.' This is one of the greatest sentences in the whole Bible. I'll just go through it . . .
CD18.4	The 'Word' is the Son of God And being 'made flesh' means getting skin and muscle and bone and
CD18.5	becoming human. *(Put up Jesus picture)* And 'dwelt among us' means living among us, but if you read this Gospel in Greek – that's the language it was originally written in – you'd find the words coming out like this: 'And the Word became flesh and pitched his tent among us.' Jesus pitched His tent among us. Let's put up a Jesus tent. Where should it go?

Take all answers, but make sure you construct it bang in the middle of the room

> And this time there's quite a different notice on the flap:

Put up the 'Come In' notice

When God became a Human Being, we could get near Him –
Jesus came to live among us.

BEFORE THE FINAL PRAYER

If you have a very small number of kids you could perhaps get inside the tent, otherwise you'll have to put a couple inside and gather the rest in a circle outside (rather like sitting round a campfire)

Leader   Jesus came to live with His people – and He has never left them.
He pitches His tent in every church.
We find Him at the altar in the bread and wine.
He's right there among us.

MUSIC

'Living Lord' *(first line:* 'Lord Jesus Christ, you have come to us') *works well.*

FINAL   Almighty God,
PRAYER   We thank you for sending your Son
Jesus Christ
To pitch His tent among us
And live with us, as a human being. **Amen**

BACK IN CHURCH

Go back with a large copy of a tent from **CD18.2**
The children line up down the front – the child at the very end holding the tent

Leader   Today we heard that God used to visit His people in the Tent of
Meeting.

The child holds up the tent

It was so dangerous, that the Tent was put up right away from the
other tents.

The child moves even further away

But then we read the Gospel.
And we heard that, when the Son of God became a human being,
He pitched His Tent right here among us.

The tent is passed along the line until it gets to the middle

Child   'And the Word was made flesh and dwelt among us.'

Tabernacles

If your church reserves the Blessed Sacrament in a tabernacle, you may like to take an expedition after Mass to look at it. 'Tabernacle' is simply Latin for tent, and some tabernacles look rather like tents, with little cloth covers or tent flaps at the entrance.

A tabernacle is the Christian Ark and in it we place the consecrated Bread, the Body of Jesus. We genuflect when we approach it, because Jesus is there, but it isn't scary – in fact it's a good place to kneel and pray.

(CD18.1)

(CD18.2)

(CD18.3)

Specimen cartoons for this script

Script 19   The Transfiguration of Jesus

1 before Lent (Church of England)
or Lent 2 (Roman Catholic)

St Mark 9.2–9

If you are using this session for Lent 2, the liturgical colour will be Purple and you should use the opening sequence of prayers provided on page 114 for Script 21.

THEME

One way to understand the Transfiguration of Jesus is to know something about the two men who appear beside Him on the mountain: Moses and Elijah. Moses turns up again for Lent 4, so this session concentrates on Elijah – particularly his encounter with Almighty God on the top of a mountain.

SET UP

- The liturgical colour is Green.
- Pictures of mountains – your own if you've got some, skiing pictures are fine, or the mountain photos on the CD-Rom.
- Elijah pictures from the CD-Rom.

WELCOME *the children and lead them in* **The Sign of the Cross ✠ (p. xxxvi).**

THE KYRIE   Lord Jesus, you came to call us back to God,
Lord have mercy
Lord have mercy

Lord Jesus, you came to forgive us our sins,
Christ have mercy
Christ have mercy

Lord Jesus, you told sinners how much God loved them,
Lord have mercy
Lord have mercy

OPENING   God our Father,
PRAYER   James, John and Peter once heard your voice on a mountain top.
           Today help us to hear your voice in the Gospel of your Beloved Son,
           Jesus Christ. **Amen**

BEFORE THE GOSPEL

Mountains

Leader   Today I'd like to talk about mountains.
           Anyone ever been up one?

Take what comes, see if anyone has been on a mountain walk, or skiing

           Was it fun? Was it scary?
           Let's look at some.

*Show them some classic mountain shots – green meadows, rocky peaks, snow and
blue sky – then put up a picture of a mountain covered in cloud (there is a selection of
seven photos on the CD-Rom* (**CD19.1–CD19.7**), *19.5 is the cloudy one)*

           Which one would you like to go up?

*Go with the flow – perhaps some kids wouldn't like to go up any of them, that's fine
Draw your way through the following section (templates provided)
Ask the children to help you*

CD19.8   OK, let's sort out the good things and bad things about mountains.

*Good things include: the fun of climbing up, and skiing down, and the great view at
the top
Bad things include: freak storms, clouds blotting out the view (and the path), being
hit by a rock, or getting caught in an avalanche*

           Mountains are exciting things, they are grand, beautiful and
           dangerous.

Escaping to the Mountains

Leader   In the old days people didn't like mountains very much. They thought
           they were just lumps of rock, but sometimes they found them useful
           – especially when they were running away from something.
           If you had enemies after you, you could climb up a mountain – and
           disappear.
           But, of course, you would be on your own.
           And that's when a mountain might begin to feel weird.
           There you were, all alone, between earth and the sky. Suddenly God
           might seem to be very close indeed.

Elijah

Leader   Once there was a man who climbed a mountain to find God, and he
                  really did find Him – but not in the way he expected.
                  He's the chap in these pictures

Refer to the first three pictures

                  Let's hear his story
                  Ages ago, God sent a prophet to His people, the Israelites.
CD19.9   His name was Elijah.
                  The Israelites needed a prophet as they were being ruled by bad King
CD19.10   Ahab – who didn't believe in God and was persecuting those who
CD19.11   did. Elijah heard that Ahab was after him so he fled –

Re-position **CD19.9** *after* **CD19.10**

Then **CD19.12**   And got to the top of Mount Sinai – and then realized he was all
Then **CD19.13**   alone.
                  Elijah ducked down from the top, and found a cave in which to
CD19.14   spend the night. God spoke to him. 'What are you doing here,
                  Elijah?'
                  Elijah suddenly felt very sorry for himself, 'I'm here,' he said,
                  'because the Israelites have forgotten you *and* broken your altars
                  and killed anyone who believes in you – and I'm the only one left!'
                  'Go and stand before me on the top of the mountain,' said God.
                  So Elijah went to the top again – and God sent a furious wind that
CD19.15   split the rocks, but God was not in the wind. *(Remove* **CD19.15***)*
CD19.16   Then God sent an earthquake which shook the summit, but God
                  was not in the earthquake. *(Remove* **CD19.16***)*
CD19.17   Then God sent a fire that roared round Elijah but God was not in the
                  fire. *(Remove* **CD19.17***)*
CD19.18   And after the fire there was a still, small, voice.
                  And Elijah realized that God was in the quiet voice, and he covered
                  his face in his cloak, and listened hard. And God told him to go back
                  to the Israelites, find them another king – and cheer up, 7,000 of
                  them still believed in God.

Sum up

Leader   So Elijah did find God on the mountain top – or at least he heard
                  Him.
                  What did God sound like? (**Quiet**)
                  I think that's interesting. You see, there *is* something funny about
                  mountains, you can feel very close to God up there. But God isn't

like a mountain, He doesn't crash around. You have to listen hard. Jesus went up a mountain once – we'll hear about it now.

THE GOSPEL PROCESSION *if you are using this on the Sunday before Lent.*

(If you are using this for Lent 2, there is no Gospel Procession. *Ask a child to bring the Gospel book up to the front)*

THE GOSPEL *St Mark 9.2–9*

AFTER THE GOSPEL

After you've read the Gospel, draw a large basic mountain and make sure that Jesus **(CD19.19)**, *Elijah* **(CD19.9)**, *Moses* **(CD19.20)**, *and the Voice* **(CD19.21)** *are to hand. Run through it.*

Leader	Jesus went up a mountain with Peter and James and John. What happened? (**Jesus changed, His clothes shone white**)

CD19.19 *Add Jesus picture*

And did you hear who came to talk to Him? (**Elijah and Moses**)

CD19.9, CD19.20 *Add the Elijah and Moses picture*

Elijah and Moses had been dead for centuries. No wonder Jesus' friends were frightened. Then a cloud covered the mountain, and out of the cloud came a Voice.

CD19.21

Add the Voice picture

CD19.22	Who do you think was speaking? (**God**)

Yes, God the Father.

Then everything went back to normal. Jesus looked ordinary again, and they all went down.

That's a very strange story – and the disciples never forgot it. For a moment they had seen Jesus as He really was, talking to great saints from the past. And it all happened on a mountain.

ACTIVITY

Today is the day when the Church joins Peter, James and John on the mountain to hear the Voice of God telling us that Jesus is 'His Beloved Son'.
Ask the children to add the three disciples and themselves to the picture. The disciples are provided **(CD19.23)**, *the children should draw themselves into the picture or add their names.*

REHEARSAL

Practise your presentation for when you go back into church (see below).

FINAL	Today is all about listening.
PRAYER	Let's put our hands together, shut our eyes – and listen.
	Listen to the noises around us.

Ad lib on any noises you can hear – traffic, police sirens, people talking – or peaceful noises like birds, rain, or nothing at all. Any of these can be linked to the experiences of Elijah and the disciples. Loud noises aren't a problem, they needn't bother us: we hear God in quietness – actual quietness or the stillness of our hearts

> God our Father,
> Today you told us that Jesus is your Beloved Son.
> Help us to hear your Voice
> And listen to Him. **Amen**

BACK IN CHURCH

Bring in the Transfiguration picture, two kids hold it up
Point out the various components of the picture as they are mentioned

Leader	Today we've been hearing about mountains:
Child 1	Jesus climbed a mountain . . .
Child 2	With His friends, Peter, James and John.
Child 3	There they saw Moses and Elijah . . .
Child 4	And they heard God telling them that Jesus was His beloved Son.
Child 5	We decided to join Peter, James and John, so we could hear God's voice as well.

Specimen cartoons for this script

(CD19.9)   (CD19.10)

Script 20   Jesus Goes into the Desert

Lent 1

St Mark 1.12–13

Lent

It is a good idea to get children used to the variety of the Church year by giving some seasons a special character. Christmas and Easter have such strong traditions they always stand out, but the 'Purple' seasons that set them off are another matter. Lent particularly benefits from having its own traditions (a mini-desert, Lenten prayers) that turn up year after year.

You'll find that the children often do a mock wail when their candles and bells are emphatically buried on Lent 1 but, next Lent, they'll look forward to burying them again.

THEME

This session marks the break between the rest of the year and Lent as we follow Jesus into the desert at the start of His ministry. A lay 'ashing' is provided in this session if you think some of the kids weren't ashed on Ash Wednesday. But check this with your priest first.

SET UP

- The liturgical colour is Purple.
- Try to wear a purple top or tie – even socks will do.
- Stuff to make a desert:
  - A deep baking tray filled with sand.
  - Some rocks or large stones.
  - Mini cacti, or candle cacti from a florist.
  - Any suitable extras – like a toy camel.
  - Plus a large candle, that will stand by itself in the sand, to represent Jesus.
- A large box to bury your candlesticks and bells in: covered with purple paper if you've got the time.

- Large red, yellow and blue marker pens.
- Pictures from the CD-Rom.

Optional

- Ash – either see if there is any left from Ash Wednesday, or make some by burning the charcoal used for incense (it'll take a good 15 minutes) or burning up some small dry twigs. Cool the ash down with water. (You'll need a spot of water anyway to add to the ash and make it stick.)

WELCOME *the children and lead them in* **The Sign of the Cross** ✠ (**p. xxxvi**).

Leader	Did anybody notice the colour in church today? (**Purple**)
	What colour are my socks [or whatever . . .]? (**Purple**)
	We're in Purple time.
	Does anyone know what purple means in church?

Take all answers, end up by establishing . . .

Purple is a dark, serious colour, and the Church always goes into purple when we're about to get ready for something.
What are we getting ready for?

Give some hints – it's almost impossible to trigger the word 'Easter' without mentioning chocolate

(**Easter**)

Absolutely, Easter – ages away, not for another six weeks.
But Easter is so important that we start getting ready six weeks before.
Those six weeks have a special name – does anyone know it? (**Lent**)

OPTIONAL ASHING

Leader	Lent started last Wednesday when people came to church to be 'ashed'.
	We start Lent by putting a cross on our foreheads.
	It's made of ash *(show them the ash)*
	We do this to show:
	This is Lent,
	We're sorry for the things we've done wrong,
	And we're going to return to God.
	This is how you ash somebody . . .

Another Leader ashes you with the words 'Return to God'

Leader   Amen.

Ash the children . . .

                    Return to God.
Children   Amen.

Finish with **The Kyrie**

If you haven't ashed the children, introduce the Kyrie by saying:

                    As we start the holy season of Lent, let us call to mind the things
                    we've done wrong and ask God to forgive us.

THE KYRIE   Lord Jesus, you came to call us back to God,
                    Lord have mercy
                    Lord have mercy

                    Lord Jesus, you fasted in the desert,
                    Christ have mercy
                    Christ have mercy

                    Lord Jesus, you told sinners how much God loved them,
                    Lord have mercy
                    Lord have mercy

Ask the children to repeat **The Prayer for Forgiveness** *after you* (**p. xxxvi**).

There is no Opening Prayer, go straight into the Lent procession

Leader   OK, Lent is such a serious time that we get rid of some of the fun
                    things we do in church.
                    This morning we're going to bury our bells and candles in that box
                    over there.

Somebody holds up the box at the other end of the room
*Dish out the bells and candles and practise killing the bell sound by cueing the children
in, and stopping them with the 'kill that!' cue (a finger across throat). Make sure you
give the cue bang in the middle of a ding*
Set up a procession of kids to take the bells and candles to the box

LENT PROCESSION

The children hold the candles high and ring the bells
Everything goes silent as the objects go into the box

Leader   Right, now we're ready for Lent.
                Jesus understands about getting ready.
                Before He began His ministry, He got ready Himself,
                let's hear how He did it.

There is no Gospel Procession in Lent
One child brings the Gospel up from the back

THE GOSPEL *St Mark 1.12–13*

Start the Gospel reading with the words 'After Jesus was baptized . . .'

AFTER THE GOSPEL

Deserts
Leader   So, after His Baptism, the Spirit sent Jesus off into – where did He
                go? (**The desert**)
                You're right, the desert.
                Let's think about deserts – can anyone draw one for me?

Offer the volunteer a choice of marker pens, blue, red, yellow

                Which do you think the best colour would be?

Yellow probably, unless they've seen the red deserts of Australia or the USA
The child normally draws a bumpy yellow line – comment on whatever you get and
establish that deserts are bare and dry

                Has anyone been to a desert?

See if you can elicit a desert story – one of the other Leaders may have one – this is
one that I use. Ask another Leader to tell it

Gary in the Desert

Leader 2   My friend Gary once tramped through a desert in Israel.
CD20.1   He was with a group of friends and they went further than they
                meant and found night was falling before they could get back. One
                of the odd things about deserts is that, though they're very hot in
                the daytime, they cool down fast at night, so Gary looked round for
                some shelter, and saw a ruin on the horizon.
                He and his mates went towards it and found an old Crusader castle.

CD20.2

It was nothing but crumbling stone, no doors or windows, but it was better than sitting out on the sand, so they huddled against an ancient wall.

The sun went down, the stars came out, and Gary thought the desert seemed even more lonely than usual. Then he began to hear things: wind blowing through the gaps in the wall, a dead tree creaking, and – far off – this noise *(imitate the howl of a wolf)* . . .

'Ow-ow-ow . . .' What do you suppose that was?

Take all answers – establish that it's the sound of a wolf

Gary and his friends looked at each other. 'Wolves!' they said, 'what shall we do?'

Well, Gary had read *The Hobbit* as a little boy and he remembered that Bilbo and the dwarfs kept some wolves at bay with a camp fire. 'Why don't we burn that dead tree?' he said. 'Good idea!' said the others and they broke it up and set light to it.

It was the worst thing they could have done.

The wolves, when they saw the light, ran to the castle to see what was happening.

CD20.3

And, the next thing Gary and his friends knew, they were surrounded by dozens of yellow eyes all glinting in the firelight.

I was horrified when Gary got to this bit of the story and said, 'What did you do, Gary?'

'Oh well,' said Gary, 'You can't sit up all night worrying about wolves so we all fell asleep . . .'

And that's the story. I don't know what happened to the wolves but,

CD20.4

as Gary lived to tell the tale, I suppose they fell asleep too.

ACTIVITY

If you elect to tell the above story, you can refer back to the Gospel and discover that there were wild beasts in Jesus' desert. Fortunately He had angels on hand to help Him as well.

Leader

Deserts can be scary places – but they are beautiful in a bare sort of way.

Let's make one.

Bring the 'Desert Tray' forward filled with sand only

This is our desert . . .

Run the sand through your fingers

It's very dry . . .
The only things you'd see there would be **rocks** . . .

Get the kids to put in the rocks

The only things that grow would be **cactuses** . . .

A child puts in the cactus

The only animals that could live there would be weird things like **camels** . . .

In goes the camel

But there's Jesus, praying in the middle of it – this **candle** represents Jesus.

A child places the candle

BEFORE THE FINAL PRAYER

Gather the kids round the desert, light the candle

Leader   So that's the desert, it's very rocky, and lonely – and Jesus was there for 40 days.
It's very good prayer – and very short.
Why do you suppose He did that?

Take all answers. Establish that Jesus wanted some time to be alone with God

Jesus took time out to pray.
That is something we could try.
How about us all making the Sign of the Cross when we get up or go to bed this Lent?
It's a very good prayer – and very short.

REHEARSAL

Practise your presentation for when you go back into church (see below).

FINAL PRAYER

Lead the children in **The Sign of the Cross** ✠ (**p. xxxvi**).

Ask the children to repeat the following prayer after you

Lord Jesus,
This Lent, help us to return to you
To pray to you
And love you.

Help us to see you more clearly,
Love you more dearly,
And follow you more nearly,
Day by day. Amen

MUSIC

The traditional hymn 'Forty days and forty nights' *(verses 1, 2 and 6) gives a graphic account of Jesus in the desert.*

BACK IN CHURCH

You will need a Leader, three children and the desert

Leader	This Lent we are going to follow Jesus into the desert . . .

Bring the desert forward

Child 1	This is our 'desert'. *(She runs some sand through her fingers)*
Child 2	It's dry, and rocky and very lonely. *(Holds up a rock)*
Child 3	And it's full of strange animals. *(Holds up the camel – or whatever you've got)*
Leader	But Jesus is there in the middle. *(Lifts up the lighted Jesus candle – careful of the wax . . .)*

(CD20.4)

(CD20.1)

Specimen cartoons for this script

Script 21   Following Our Leader

Lent 2 (Church of England)

St Mark 8.31–34

The Gospel read in the Roman Catholic Church today is St Mark 9.2–9: you will find it in Script 19.

THEME

Following a leader can be fun, especially if it's a game, and following Jesus was obviously a wonderful adventure for the first disciples. Today's Gospel marks the moment when He warned them that following Him was tougher than it looked.

SET UP

- The liturgical colour is Purple.
- No candles or bells.
- 'Desert Tray' plus the Jesus candle to hand.
- Ask a lively grown-up, or reliable kid, to lead the game (see below).
- Some pitta bread or anything that's quick and easy to divide up and eat.
- Small processional cross.

LEAVING CHURCH

Whatever you do on other Sundays, this Sunday make sure the children process out behind the Gospel book.

WELCOME *the children and lead them in* **The Sign of the Cross** ✠ **(p. xxxvi).**

THE KYRIE   Lord Jesus, you came to call us back to God,
Lord have mercy
Lord have mercy

Lord Jesus, you fasted in the desert,
Christ have mercy
Christ have mercy

Lord Jesus, you told sinners how much God loved them,
Lord have mercy
Lord have mercy

Ask the children to repeat **The Prayer for Forgiveness** *after you* (**p. xxxvi**).

Run a brief résumé on Lent – the colour in church and the fact we're getting ready for Easter (see Script 20)

Leader   This Lent, we're thinking about Jesus, praying in the desert.

Bring the 'Desert Tray' forward

This is our desert – *(Run the sand through your fingers)*
It's very dry,
Very rocky,
Very lonely,
But Jesus is there in the middle. *(Place the Jesus candle)*
Jesus prayed in the desert
So let's copy Him.

Light the candle and ask the children to repeat after you:

OPENING   Lord Jesus,
PRAYER   **This Lent, help us to return to you**
                            To pray to you
                            And love you.

                            Help us to see you more clearly,
                            Love you more dearly,
                            And follow you more nearly,
                            Day by day. Amen

Follow My Leader

Leader   Today is about being a follower. *(Ask the children to form a line)*
                            Right, if you're a follower, you need someone to follow.
                            Follow me!

Lead them round the room in the game 'Follow my Leader'. The children have to copy exactly what you do. Do fairly sedate things – like hopping, walking backwards – all at a moderate pace

                            Yup, you've got the idea. Actually, I think it's easy to follow me –
                            supposing I turn you over to *Name?*

Hand over to an energetic Leader. He starts with hands outstretched like an aeroplane and gets the line to swoop a bit, then moves on to whatever strikes him as fun (head over heels, pretending to be a train, cartwheels, anything). Don't go really fast until the end, then bring them to an abrupt halt
Congratulate the children and ask them to sit down

You might have noticed I didn't follow *Name* – it was much too difficult.
Now Jesus' friends were often called His Followers – and they loved it.
They followed Jesus round Galilee, listening to Him teach and watching Him heal people. But there came a day when Jesus told them that following Him was much tougher than they realized.
We'll hear about that in the Gospel.

There is no Gospel Procession in Lent. Ask a child to bring the Gospel book down to the front

THE GOSPEL *St Mark 8.31–34*

AFTER THE GOSPEL

Run through the Gospel with the children

Leader   What did Jesus say would happen to Him?
          (**He'd be rejected/killed**)

Some children may have spotted He also said **He'd come back to life**

Which bit of that do you suppose upset St Peter?
(**Jesus would be killed**)
Peter didn't want to hear that Jesus would be killed, he told Jesus to be quiet – and Jesus had to be very tough indeed.
'Peter,' He said, 'you are talking like Satan – get away from me!'
Well, Peter stuck with Jesus, but from that moment onwards he realized it might be dangerous.
Let's follow our Leader again, but this time the Leader is Jesus.

FOLLOWING JESUS

Another Leader goes to the other end of the room

Leader 2   Follow me and I will make you fishers of men.
Leader 1   OK, let's run over to Jesus. *(The kids do so)*
Leader 2   Right, I want you to do what I do:
          If I kneel to pray – so do you

> If I walk round Galilee, follow me
> If I stop for something to eat, gather round

Leader 2 takes the children round the room, comments on what he or she is doing as they go round Galilee – jumping brooks, climbing hills, rowing across the lake – the children follow all these actions. Stop every now and then to pray
Lap the room a couple of times, and finish at the end of it. Ask the children to sit down and have a picnic with you (divide some pitta bread among them)

Leader 1   But there came a moment when Jesus did something else – just watch him.

Leader 2 stands – the kids stay sitting

He went to Jerusalem – and was handcuffed.

Leader 2 puts his wrists together

He was beaten up.

Leader 2 flinches and tries to protect his face

And He was given a cross to carry through the streets.

Somebody hands Leader 2 the cross, he walks over to the children carrying it

And Jesus' friends remembered how Jesus had said,
'If anyone wants to come with me, he must forget himself, carry his cross and follow me.'
Let's follow Jesus.

The children follow the cross to the front, and gather round

REHEARSAL

Practise your presentation for when you go back into church (see below).

FINAL   Let's kneel before the Cross of Jesus.
PRAYER   *(Ask the children to repeat this prayer after you)*

Lord Jesus Christ,
By your Holy ✠ Cross
You have saved the world. Amen

As the message today is rather sobering, you may want to reassure the children that, however difficult following Jesus may be, He'll always be beside us. Two hymns pick up these themes very well:

MUSIC

The traditional hymn 'Take up thy cross', *particularly verses 1, 2 and 4, or the modern hymn* 'Do not be afraid' *which is excellent, verses 1 and 5.*

Form up behind the crucifix and go back to church

BACK IN CHURCH

The children process into church behind the crucifix

Child 1	At the start of Mass we all processed out of church behind the Gospel.
Child 2	But we've come back behind the cross.
Child 3	That is because, in the Gospel today, Jesus told us to 'take up our cross and follow Him'.

Script 22   Cleansing the Temple

Lent 3

St John 2.13–22

THEME

A straightforward telling of the Gospel story. The children imitate Jesus by finding, then ejecting, all the sheep hidden round the room.

SET UP

- The liturgical colour is Purple.
- No candles or bells.
- The 'Desert Tray' plus the Jesus candle to hand.
- Any toy farm animals you can gather, the larger the better: sheep, cows, goats (no pigs!).
- Pictures from the CD-Rom. Two are of doors into a church and the Temple. Try to make these fairly big, so you can slit them down the middle and open them as you would a door.
- Set up a Sheep Hunt: print up the sheep from the CD-Rom **(CD22.1)** and hide them round the room – Blu-Tacking them along the skirting board, under the chairs and so on.
- Shoe box or similar to put the sheep in.

WELCOME *the children and lead them in* **The Sign of the Cross** ✠ **(p. xxxvi).**

THE KYRIE   Lord Jesus, you came to call us back to God,
Lord have mercy
Lord have mercy

Lord Jesus, you fasted in the desert,
Christ have mercy
Christ have mercy

Lord Jesus, you told sinners how much God loved them,
Lord have mercy

Lord have mercy

Ask the children to repeat **The Prayer for Forgiveness** *after you* (**p. xxxvi**).

Résumé on Lent

Leader	Well, we're still in Purple time.
	Can anyone remember what this season is called? (**Lent**)
	Quite right, Lent.
	Lent is a time when we give up things – we've given up our bells and candles.
	Some Christians give up eating chocolate, or watching TV.

Ask a couple of leaders what they have given up . . .
(Check this first – it's not the moment to discover they haven't given anything up at all)
The children may want to tell you what they have given up – but don't quiz them, some kids may be rather panic-stricken at the idea

Lent is a time when people give up things, or come to church a bit more, or read their Bibles. We do this to get ready for Easter.
We're getting ready for Easter by thinking about Jesus praying in the desert. *(Bring the 'Desert Tray' forward)*
This is our desert. *(Run the sand through your fingers)*
It's very dry
Very rocky
Very lonely
But Jesus is there in the middle.

Place the Jesus candle
Light the candle and ask the children to repeat after you:

OPENING PRAYER	Lord Jesus,
	This Lent, help us to return to you
	To pray to you
	And love you.
	Help us to see you more clearly,
	Love you more dearly,
	And follow you more nearly,
	Day by day. Amen

BEFORE THE GOSPEL

Walking into Church

Put up the two large doors from the CD-Rom which you have placed on top of two disgraceful scenes: footballers celebrating a victory in the church, and loads of sheep and shopkeepers making a row in the Temple

Leader	I've got two doors behind me. This one is the door to a church.
	Now, supposing it's Sunday, I come along to church – open the
CD22.2	door *(Open it)* What do I find? Good heavens, blokes
CD22.3	singing football songs! Disgraceful! What do I do?

Take all answers; the little ones will probably tell you to walk in and tell them to be quiet, older kids will suggest you tiptoe away

I think I'll just shut this door *(do so)* and slip away.

Move over to the other set of doors

CD22.4	Right, now *these* are the doors to the Temple in Jerusalem.
	One day Jesus went to the Temple to pray and He opened the doors – *(Open them up)*
CD22.5	Good heavens! The Temple is full of animals!

Move away from the picture as you explain it

Actually people used to bring animals to the Temple to sacrifice them to God.
They could buy animals there as well – and the entrance was jammed up with sheep pens, and bird cages, and shopkeepers.
All making the most horrible noise.
Let's hear what it sounded like:

Temple Noises

Get one set of kids to moo like cows; another to baa like sheep. Add any other noises that seem appropriate
Ask the other Leaders and grown-ups to shout 'shopkeeper remarks' like:
'Three lambs for the price of two!'
Practise cueing them in: cows first; then sheep; then shopkeepers
Kill the noise with a finger across the throat

Leader	Right, let's re-run that moment when Jesus went up to the Temple to pray. *(Shut the doors)*
	When I open them, off you go . . .

Open the doors – pandemonium – then kill it

Yup, that sounded ghastly!

What do you suppose Jesus did when He heard it? I can't imagine Him tiptoeing away. We'll find out in the Gospel.

There is no Gospel Procession in Lent. Ask a child to bring the Gospel book down to the front

THE GOSPEL *St John 2.13–22*

Optional Paraphrase

Now the feast of Passover was about to happen and Jesus went up to Jerusalem. And in the Temple He found people selling oxen and sheep and pigeons, and other people changing money. Making a whip of cords, He drove all of them, sheep and oxen, everything, out of the Temple, and He knocked over the coins of the money-changers and overturned their tables. And He told those who sold the pigeons, 'Take these things away; you are not to make my Father's house a market place!'

AFTER THE GOSPEL

Leader   Jesus was really angry. What did He do?
                (He whipped out the shopkeepers, and the animals, and turned over their tables)
                Right, let's get rid of these things from the Temple.

Remove the animal/shopkeeper picture from the Temple and put it in a shoe box or something similar

                Hmm, I'm pretty sure I haven't got rid of all the animals . . . Aha!

Find a sheep that has mysteriously got itself Blu-Tacked to the underside of a chair

                Let's find the rest.

Send the children off to hunt sheep

The Sheep Hunt

Once it's all over, dump the sheep into the shoe box

Leader   That's what's called 'Cleansing the Temple' . . .
                Jesus cleaned up the Temple. Why did He do that?

Take all answers. Establish that a church is a quiet holy place, where people come to pray

REHEARSAL

Produce the animal toys and hand them to some of the children. Practise your presentation to take back into church (see below). (If you haven't managed to acquire any toys, use some sheep from the sheep hunt.)

FINAL PRAYER

Settle the children for prayer.

MUSIC

If you have the resources, some quiet music on a CD player, or the song 'Be still, for the presence of the Lord' *will help to create the right atmosphere.*

Leader	Have you ever gone into church when there's no service going on? It's very quiet. Let's see how quiet we can be . . . *(Give them a chance to be quiet)*
	Lord Jesus You prayed to your Father in the quiet of the desert, Help us to be still To cut out the noise And pray to God in the quiet of our hearts. **Amen**

BACK IN CHURCH

Place two sets of children on each side of the sanctuary step: one set hold the toy animals

Leader	Today we cleansed the hall. We found all these people in it, selling sheep and making a dreadful noise . . .

The kids with the animals hold them up and start baa-ing (put some grown-ups with them, they may have stage-fright). Kill the noise

And we chased them out . . .

Cue in the noise, and then cue the other group of children to flap their arms and say 'Shoo!'. *The first set of kids put the animals behind their backs and fall silent*

We did this because Jesus said that His Father's House should be a House of Prayer.

Script 23 Mums and the Brass Snake

Lent 4 or Mothering Sunday

St John 19.25b–27 (Church of England)
or St John 3.14–16 (Roman Catholic Church)

THEME

Today is a 'Pink' Sunday, when the vestments and the liturgy lighten up. The traditional sentence that begins Mass today starts with the word 'Laetare' (Latin for 'Rejoice!') and this Sunday is sometimes known as Laetare – but it's just as likely to be called Lent 4, Mothering Sunday or Refreshment Sunday.

There are two possible Gospel readings for today. Check with your priest as to which your church is going to use.

This session uses both Gospels: one is about the Virgin Mary standing at the foot of the Cross, and the other records Jesus' saying about Moses and the Brass Serpent. (Not an obvious choice for a Pink Sunday perhaps, but children are always intrigued by snakes.)

SET UP

- The liturgical colour is Rose, though the churches that don't have a rose set of vestments will still be in Purple. If you flag up the changes in liturgical colour in your Children's Church, try to find a pink drape.
- Wear a pink garment.
- The 'Desert Tray' plus the Jesus candle to hand.
- Pictures from the CD-Rom.
- An image of the Virgin Mary – an icon, a little statue, poster or a postcard.
- A Bible scroll – make this by sticking the text of Numbers 21.6–8 on to a large stiffish bit of paper and rolling it up.

Paste in the Bible text

roll the scroll from both ends

Tie with ribbon

- A toy snake (joke and party shops sell them).
- A crucifix or a small processional cross.
- The 'Hail Mary' cards (see page xxii), or the materials to make them (see page 128): 10 pieces of card and some brightly coloured marker pens. (An alternative to the 'Hail Mary' is provided below.)

WELCOME *the children and lead them in* **The Sign of the Cross** ✠ (**p. xxxvi**).

THE KYRIE   Lord Jesus, you came to call us back to God,
                     Lord have mercy
                     Lord have mercy

                     Lord Jesus, you fasted in the desert,
                     Christ have mercy
                     Christ have mercy

                     Lord Jesus, you told sinners how much God loved them,
                     Lord have mercy
                     Lord have mercy

Ask the children to repeat **The Prayer for Forgiveness** *after you* (**p. xxxvi**).

Leader   We're in Lent, there are no candles or bells today, instead
                     we've got our desert.

Bring the 'Desert Tray' forward
                     We've been in the desert for three weeks.

Run the sand through your fingers
                     It's very dry
                     Very rocky
                     Very lonely
                     But Jesus is there in the middle.

Place the Jesus candle
                     Jesus prayed in the desert
                     So let's copy Him.

Light the candle and ask the children to repeat after you

OPENING
PRAYER

Lord Jesus,
This Lent, help us to return to you
To pray to you
And love you.

Help us to see you more clearly,
Love you more dearly,
And follow you more nearly,
Day by day. Amen

Leader

OK it's still Lent, we're still fasting

Optional Pink Moment

Leader

But something's changed, what is it?
Yes, the altar *(or whatever)* is draped in pink.
I'm in pink, *Name* is wearing his pink socks – *Name* is in pink and so is *Name (choose any child you see in pink)*.
It's a Pink Sunday, there's one in Advent and one in Lent.
It's a moment to lighten up.

Mothers

Leader

There's some people who are feeling very cheerful today, can you guess who they are? *(Give some hints)*
Is there anyone at home who got a card today, or some flowers?
Yes, our mothers.
Today is Mother's Day, or Mothering Sunday.
I'd like to think about mothers for a moment, especially Jesus' mother.

CD23.1   Who was it who told Jesus to tidy His bedroom?
CD23.2   Or eat up His nice chicken soup?
CD23.3   Or do His homework?

His Mother. *(Image of the Virgin Mary)*
What was Jesus' mother's name? (**Mary**)
And what do we often call her? (**Our Lady**)
Now, I imagine that Jesus only had to be told once to do any of these ghastly things, but we can be quite sure that Our Lady brought Him up properly. I bet she made sure He read His Bible.
One reason I'm sure of this is that Jesus knew His Bible so well, even the odd bits: the sort of things you'd only know if you read a book over and over again.

Jesus' Bible would have looked like this *(Produce the scroll)*
And in it He would have found this strange story:

Open up the scroll – and read Numbers 21.6–8

Optional Paraphrase

When the Jews were wandering in the desert, poisonous snakes came among them and bit them, and many died. But God commanded Moses to make a brass snake, and put it on a pole, and lift it up. And anybody who looked up at the brass snake got better.

Leader	That's a weird story.
I expect Jesus thought it was odd too.
But He never forgot it.
What seems to have interested Him was that something that hurt you – like a snake – could be turned by God into something that healed you.
In fact God could even use a pretend snake to heal His people.
We've got a snake here . . . *(Make it hiss and lunge at the kids)*
Is it really dangerous? (**No!**)
Why not? (**Because it's pretend**)
Yup, it's only made of plastic *(Or whatever)*
And the one Moses showed the Jews was made of brass. It was a snake that looked as dangerous as a real snake, but once it was lifted up *(Lift it up, this is important!)* it could heal people.
Let's see what Jesus made of that in the Gospel.

There is no Gospel Procession in Lent. Ask a child to bring the Gospel book down to the front

THE GOSPEL *St John 3.14–16*

Optional Paraphrase

Jesus said, 'Just as Moses lifted up the brass snake in the desert, in the same way shall I be lifted up. So that everyone who believes in me may have eternal life. For God so loved the world that He gave His only Son so that everyone who believes in Him, should not die but have eternal life.'

AFTER THE GOSPEL

Leader	Well, that's a rather odd Gospel too.
Jesus said that just as the snake would be lifted up . . .

Get another Leader to lift the snake

> He would be lifted up.

> And, just as the snake healed people,
> He would give those who believed in Him eternal life.
> What could He mean. When was Jesus lifted up?

Take all answers, bring forward the crucifix, lift it up

> Jesus meant His crucifixion.
> The cross was a horrible thing, people died on it.
> But, even so, the moment Jesus was nailed to the cross, it turned into
> something that could heal.

BEFORE THE FINAL PRAYER

Hold the cross above the children

Leader 1   The Gospel today said that Jesus would be lifted up.
Here He is, lifted above us.
When He was on the cross He looked down and saw two people
standing below Him.
Does anyone know who they were? (**Mary and John**)
Yes, His mother Mary and His friend John.
And Jesus spoke to them:

Leader 2   *Reads St John 19.25b–27*

Leader 1   So even on the cross, Jesus remembered His mother.
Let's remember her too.

ACTIVITY

Either see how fast the children can assemble the 'Hail Mary' cards – or ask the children to make a set themselves, shuffle them, and reassemble them at speed. The Hail Mary prayer is split into these sections:

1 Hail Mary
2 Full of Grace
3 The Lord is with thee
4 Blessed art thou among women
5 And blessed is the fruit of thy womb, Jesus
6 Holy Mary
7 Mother of God
8 Pray for us sinners
9 Now, and at the hour of our death
10 Amen

If the Hail Mary is not a prayer used in your church, use this one instead:

1 God our Father
2 We thank you
3 For the Virgin Mary
4 Help us to love her
5 Just as your Son loved her
6 And grant that one day we will
7 Join her in Heaven
8 And live with you and your saints
9 For ever
10 Amen

REHEARSAL

Practise your presentation for when you go back into church (see below).

FINAL PRAYER

Hail Mary . . .

Or the alternative

BACK IN CHURCH

Line up ten children down the front with the cards, blank side towards the congregation. The rest of the children are on the side.

Leader   Today we thought about Our Lady.
             How she brought Jesus up
             How she was with Him in Jerusalem
             And stood at the foot of the Cross.
             The children have made this prayer for her.

The children whip up the cards in order as they all say the prayer

Script 24 A Grain of Wheat

Lent 5

St John 12.23–24

THEME

The Gospels in Lent can be quite distressing as we realize that Jesus has set His face towards Jerusalem and is walking steadily to His death. But Jesus wasn't death-haunted; all His predictions of the Passion have seeds of hope in them. This session introduces the children to the idea that death couldn't hold Jesus and, as a result of His victory, it can't hold us either.

SET UP

- The liturgical colour is Purple.
- The 'Desert Tray' plus the Jesus candle to hand.
- Pictures from the CD-Rom.
- Packet of seeds.
- Paper flower shapes from the CD-Rom. Try to replicate them on quite heavy paper. They are such an easy shape to draw, you or the kids may make some yourselves.
- Large glass bowl, jug of water.

WELCOME *the children and lead them in* **The Sign of the Cross ✠ (p. xxxvi).**

THE KYRIE   Lord Jesus, you came to call us back to God,
Lord have mercy
Lord have mercy

Lord Jesus, you fasted in the desert,
Christ have mercy
Christ have mercy

Lord Jesus, you told sinners how much God loved them,
Lord have mercy
Lord have mercy

Ask the children to repeat **The Prayer for Forgiveness** *after you* (**p. xxxvi**).

Leader　　　　　　We're coming up to the end of Lent
　　　　　　　　　And we're still with Jesus in the desert.

Bring the 'Desert Tray' forward and run the sand through your fingers

　　　　　　　　　It's very dry
　　　　　　　　　Very rocky
　　　　　　　　　Very lonely
　　　　　　　　　But Jesus is there in the middle *(place the Jesus candle)*
　　　　　　　　　Let's say our Lent prayer together.

Light the candle and ask the children to repeat after you

OPENING　　　　Lord Jesus,
PRAYER　　　　　This Lent, help us to return to you
　　　　　　　　　To pray to you
　　　　　　　　　And love you.

　　　　　　　　　Help us to see you more clearly,
　　　　　　　　　Love you more dearly,
　　　　　　　　　And follow you more nearly,
　　　　　　　　　Day by day. Amen

BEFORE THE GOSPEL

Leader　　　　　　We've got to the Fifth Sunday of Lent.
　　　　　　　　　This is the moment when Jesus decided to go to Jerusalem and finish
　　　　　　　　　the job God had sent Him to do.
　　　　　　　　　He knew He'd probably be killed, but He knew something else –
　　　　　　　　　that His death would bring life to everyone else.
　　　　　　　　　Let's hear that in the Gospel

There is no Gospel Procession in Lent. Ask a child to bring the Gospel book down to the front

THE GOSPEL *St John 12.23–24*

Optional Paraphrase

Jesus said to His friends, 'The time has come for the Son of Man to be glorified. Truly, truly, I say to you if a grain of wheat falls on the ground, it will never be more than one grain unless it dies. But if it dies it will produce many grains.'

AFTER THE GOSPEL

Leader	Bits of this Gospel are quite difficult.
	Let's think about that first sentence:
	'The time has come for the Son of Man to be glorified.'
	Well, the Son of Man is Jesus, so He must be saying,
	'The time has come for me to be glorified.'
	But what does *glorified* mean?
	Here are some pictures of people being *glorified*.

Put up pictures from the CD-Rom of people getting medals, hearing their exam results, shaken, getting wreaths and so on. Talk them through

CD24.1	These people have won races, or been brave in battle, or even got
CD24.2	to Heaven. This is the moment when they make it – everyone can see
CD24.3	they've won.
and CD24.4	Being glorified is great.
	But when Jesus said He'd be *glorified*, He meant being nailed to the Cross. How can that be anything to do with glory?
	Well, on the Cross, we believe that Jesus faced the powers of evil and dared them to do their worst. And they did: He died.
	But what the powers of evil didn't realize was that killing Jesus meant He entered the world of the dead.
CD24.5	*Jesus in His tomb*
and CD24.6	*A separate stone*
	There He is, safely dead. All you have to do is roll a stone over the opening *(do so)* and that's that.
	But death was far too weak to contain Jesus.
	What happened next? (**He rose from the dead**)
	Yup, He bust out of that tomb.
CD24.7	*Jesus busts out*
	And in doing so destroyed death.
	On the Cross, Jesus realized He'd won. He called out 'I've done it!'
	That was the moment He was glorified.
	Now how was He going to get His disciples to understand?
	Well, He took some seeds.

Hold up a packet, pour some seeds into your hand

	Look at them, really dry and shrivelled, they look half-dead already.
	Now if you bury a seed, what happens? (**It'll grown into a plant**)
	Yes, but what happens to the seed? If you dug the plant up,

would the seed still be there? (**No**)

The seed would have gone. When a seed turns into a plant, it splits and bursts open, and a shoot comes up one way, and a root the other way.

Draw this. Template provided **(CD24.8)**

And the seed disappears. It's as though it has died.

But when you look at the plant . . .

Draw an ear of wheat **(CD24.9)** *template*

And pull off a grain, what do you find? (**More seeds**)

So, by dying, one seed has produced something bursting with life.

Jesus was telling His friends that He was like that seed.

He'd have to die, but His death was the beginning of more life, loads of life. Jesus springing out of the grave and all those little seeds (that's us!) able to beat death too.

ACTIVITY

Leader

Now we've got to explain this to the people back in church.

We haven't got time for a grain of wheat to grow, so we'll do something a bit faster.

Bring forward a glass bowl, fill it with water. Show the children one of the flower shapes. You will have already folded it tightly up (instructions on **CD24.10***) so they won't realize what it is*

OK, here's a really tightly folded bit of paper.

Look at it, all scrunched up and unhappy.

Hold it to your ear

Yup, I can hear it's really miserable.

I think it needs a bit of help from us.

Float the shape on the water, its petals will open as if by magic

Can you do that?

Offer the children some more tightly folded shapes. Watch the petals opening

You see life always wins – even with little paper flowers. They have to open up, look good, and cheer up.

Ask the children to make their own flower shapes. If there's time, they can write negative words like 'Anger' or 'Grief' on one side of the flower, with positive equivalents ('Joy', 'Love') on the coloured side. Make sure they fold them so that the cheerful message is the one that opens up

Sum up

Leader   Jesus said, 'Truly, I say to you, if a grain of wheat falls on the ground, it will just stay one grain – unless it dies. But if it dies, it will produce many grains.'

FINAL   Eternal God,
PRAYER   You sent Jesus to destroy death.
We pray that, by His victory, we too may overcome death
And live with you for ever
In your heavenly Kingdom
Where you live with the Son and the Holy Spirit. **Amen**

BACK IN CHURCH

Take the bowl and some fresh water back to church, plus the children, all armed with their folded-up flower shapes

Leader   Today we heard Jesus saying that if a grain of wheat fell into the ground and died, it would produce many more grains.

Child 1   We thought that Jesus was telling us that He was like that grain of wheat.

Child 2   And we thought we'd show you how quickly things can come back to life.

Child 3   *Holding up its folded-up flower*
We've all got little bits of paper folded up:
Watch this!

Someone pours the water into the bowl. The children float their flower shapes
They open up

Child 4   You see, we've got a bowl full of flowers!

(CD24.1)   (CD24.2)   (CD24.3)

Specimen cartoons for this script

Script 25   Palms to Crosses

Palm Sunday

St John 12.12–16 (Church of England),
St Mark 11.1–10 (Roman Catholic Church)

THEME

This session will use the Gospel, read at the beginning of the service, which describes Jesus' Entry into Jerusalem. Two Palm Sunday Gospels are on offer – one from St John and the other from St Mark – check whichever your church is using.

You will obviously have to fit round whatever your church does on Palm Sunday: the priest will probably bless and distribute palm crosses at the beginning of the service and there might be a procession.

In this session the children will re-tell the story of Palm Sunday by making a donkey, a palm to lay at its feet and (by an adroit set of origami folds) a little paper cross from their palm drawing.

SET UP

- The liturgical colour is Red – make sure there is something red in the hall, even if it's only your jumper.
- The 'Desert Tray' minus the candle.
- White or purple cloth to lay on top of the desert (see below).
- (If you have other devotional objects in the hall, cover them up with a white or purple cloth.)
- Arrange the room for a craft session: setting up tables, or clearing a bit of the platform.
- Donkey cut-outs from the CD-Rom.
- Enough strands of wool and wooden clothes pegs for each child to make a donkey (instructions on the CD-Rom).
- A5 sheets of paper, green marker pens for the palms (template on the CD-Rom). The template also includes instructions for making some origami folds to turn the palm into a cross. It is dead easy, and the transformation looks like magic.
- One A4 sheet of paper, on which you have drawn some palm leaves, for an origami demonstration.

- Scissors (some of them child-friendly).
- Palm crosses.

WELCOME *the children and lead them in* **The Sign of the Cross** ✠ (**p. xxxvi**).

THE KYRIE	Lord Jesus, This week you allowed your enemies to capture you, Lord have mercy **Lord have mercy**
	Lord Jesus, This week you carried your cross, Christ have mercy **Christ have mercy**
	Lord Jesus, This week you died on the cross for us, Lord have mercy **Lord have mercy**

Ask the children to repeat **The Prayer for Forgiveness** *after you* (**p. xxxvi**).

OPENING PRAYER	Lord Jesus, Today you entered Jerusalem on a donkey As you did so, the Jewish children sang your praises Help us follow their example And sing your praises this morning. **Amen**

BEFORE THE GOSPEL

Leader	This is the last Sunday in Lent, and suddenly the colour has changed. Did anyone spot the new colour in church?

Give them a hint – what colour is my jumper? (**Red**)

Red is the colour we use when we remember Christians who've died for their faith. But today we use it to remember Jesus Himself, because today is the start of Holy Week, the last week of Jesus' earthly life.

The Church goes into mourning this week and we cover up all our pictures and crucifixes and statues, so we can concentrate on Jesus Himself.

I guess we'd better cover up our desert. *(Pull it out)*

Here it is, with its rocks and sand and cactuses.
Can anyone see what's missing? (**The Jesus candle**)
Yes, Jesus has moved on.
We'll find out where He is in a minute, but first we'll put the desert away. *(Ask a child forward to lay the cloth over the desert)*

Put the desert away

OK, where did Jesus go today? Let's find out in the Gospel.

Ask a child to bring the Gospel to the front

THE GOSPEL

Either St John 12.12–16 (Church of England) or *St Mark 11.1–10* (Roman Catholic Church).

AFTER THE GOSPEL

Leader   That's one of the great Gospels.
Jesus borrows a donkey and rides into Jerusalem, with everyone cheering, and waving palm branches, and throwing down their coats in front of Him.
All over the world Christians are waving palm branches today – and some lucky churches even have a donkey to process round with.
I think our church ought to have some donkeys. Let's make some.

ACTIVITY

Settle the children for a craft session and dish out the stuff they need to make donkeys **(CD25.1)**. *You may have to help the little ones with the tail.*
*Once the donkeys are made, ask the children to draw palm branches (in green) on both sides of their sheets of paper (***CD25.2*** offers a variety of palm shapes).*
Set up a donkey procession, make a pathway with the palm branches and stand back to admire the effect.

OPTIONAL MUSIC

If you have a musician to hand, a Palm Sunday hymn would fit in well here. (The first three verses of 'All glory, laud and honour' for example.)

Leader   That looks really good.
Jesus rode into Jerusalem, listening to the shouts, looking at the palm branches – yet knowing all the time the people weren't always going to be so happy and friendly.

Today, Palm Sunday, they waved palms *(Hold up your A4 sheet)*
But by the end of the week they didn't want to give Jesus palms
They wanted to give Him this . . .

Origami demo **(CD25.3)**: *fold and cut the A4 sheet so it becomes a cross*

A cross. Can you do that?

MAKING CROSSES

*Gather the children round and do another demo with a blank piece of paper.
Let them have a go with their pictures of palms: you may have to help the little ones
with the scissors. Admire the result.*

FINAL PRAYER

*Ask the children to sit down, with their crosses in front of them. Bring forward a
palm cross*

Holy Week starts today on Palm Sunday, and for the rest of this
week the Church will be hearing about the things Jesus did in the
last week of His life until we get to Good Friday, when He died on
the Cross.
That's why our palms *(show them)* are made in the shape of a cross.
But Holy Week doesn't stop at Good Friday, it goes on to Easter
Sunday, the day Jesus conquered death and rose from the dead.
So you see, the crosses we've made look like crosses, but they are
also bright green. Green is the colour of life and a green cross shows
that Jesus brought life back from the tomb.*

Ask the children to say the following prayer after you

Lord Jesus
By your Holy Cross
You have saved us all. Amen

Let's finish by making the Sign of the Cross
✠ **In the Name of the Father, and of the Son, and of the Holy Spirit.**
Amen

---

* Leaders may be interested to know that in mediaeval stained glass Jesus is usually shown on a green
cross, for the same reason.

BACK IN CHURCH

The children line up down the front with their crosses

Leader   Today we drew some palm leaves, and then turned them into crosses.
Our crosses are bright green to show that, though Jesus died on the
cross, His death brought life to us all.
We'd like to share a prayer with you.

The children hold up their crosses as one of them says

Child   Lord Jesus
By your Holy Cross
You have saved us all. **Amen**

1) Cut donkey shape from card—it should be about 4" long from
    nose to back.

2) Wrap some wool round a piece of card about 2" inches wide.

3) Slide the wool off and knot at one end

4) Cut wool at the other end and
glue on to the back of the donkey.

5) Fold over a piece of paper, about 3" long, colour it brightly

6) Clip on wooden clothes pegs for legs. The donkey should end up
looking like this:

(CD25.1)

Script 26   The Race to the Tomb

Easter Sunday

St John 20.1–9

THEME

The Gospel for Easter Sunday is the Empty Tomb. Some churches add Mary
Magdalene's encounter with Jesus in the garden, but the Empty Tomb is, in its
way, more startling. It's like a news story just hitting the headlines which no one
knows what to make of.

Given the dashing about in St John chapter 20, the children are encouraged to
work off their Easter joy (and those Easter eggs) in a race.

SET UP

- The liturgical colour is White or Gold.
- Candles, bells – and flowers if you can manage some.
- A line of tape at the end of the room, marking the finishing line for the race.
- Pictures from the CD-Rom.
- Check out the presentation (see below) with your priest.

THE KYRIE

Leader	Lord Jesus, when you rose from the dead, you defeated evil,
	Lord have mercy
	Lord have mercy

Lord Jesus, when you rose from the dead, you washed away our
sins,
Christ have mercy
Christ have mercy

Lord Jesus, when you rose from the dead, you set us free,
Lord have mercy
Lord have mercy

Ask the children to repeat **The Prayer for Forgiveness** *after you* (**p. xxxvi**).

THE EASTER GREETING

Teach the children the Easter Greeting

Leader	Alleluia! Christ is risen!
Children	**He is risen indeed! Alleluia!**

BEFORE THE GOSPEL

Leader   At last, we've got to Easter.
The church is shining in white and gold.
The candles are back, so are the bells, and the Gospel this morning
is so amazing that we're going to hear it right now.

THE GOSPEL PROCESSION

THE GOSPEL *St John 20.1–9*

AFTER THE GOSPEL

Leader   So let's get this straight:
Who arrived at Jesus' Tomb first? (**Mary Magdalene**)
What did she do? (**Went and told Peter and John**)
And what did they do? (**Ran to the tomb**)
Who got there first? (**John**)
OK, let's run the Gospel again, this time using the whole room.

GAMES

The Race to the Tomb

Line the children up into relay teams, have a 'Mary Magdalene' from each team at the other end of the room to start the race. After she has run back and touched the first kid in her team, run the race like a normal relay race.
However, as the finishing line represents the Tomb, every child that gets there should kneel before running back to touch the next kid. Children only run once and the first team to finish wins.

Leader   Right, so this team won – they are all 'Johns'. And the rest of you got
there later – you're all 'Peters'. *(Ask the children to sit down)*

CD26.1   Let's think about these guys *(Put up the John picture)*
John got to the Tomb first, but he didn't go in – he just looked
through the entrance. I don't think he was afraid. I think he realized
that something very holy had happened.

CD26.2   *Put up the Peter picture*

Peter was so anxious about Jesus that he looked inside and saw the grave clothes neatly folded.
Neither of the men quite knew what to make of it.

CD26.3   *Put up the Mary picture*

What about Mary Magdalene?
She actually got there before John – and it was she who ran to tell the others.
Now very soon, Jesus is going to be back with His friends, telling them to give the whole world the message that He is alive. They were to be His messengers, His Apostles.
But Mary was the first person to carry the message of the Empty Tomb to the disciples. She told Peter and John – so she is called the Apostle to the Apostles.
It's up to us to be Apostles too. We're going to start right away and share the good news about Jesus with the grown-ups.

REHEARSAL

Practise your presentation for when you go back into church (see below).

Leader   OK, we're ready to be Apostles.
But first we'll pray to Jesus, risen from the dead.

FINAL PRAYER

Ask the children to stand extra straight and pray with open arms and hands

Christians are so happy today, they can't sit or kneel for long.

Lord Jesus,
You rose from the dead
And filled the hearts of your friends with joy.
Your church is full of happiness today.
Help us to share our joy with other people. **Amen**

MUSIC

Any Easter hymn is suitable, try to choose one with a swing to it.
'Thine be the glory' *among the traditional hymns, or* 'I danced in the morning', *verses 1, 3 and 5, among the moderns.*

BACK IN CHURCH

If the aisle is clear, and the priest can stand it, the kids should race down to the front.
Gather them at the back of the church to run down to the front – at a given signal.
One of the Leaders goes down the front first

Leader	This morning we heard about Peter and John running to the Tomb, so the children thought they'd run in to tell you the good news. Here they come!

The children run down the aisle

Leader	OK kids, Peter and John ran to the Tomb. What was inside?
Kids	**Nothing!**
Leader	What's happened to Jesus?
Kids	**He is risen!**
Leader	I think that's the best news we have ever heard. The children have got a special acclamation for you I hope you know the reply *(the priest will!)*
Kids	**Alleluia! Christ is risen!**
Congregation	**He is risen indeed! Alleluia!**

(CD26.1)

HEY!

(CD26.2)

(CD26.3)

Script 27 Doubting Thomas

Easter 2

St John 20.19–20, 24–29

THEME

How lucky we are that St Thomas had his doubts, as a result we know that the Risen Jesus could be touched. And how wonderful to hear Jesus' words, 'Blessed are they who have not seen and yet believed' – because that's us. This session the children are given a graphic demonstration of what it is like not to see, but be able to trust, in the Deadly Swamps game.

SET UP

- The liturgical colour is White or Gold.
- Pictures from the CD-Rom.
- Blindfold.
- Some chairs or similar for an obstacle course.

WELCOME *the children and lead them in* **The Sign of the Cross** ✠ (**p. xxxvi**).

THE KYRIE   Lord Jesus, when you rose from the dead,
you defeated evil
Lord have mercy
Lord have mercy

Lord Jesus, when you rose from the dead,
you washed away our sins
Christ have mercy
Christ have mercy

Lord Jesus, when you rose from the dead,
you set us free
Lord have mercy
Lord have mercy

Ask the children to repeat **The Prayer for Forgiveness** *after you* (**p. xxxvi**).

THE EASTER GREETING

Run this three times, softly, louder, very loud indeed

Leader   Alleluia! Christ is risen!
Kids   **He is risen indeed! Alleluia!**

BEFORE THE GOSPEL

Leader   Well, it's been a week since Easter Sunday and, 2,000 years ago, this was the most exciting week of the disciples' lives.
You never knew when Jesus was going to turn up.
Sometimes He appeared in your room, without apparently opening the door.
Sometimes you found Him beside you as you walked home.
Sometimes He made a private visit to a friend, like Peter.
The disciples had started the week looking like this:

CD27.1   *Picture of miserable disciples*

But they ended it looking like . . .
How do you think they looked?

CD27.2   *Template of disciples*

Can you make them look cheerful?

Ask the kids up to draw smiles on the Disciples' faces

But there was one disciple who didn't cheer up.
His name was Thomas, and he looked like this . . .

CD27.3   *Picture of sceptical Thomas*

The disciples all buzzed round him, telling him that Jesus had come back from the dead – and Thomas just narrowed his eyes.
'Oh yeah?' he said, 'prove it . . .'
'I felt Jesus was in the room,' said James.
'Indigestion,' said Thomas.
'I saw Jesus walk through that door!' said Philip.
'A ghost,' said Thomas.
'Peter saw Him, Mary saw Him, Cleophas saw Him . . .' said everyone.
'Listen guys,' said Thomas, 'unless I see Jesus with my own eyes *and* touch His hands *and* feel the wounds the nails made, I won't believe a word of it. You've all gone crackers!'
But a week later, Thomas was in the room with the others when . . .
Let's hear about it in the Gospel:

THE GOSPEL PROCESSION

THE GOSPEL *St John 20.19–20, 24–29*

AFTER THE GOSPEL

Leader	So Thomas ended up believing in Jesus, and he stopped looking suspicious and cheered up. Let's give Thomas a new face.
CD27.4	*Template of Thomas. Ask a child to add a smile to the picture* What made Thomas change his mind? (**He saw and touched Jesus**) Yup, we ought to be very grateful to Thomas: because of him we know that Jesus could be touched and that He wasn't a ghost. Even so, Jesus thought it was a pity that Thomas was such a doubter. He said, 'You believe in me because you have seen me, blessed are those who have not seen and yet believed.' Jesus knew He wasn't going to be on Earth much longer, and He wanted His friends to trust Him, even when they couldn't see Him. And I must say, it is very difficult to trust someone when you can't see them. Let's think about that . . .

GAMES

Deadly Swamps

Leader	Supposing this hall turned into a set of deadly swamps and *Name* over there had to get across, and it got so dark that she couldn't see her hand before her face . . . How would she manage? I'll tell you, she'd have to rely on my amazing knowledge of the death-dealing swamps to get across.

Set up an obstacle course – not too large – blindfold Leader 2 and get him/her across the room by telling him/her to go three steps to the left and so on. (Don't take too long.) If he/she inadvertently knocks a chair, make a ghastly sucking noise – 'Blimey, that was close' – but make sure nothing fatal happens

Leader 1	Could any of you do that?

Let the children guide some other victims across. Give each kid a chance to call out an instruction as there probably won't be time for every child to have a complete turn. Collisions are not deemed fatal, just yell 'Stop!' if a kid bangs into something. Make sure one of the Leaders is terrible at instructions. Review the game

Leader 1	You see how scary it is to be blindfolded like that? You just have to trust your guide. And I must say, if I really had to cross a swamp I'd have to have a lot of trust before I let old *Name (mention the duff Leader)* get me over.

Sum up

Leader	Jesus knew how difficult we'd find it to trust Him when we couldn't see Him. So He left us some things to help us. One of the most precious things He left us was the Eucharist. In the Eucharist the priest takes bread, blesses it, and it becomes for us the Body of Jesus. We can touch it, just as Thomas did 2,000 years ago and we can say with him, 'My Lord and my God'. Let's pray to St Thomas now.
FINAL PRAYER	Holy Thomas, Friend of Jesus, **Pray for us** When we feel doubtful **Pray for us** When we come to church **Pray for us** When we receive Communion **Pray for us** Holy Thomas, may we say with you 'My Lord and my God'. **Amen**

End with a **Glory be . . . (p. xxxvii)**.

BACK IN CHURCH

The children go in with the cheery Apostle pictures and the two Thomas pictures. All the pictures are turned away from the congregation so the kids can turn them on cue. If the kids are up to it, you can ad lib the following exchanges with them. The other Leaders should be on hand to prompt.

Leader	Today we learnt that Jesus' friends really cheered up at Easter.

The kids turn the disciple pictures

Leader	All except this one. *(The first Thomas picture is turned)* What was his name?
Child 1	Thomas

Leader	What was his problem?
Child 2	He didn't believe Jesus was alive
Child 3	He said he wouldn't believe until he touched Him
Leader	And did he touch Him?
Everyone	**Yes!**
Leader	So Thomas cheered up *(turn second Thomas picture)*
	And he gave us a prayer.
	When Thomas realized that Jesus really was alive he said:
Everyone	**My Lord and my God!**

(CD27.3)

(CD27.4)

Specimen cartoons for this script

Script 28 Jesus Eats Some Fish

Easter 3

St Luke 24.36–43

THEME

A wonderful low-key Resurrection story. Jesus turns up: He points out that He's got the usual hands, feet and bones, and eats some fish. Happy Endings are like that – life returns to normal.

SET UP

- The liturgical colour is White or Gold.
- Pictures from the CD-Rom.
- Marker pens for the children – or just the Leader if you do the activity as a group.
- Prime the grown-ups to talk about things that make them afraid – nothing too awful.

OPTIONAL

- Picture of the 'Flying Scotsman' if you use the train story below. (You will find lots of images online.)

WELCOME *the children and lead them in* **The Sign of the Cross** ✠ **(p. xxxvi).**

THE KYRIE Lord Jesus, when you rose from the dead,
you defeated evil
Lord have mercy
Lord have mercy

Lord Jesus, when you rose from the dead,
you washed away our sins
Christ have mercy
Christ have mercy

Lord Jesus, when you rose from the dead,
you set us free
Lord have mercy
Lord have mercy

Ask the children to repeat **The Prayer for Forgiveness** *after you* (**p. xxxvi**).

THE EASTER GREETING

Run this three times, softly, louder, very loud indeed

Leader   Alleluia! Christ is risen!
              He is risen indeed! Alleluia!

BEFORE THE GOSPEL

Leader   Has anyone here ever been afraid? Just put your hands up . . .
              Hmm, quite a lot of us.
              What sort of things are frightening? (**Loud noises, scary films,
              somebody putting the lights out, mad axemen . . .**)

Go with the flow and pick up on any sensible fright

              Actually, it's very sensible to be frightened sometimes.
              But what about being frightened of nice things?

*This is the moment when you use a story in which something is so super that it's
almost frightening. It can be as simple as realizing that Father Christmas really has
come. You can feel the sock full of goodies, but you hardly dare open them. I use the
Flying Scotsman story.*

Flying Scotsman *story*

When my brother and I were very little, we were sometimes taken to see the trains coming into the station at King's Cross. They were steam trains in those days, and they came down the track puffing and hissing, and sometimes the driver pulled something in his cabin and set off a hideous screeching whistle. It was all very exciting.

The most exciting train of all was the *Flying Scotsman*. It went from London to Edinburgh (and back), and was bright green and enormous. We learnt its number (4472) and one glorious day we talked to the driver. He looked down at us from the engine cab and said, 'Would you like to come up?'

Our Dad was just about to lift us on to the footplate, when we both hid behind him. The *Flying Scotsman* was big and green, and still snorting and hissing to itself, and it was all so wonderful we just couldn't cope.

So my brother and I just shook our heads and looked weedy, and we never got the chance to stand beside the driver of the *Flying Scotsman* ever again.

Leader
Some things can be so big and exciting that we are too scared to enjoy them. I think that's how the disciples felt about Jesus coming back from the dead.

It was so lovely – it couldn't be true.

Jesus dealt with their fright in a very interesting way, let's hear about it in the Gospel.

GOSPEL PROCESSION

THE GOSPEL *St Luke 24.36–43*

AFTER THE GOSPEL

Leader
The disciples were so amazed and happy they couldn't believe Jesus had come back from the dead.

So what did Jesus do? (**He showed them His hands and His feet; He ate some grilled fish**)

Yup, He did ordinary things.

'Look,' He said, 'I'm normal – same old hands and feet.'

Then He looked round,

'Have you got anything to eat?' He said. 'Great! Grilled fish – it tastes good.'

Jesus didn't come back with a squadron of angels and blazing lights. He just turned up, looking ordinary.

That's because happy things *are* normal: it's the way God intended the world to be.

ACTIVITY

The children are given some comic strips to finish, the templates are on **CD28.1**. *A couple of frames set up a story and the last frame is left blank for the child to finish by drawing a picture or writing the last line* (**CD28.2**). *(Ask the children to rein in the tragic muse and do their best to come up with a happy ending.) The strips are in black and white so they can be coloured in.*

If you are running out of time, or the group is too large, you can enlarge the comic strips and do the activity as a group. Leave time to admire the complete strips.

FINAL
PRAYER
Lord Jesus Christ

When you rose from the dead,

You filled the hearts of your friends with joy.

Fill our hearts with joy this morning

As we go back to church to greet you

In Bread and Wine and Blessing. **Amen**

BACK IN CHURCH

The children take in the completed comic strips

Child 1   Today we thought about happy endings – and drew a few . . .

The leader (or priest) ad libs through a couple of the stories

Child 2   The Gospel today told us how happy the disciples were when they realized that Jesus really had come back from the dead.

Child 3   We think that's the best Happy Ending of all.

(CD28.1)

Script 29   The Good Shepherd

Easter 4

St John 10.3, 5, 14–16

THEME

Jesus clearly knew all about sheep farming in the Holy Land. He knew how the sheep pens were constructed, how seriously the shepherds took their job, and how they called their sheep. Actually, it's very unlikely that Galilean shepherds gave actual names to their sheep, but that doesn't stop Jesus knowing every one of His sheep by name. To stop this all getting too cosy, we reflect on the sheep who are outside the fold at the end of the session.

SET UP

- The liturgical colour is White or Gold.
- Some chairs, out of which you'll make a sheep pen.
- Ask some grown-ups, or older kids, to be spare sheep (see below).
- A couple of toy sheep.
- A crook – an old-fashioned wooden walking stick is fine.
- Typing 'Good Shepherd icon' into Google images will produce lots of images of Jesus the Good Shepherd which you may be able to download.

WELCOME *the children and lead them in* **The Sign of the Cross** ✠ **(p. xxxvi).**

THE KYRIE   Lord Jesus, when you rose from the dead,
                         you defeated evil
                         Lord have mercy
                         Lord have mercy

                         Lord Jesus, when you rose from the dead,
                         you washed away our sins
                         Christ have mercy
                         Christ have mercy

Lord Jesus, when you rose from the dead,
you set us free
Lord have mercy
Lord have mercy

Ask the children to repeat **The Prayer for Forgiveness** *after you* (**p. xxxvi**).

THE EASTER GREETING

Run this three times, softly, louder, very loud indeed

Leader   Alleluia! Christ is risen!
Children   **He is risen indeed! Alleluia!**

BEFORE THE GOSPEL

Leader   *Grab a chair and sit down in story-telling mode*
             Let's start with a story.

Sheep Calling

Over a hundred years ago, an English explorer, called George Smith, was sitting by
an oasis in the Holy Land. Three shepherds turned up, with their three flocks, to have
a drink of water and – in about two minutes flat – the oasis was full of shepherds and
sheep, all mixed up.
George looked at the muddle and wondered how they were ever going to disentangle
their sheep again.
But when every sheep had drunk its fill, the shepherds moved back a bit and sat on
three little hillocks. Then they began to call. It sounded a bit like yodelling, but each
shepherd had a different yodel, and the sheep pricked up their ears, heard their master's call, and trotted over.
And in less time than it takes to tell this, all the flocks had sorted themselves out and
gathered round their own shepherd.
The sheep knew their master's voice.

Leader   Jesus probably saw this happen loads of time in Galilee, and He
             thought the way shepherds called their sheep was very like the way
             He called His friends. Let's hear that in the Gospel.

THE GOSPEL PROCESSION

THE GOSPEL *St John 10.3, 5, 14–16*

Verses 3 and 5 are inserted slightly out of sequence in this optional paraphrase:

Jesus said: 'I am the good shepherd, I know my own and my own know me. I call my sheep by name and lead them out. A stranger they will not follow, they will flee from him, for they do not know the voice of strangers.
And I lay down my life for the sheep.
But I have other sheep, that are not of this fold, I must bring them also, and they will listen to my voice. So there shall be one flock, one shepherd.

AFTER THE GOSPEL

Leader   Jesus says He is the good shepherd.
              He didn't really go round Galilee looking after sheep, did He? (**No**)
              Who are His sheep? (**Us**)
              OK, if we're His sheep, we must know His voice.
              Let's see.

Make a sheep pen out of chairs with an obvious entrance, put the children inside
Make sure there are a few people outside the fold – preferably spare grown-ups, or a couple of older kids who are prepared to stand at the back and look moody

              OK, you're sheep – and outside there is Jesus (**Leader 1**), who knows you all, and a bad guy (**Leader 2**) who's trying to steal you. You can tell the difference because only the good guy knows your name – and you must *only* leave the sheep fold when somebody calls you by name . . .

Leader 1 calls out the children by name, while Leader 2 does a pantomime bad guy: 'No, no, come over here . . .'
Leader 2 never uses a name, it's always 'that little boy – in the red sweater . . .' Pull out the stops: act like the Child Catcher in Chitty Chitty Bang Bang *– 'Come on, kids, you can trust me . . .' and make ineffective attempts to get a kid as it comes out to join Leader 1. Try to sneak round the back of the pen. Encourage the children to shout out if the bad guy gets too near*
None of the children is likely to be fooled; congratulate them on being excellent sheep. Sit them in a huddle down the front

Wandering Sheep

Leader   Right, well you're all really good sheep.
              But you know real sheep aren't as clever as you.
              Look at this – here's my flock. *(Produce the toy sheep)*
              I keep them close to me with this crook.

Produce crook – and yank a toy sheep near you

> But they will wander off . . .
> Sheep are silly. They don't know what they're doing, and the moment I take my eyes off them, one goes missing . . .

Leader 2 scoops one up as you look the other way

> Oh no! Now I've lost a sheep.

Get it back, and run the gag a couple of times

> Jesus would never let that happen to any of His sheep.
> He's always looking round to make sure that none of His sheep has gone missing.
> And if He sees any that have wandered off, He calls them back.
> Like those guys over there *(Indicate the separate sheep)*
> He knows the name of everyone in the world, and wants them all to be part of His flock.

The Jesus character calls the names of the people at the back, a couple respond

> Of course, they don't always listen. I wonder if any of us could ask them over?

Send some children across and invite the standees to join the rest. (Small children usually stand no nonsense and drag them over.) Everybody ends up at the front

FINAL PRAYER

Optional Icon

Show the children a picture of the Good Shepherd, go through it with them. If there are Greek words on the picture they are probably 'O Poimeen Kalos' (pronounced 'Ho Poimeen Kalos'). The literal meaning is 'The Shepherd, Good'. Point out Jesus' crook and the sheep He's carrying on His shoulders
If you haven't got a picture put the crook and toy sheep on the ground and gather round them in a circle

Leader   Jesus is the Good Shepherd: He loves us and He laid down His life for us. Let's pray to Him

> Lord Jesus,
> Good Shepherd of the sheep,
> Help us to know your voice.
> And grant that other people will learn to hear your voice as well
> So that all your sheep will follow you
> And get safely home to your Kingdom. **Amen**

BACK IN CHURCH

Line the children down the front

Leader   Today we discovered the names of some of Jesus' flock. They are:

The children call out their names, one by one, keep it snappy

And we found out that Jesus knew all these names – and lots of others too.

Kids, can you see any other sheep from Jesus' flock round here?

See if the kids can come up with the priest's name, or one of the servers, or anyone near them

How about the people at the back?

Kids shake their heads

No, I can't remember everyone's name either.
But someone can, who's that?

Kids   **Jesus!**

Leader   Yup, Jesus knows His entire flock by name.

Script 30   Jesus the True Vine

Easter 5

St John 15.1–4

THEME

Another session on first-century farming. This time we work out what Jesus meant by saying He was the True Vine by acting out the whole business of vini-culture, from planting the first seed to producing a bottle of wine.

SET UP

- The liturgical colour is White or Gold.
- Pictures from the CD-Rom.
- Sound FX flash cards – on the CD-Rom.
- Spade, a toy one is fine.
- Scrunched-up balls of newspaper to represent rocks.
- A couple of bunches of dark grapes.
- Bottle of wine, relabelled 'Chateau St *Name*' (add the name of your church).
- A Bible with the Isaiah passage (see below) inserted in it.

WELCOME *the children and lead them in* **The Sign of the Cross ✠ (p. xxxvi).**

THE KYRIE   Lord Jesus, when you rose from the dead,
you defeated evil
Lord have mercy
Lord have mercy

Lord Jesus, when you rose from the dead,
you washed away our sins
Christ have mercy
Christ have mercy

Lord Jesus, when you rose from the dead,
you set us free
Lord have mercy
Lord have mercy

THE EASTER GREETING

Run this three times, softly, louder, very loud indeed

Leader   Alleluia! Christ is risen!
Children   **He is risen indeed! Alleluia!**

BEFORE THE GOSPEL

Leader   Right, Easter is the time when we try to work out just what sort of
                person Jesus is. He helps by telling us things about Himself. Last
                week He said He was like a Good Shepherd – this week He says He's
                like something else.
                Listen to the Gospel and see if you can tell me what it is.

THE GOSPEL PROCESSION

THE GOSPEL *St John 15.1–4*

AFTER THE GOSPEL

Leader   What does Jesus call Himself in this Gospel? (**A Vine/True Vine**)
CD30.1   OK, well here's a picture of a vine.
                Jesus said He was like this – but I don't think He meant He stood in
                the ground and grew leaves.
                Let's think about vines.

Vines

                What grows on them? (**Grapes**)
CD30.2   Yup, grapes
                Often we just eat grapes, but sometimes we use them to make a
CD30.3   drink – anybody know what? (**Wine** – *someone may say* '**grape juice**'
                *to which the response is: 'Absolutely right, and you can turn grape
                juice into another drink. Anyone know what it is?'*)
                So when you grow a vine, you start with grapes and end with wine.
                But you can't just plant it, go away, and come back in three months
                to find everything OK. Vines need looking after.
                You have to plant them in the right place – on a hillside, facing
                south, with good soil and no stones.
CD30.4   Look at this map, where do you think would be a good place to
                plant a vineyard? *(It will be very obvious)*
                Then you have to prune the vine.
                That means clipping it: you don't want the vine to waste its energy

by growing tall. You want a few branches, growing sideways, with loads of grapes.

Point out the way the vine is growing in the vine picture

So the farmer chops off the top, and some of the shoots, and spreads the branches out. Then he watches: if it rains, he prunes it a bit, and if it's sunny he watches the grapes ripen – and shoos off the birds – and it's all very tense until the moment the grapes are just right and he can harvest them.
The farmer ends up really loving his vineyard.
Somebody in the Bible wrote a poem about a vine.

Pick up a Bible and read the inserted text below

Isaiah 5

Leader   I will sing a song about a vineyard.
My friend had a vineyard
On a fertile hill.
He dug it over
And cleared it of stones
And planted the land with vines.
Then he built a watchtower
and made a wine press.
He was hoping for a crop of good grapes.

REHEARSAL

We're going to act this poem: it'll help us understand what Jesus is saying to us in the Gospel today.

Cast the farmer and give him/her the spade

Name is going to be the farmer, and the rest of us are going to be branches and the sound effects (FX) and the people who make wine. We'll get that sorted now.
Let's start with the Sound FX.
When I hold up a card you make the correct noise.

CD30.5   Rain. *(Fingers clicking)*

CD30.6   Thunder. *(Stamping feet)*

Practise a slick start and quick cut-off as you bring in and 'kill' the FX

OK, now I need a tall person to be the main plant.

Ask a tall kid to be the main plant – put a chair near him, and scatter a few of the newspaper rocks round about.

> The rest of you are going to be branches.

Arrange the other kids to flank the trunk

> During the poem the vine grows – how are you going to act 'growing'?

The kids crouch down and slowly get bigger

> And the vine spreads – how are we going to do that?

They extend their arms – make sure they touch. If the kids are very clued up, they could grow in sequence, the ones nearest the 'stem' growing first

> OK, stand up to begin with, and we'll see if we can put the whole thing together.

Vineyard Play

The flash card person and the Narrator are distinct

Narrator   I will sing a song about a vineyard.
A farmer had a vineyard . . .

Enter farmer   On a fertile hill.
He dug it over . . . *(Spade acting)*
And cleared it of stones . . .

He clears the rocks

> And planted the land with vines . . .

The farmer places the main plant

> Then he built a watchtower . . .
And watched.

Farmer stands on a chair near the plant

> If it rained . . . *(Sound FX)*
The farmer would prune the plant.

The farmer gets off the watchtower and does some snip actions over the head of the main plant: the main plant hunches up

> And if it thundered . . .

Thunder FX, the farmer puts his hands over his ears

> He'd get very worried.
But when the sun shone he cheered up, the vine began to grow.

The kids crouch down and begin to grow

> Then the vine began to spread . . .

The branches spread out by extending their arms, keep them touching each other

> Until it was time for the harvest.

Hand some of the bunches of grapes to the kids at the end

Wine Making

Leader	Right, the poem doesn't go on to the next bit, but we will.
Narrator	The farmer picks the grapes.

He does – a Leader takes possession of them

> Then he and everyone on his farm throw the grapes into a tub and jump on them. That would get the juice out.
> So let's jump in a tub . . .

The children form a tight circle

> And mash those grapes up. Let's see you stamp.

The kids start stamping

> You'll have to stamp harder than that.

More stamping

> How about jumping?

Let them do a couple of jumps and stop

> And the farmer collected the juice, left it to ferment, and the juice became wine.

Produce the bottle of wine

ACTIVITY

Leader	I think the grown-ups would like to see our play – but I expect they haven't got time for the whole thing. Let's see how quickly we can do one for them.

A speeded-up version of this epic is provided below for your presentation back in church.
You might like to run through this before the next section

BEFORE THE FINAL PRAYER

Ask the children to sit round you in a circle, put the wine bottle in the middle

Leader   Jesus loved wine, He liked drinking it, He liked looking at vines,
He thought the whole business of making wine was very interesting.
He thought, 'A vine is loved, and grows and spreads and is fruitful.
I'd like my Church to be like that.'
And He said, 'I am the True Vine – and you are my branches.'

FINAL   Lord Jesus
PRAYER   You are the True Vine
And we are your branches.
Your Father loves the Vine,
Just like the farmer.
Help us to stay joined to you,
And grow,
And be fruitful. **Amen**

BACK IN CHURCH

Child 1   Today we thought about vines. We heard a poem about a vineyard
from the Bible, and we listened to Jesus in the Gospel. And we made
a play about it.
It's called 'The Song of the Vineyard'.

The Song of the Vineyard

Leader   I will sing a song about a vineyard.
A farmer had a vineyard . . .

Enter farmer   On a fertile hill.
He dug it over . . . *(Spade acting)*
And planted the land with vines.

The farmer places the main plant

Then he watched:
If it rained *(Sound FX)*
The farmer would prune the plant.
But when the sun shone he cheered up, and the vine began to grow.

The kids crouch down and begin to grow

And spread . . .

The children link hands and stretch their arms

Until it was time for harvest.

Hand some of the bunches of grapes to the kids at the end

The farmer picked his grapes . . .

He does so – give them to the Leader

And put them in a tub, and got his servants to stamp on the grapes.

The kids form their circle and begin to stamp

And the farmer collected the grape juice, and let it ferment – and the grapes had turned to wine.

Produce bottle

Child 2   We think that Jesus loved vines.
He liked the way they stayed joined up, and produced fruit.

Leader   He said, 'I am the True Vine, and you are my branches.'

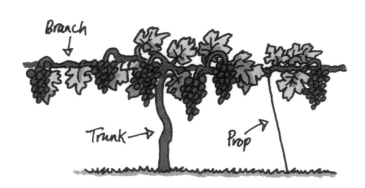

(CD30.1)

Specimen cartoon for this script

Script 31 Friends

Easter 6

St John 15.9a, 14–15

THEME

The great theme of the passage this morning is love: God's love for us, and ours for Him. Children are fine about this, but it's not a subject they usually want to linger over. Fortunately, Jesus goes on to call us His friends, which is something kids can relate to – particularly as exemplified in the story of St Ebrulf.

SET UP

- The liturgical colour is White or Gold.
- Pictures from the CD-Rom.
- Jigsaw pieces from the CD-Rom.

WELCOME *the children and lead them in* **The Sign of the Cross** ✠ (**p. xxxvi**).

THE KYRIE   Lord Jesus, when you rose from the dead,
you defeated evil
Lord have mercy
Lord have mercy

Lord Jesus, when you rose from the dead,
you washed away our sins
Christ have mercy
Christ have mercy

Lord Jesus, when you rose from the dead,
you set us free
Lord have mercy
Lord have mercy

Ask the children to repeat **The Prayer for Forgiveness** *after you* (**p. xxxvi**).

THE EASTER GREETING

Run this three times, softly, louder, very loud indeed

Leader   Alleluia! Christ is risen!
Children   **He is risen indeed! Alleluia!**

Go straight into the Gospel

THE GOSPEL PROCESSION

THE GOSPEL *St John 15.9a, 14–15*

Introduce the Gospel

Leader   This is the Sunday before Ascension Day – the day when Jesus left
                Earth and went back to Heaven. He knew His disciples were going
                to miss Him, so He said:

Optional Paraphrase

'As the Father has loved me, so I have loved you.
You are my friends, if you do what I command you.
I don't speak to you as servants – because servants don't know what their master is
doing – no, I speak to you as friends. And I have told you everything that my Father
has told me.'

AFTER THE GOSPEL

Leader   So Jesus called the disciples His friends.
                Do you know how many disciples Jesus had? (**12**)
                Yes, twelve special disciples, but lots of other people became His
                disciples too. Quite a crowd followed Him round Galilee.
                How many disciples do you think He has now? (**Millions**)
                There are millions of Christians – and they are all Jesus' friends.
                That's the nice thing about friendship, it's catching.
                I'm going to tell you a story about some of Jesus' friends and one
CD31.1   friend in particular – St Ebrulf.

St Ebrulf

Leader   Ebrulf lived a long time ago in France. He loved God so much that
                one day he decided to tuck himself away, grow his own food, and
                just get on with being alone with God.
CD31.2   So off he went, deep into a forest, and built himself a hut.
                And Ebrulf stayed there, quite alone, but very close to God.

But he didn't stay alone for very long, because people began to creep up to his hut to see what he was doing. And they liked Ebrulf so much that some of them wanted to join him in the forest.

CD31.3–31.6   *Ebrulf's new friends are drawn so they form a chain of linked hands.*

So suddenly Ebrulf had loads of friends.
And they made little huts, and prayed, and dug their vegetable patches, and sat round campfires, just like Ebrulf.
And some rather more dodgy people saw the lights and wondered what was going on in the forest. And one of them said,
'I wonder if those geezers have got anything we can nick?'

CD31.7   He looked like this.
What do you think he was? (**A robber, thief, burglar**)
Exactly.
So up he crept, with his robber band, but when they got to Ebrulf's

CD31.8   hut all they found was this –
Then they met Ebrulf and his mates, who were such a nice bunch, that the robbers asked if *they* could be friends too and stay in the forest with them. So the robbers made little huts, and settled down

CD31.9–31.10   to pray and dig and learn to love God.

Attach the robbers to the Ebrulf chain

When Ebrulf died he was made a saint and, centuries later, some English monks liked him so much that they nicked his body and

CD31.11–12   buried it in their own church in Lincolnshire.

Add the monks to the chain

I'm not saying it's a good thing to steal a saint's body, but you see how catching friendship is. Let's see whether we can make friends – fast!

ACTIVITY

Finding Friends

Two Friends

Hand out the little jigsaw pictures on **CD31.13**. *Each one has a unique join and the children have to rush round to find a partner with the other half.*

Lots of Friends

When the children have each got a partner, call in the jigsaw pieces and ask the kids (still in pairs) to spread out. Then run a game of Chain Tag. Each pair joins hands and runs round as a unit, joining up with other pairs until the whole room is in a gigantic line. See if they can make a circle, without breaking up, and ask them to sit down.

REHEARSAL

Practise your presentation for when you go back into church (see below).

BEFORE THE FINAL PRAYER

Leader   Let's just think about St Ebrulf. *(Hold up picture* **CD31.1***)*
He ended up with lots of friends, but he started off with just one.
Anyone know who that was? (**Jesus**)

Ask two kids to stand up. One holds the Ebrulf picture (**CD31.1**), *the other a Jesus picture* (**CD31.14**)

Ebrulf knew he was loved by Jesus.
And God's love is like a magnet, it draws people to you.
Look, here are the people who wanted to be Ebrulf's friends.

Give a kid the picture (**CD31.3**). *She runs across to link it to the other two.*

Then some more people felt Ebrulf's love.

Same business with the robber pictures

And even after Ebrulf died, people loved him and wanted to be friends.

Add the monks

And all the time, it was not just Ebrulf they were drawn to, but the wonderful love he had in his heart that came from Jesus.

It's because Jesus loves us that we can make friends with other people and bring His love to them.

Let's ask St Ebrulf to help us.

FINAL   Holy Ebrulf,
PRAYER   Friend of Jesus,
Be our friend too
And pray for us to God our Father,
That we may love Him, and be so full of His love
That we may draw people to His Son, Jesus Christ. **Amen**

MUSIC

'A New Commandment' *is a nice simple lyric to finish the session.*

BACK IN CHURCH

Go in with the pictures of Jesus, Ebrulf and his friends.

Leader   Today we heard about St Ebrulf . . .

Kid holds up the Ebrulf picture

Who was a friend of Jesus.

Jesus picture held up

And because Ebrulf loved Jesus, other people loved him too – ordinary people

Hold up friends

And robbers . . .

Hold up robbers

And monks . . .

Hold up monks

And people like us.

The other children link hands with the children holding the pictures. You should end up with a row of people holding hands – but don't worry if the links don't quite touch

That's the sort of thing that happens when Jesus is your friend.

Script 32   Ascension

Ascension Sunday (Roman Catholic)

St Luke 24.50–51, Acts of the Apostles 1.7–12

Ascension Day falls on the 40th day after Easter – a Thursday – however, the Roman Catholic church in some countries now celebrates on the Sunday following. If that's what you're doing, this is your script. But check with your priest first. It'll either be this or Script 37.

THEME

The Ascension is the last chapter of Jesus' earthly life and one that unnerves many adults. Did Jesus really go up? And what does that tell us about Heaven? We'll be exploring these ideas this session.

SET UP

- The Liturgical colour is White or Gold.
- *Either* A thurible, charcoal (get it lit before the liturgy), incense boat and thurible stand (open the windows . . .).
- *Or* An ordinary balloon and a helium balloon (the word 'Jesus' is written on the latter with a large black marker pen).
- Pictures from the CD-Rom.
- Prayer candle and candle snuffer if you can get one.
- For the jumping game you'll need either some small floor mats or large hoops or double spreads of newspaper – or 'jumping frogs'. (You can get packets of cheap plastic frogs from party shops, or by keying in 'jumping frog toys' into an Internet search.)

WELCOME *the children and lead them in* **The Sign of the Cross** ✠ **(p. xxxvi).**

THE KYRIE   Jesus, Son of God, you came to earth to save us from our sins,
Lord have mercy
Lord have mercy

Jesus, Son of God, you have ascended to Heaven and pray for us to
the Father,
Christ have mercy
Christ have mercy

Jesus, Son of God, you sent the Holy Spirit to be with us for ever,
Lord have mercy
Lord have mercy

Ask the children to repeat **The Prayer for Forgiveness** *after you* (**p. xxxvi**).

INTRODUCTION

Leader   Today is Ascension Day.
              Anyone know what 'Ascension' means? *(Establish that it means
              going up)*
              The church is always asking us to look up, especially when we use
              incense. Let's see that in action . . .

Incense

(There's an option for non-incense users below)
*Show the kids the glowing charcoal in the incense bowl, get a kid to add incense from
the boat*

Leader   Right, now let's watch that incense . . .
              Which way is it going? Yes, up.
              We use incense in church because it smells nice, and because we can
              see the smoke going up to God.
              There it goes – just like our prayers to Heaven.

For non-incense churches:

Balloons

Produce the balloons

Leader   Right, let's look at these balloons – this is an ordinary one. I can bat
              it around *(do so)* but eventually it just bumps along the floor.
              But this is a Jesus balloon *(the helium one)* and if I let go of it *(do so)*
              it ascends – just like our prayers to Heaven.
              Let's think about that as we pray . . .

**OPENING
PRAYER**

God our Father,
We thank you for the Ascension of your Son, Jesus Christ.
Grant that one day, we too will follow Him to Heaven
Where He lives and reigns with you,
And the Holy Spirit, for ever. **Amen**

Jumping

Leader

Ascension Day is one of the big feasts. Christians everywhere go to Mass and in some countries people have a holiday. In Italy, some kids will be up to something really weird – they'll be catching crickets.
Anyone know what a cricket looks like?
It looks like this . . .

CD32.1 *Point out its huge back legs*

Does it remind you of anything?

(Some child might be reminded of a grasshopper)

Italian children put their crickets in a little cage and take them home.
They feed them on lettuce.
Sometimes they just buy a toy one.
But why do they want a cricket on Ascension Day?
Well, I think it's the way it moves.
How do you think a cricket moves? (**It jumps**)

Add jump lines to picture

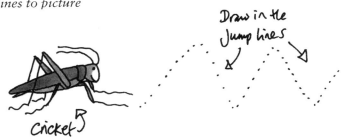

OK, how far do you get when you jump?

Jumping Games

Depending on your resources (see above) play one of the following games.

Frog Racing

Give each child a plastic jumping frog, establish a start line and a finishing line (not too far apart) and run a frog race. You'll find the frogs go everywhere, so split the kids into teams. Aim to have four children racing at any one time and run a knock-out race.

Lily Pads

In this game the children are the frogs. Set out the pads (either small floor mats or hoops or – if you haven't got either – double spreads of newspaper) in straight lines. Line the kids up in teams and get them to jump from one pad to the other. Run this as a relay race.

Measuring Jumps

At the end congratulate the winners and then cluster round a couple of frogs, or place two of your mats in the centre of the room. Establish how far (on the whole) a frog or a child can jump.

Leader	So a frog can jump from *here* to *here*.
	And a kid can jump from *here* to *here*.
	It's not very far is it?
	And I'll show you something else.
	Stand in a line for a moment,
	OK, now jump!

The children jump – watch them carefully

Yeah . . . interesting – you only stayed up in the air for a second.
Could you do it again?
Ballet dancers manage to stay up a bit longer by doing this . . .

One of the leaders stretches their arms above their head, leaps up and brings the arms down at the top of the jump. Only a ballet dancer can really pull this off: it does help them stay up a fraction longer. The children may like to try

Right, arms up, try again.
Jump!

The children jump again – look exasperated

You've done it again!
Look at you, all on the ground.
Why's that?

Encourage a child to tell you about gravity

OK, so however high we jump, we always come down again.
Well Jesus did better than that.
Let's hear about it.

If you've got incense put some more grains in the thurible for the Gospel Procession

GOSPEL PROCESSION

The leader (or a server if one of the kids happens to be one) censes the Gospel Book.

THE GOSPEL (PLUS ACTS)
St Luke 24.50–51 and The Acts of the Apostles 1.7–12

Optional Paraphrase
Jesus led His disciples out to the a place near Bethany, and He lifted up His hands and blessed them. And said to them, 'You will receive power when the Holy Spirit comes upon you, and you will be my witnesses in Jerusalem, and in all Israel, and to the ends of the earth.'
After He said this, He was taken up before their very eyes, and a cloud hid Him from their sight. The disciples stared up into the sky as He went, when suddenly two men in white robes stood beside them.
'Men of Galilee,' they said, 'why are you looking up into the sky? This Jesus, who has been taken from you into Heaven, will come back in the very same way you saw Him go.'
And the disciples went back to Jerusalem full of joy, and went to the Temple every day to thank God.

AFTER THE GOSPEL

Leader   So what was different about Jesus' jump? *(He stayed up)*
              Yes, He didn't come down again.
              But did He stay hovering in the air? **(CD32.2)** (No)
              Oh, so did He zoom out of sight like a rocket? **(CD32.3)** (No)
              How did He go? Let's look at the Bible again.

Pick up the Gospel book and read:

              He was taken up before their very eyes, and a cloud hid Him from
              their sight.
              That doesn't sound very far, I think it happened like this . . .
              (a picture of the ascension **(CD32.4)** *with detachable cloud* **(CD32.5)***)*
              Jesus left the ground, and suddenly He wasn't there any more.
              A cloud had just moved across in front of Him.
              Jesus didn't fly into the sky: He wasn't a plane.
              And He didn't launch Himself into space: He wasn't a spaceship.
              Where did He go? **(Heaven)**

Optional Session for Older Children

              Is Heaven in the sky?

(You might get a mixed response for this, establish that it isn't)

              Is Heaven in space?

*(The same response probably: the kids usually get very interested at this point and
sometimes try to establish the idea of meta-space, somewhere beyond space)*

              Heaven isn't part of this universe at all.
              It's not up (or down, or sideways).
              It's *out:* somewhere completely different.

Leader   Is Heaven very far? *(Take all answers)*
              Let's think about it.
              When you pray, how quickly does God hear you? **(He hears you at
              once)**
              Yes, there's no time delay. Heaven seems to be very close.
              It's just that we can't see it.
              When Jesus went back to Heaven He moved a little way from the
              Earth, a cloud covered Him and He'd gone. But not very far – only
              as far as God. And God is very near.

REHEARSAL

Practise your presentation for when you go back into church (see below).

FINAL PRAYER

Gather the children into a prayer circle, put a lit candle in the middle

Leader	In some churches this is the day they put out the Paschal Candle – the big candle that has been burning since Easter Day. The candle is a sign of Jesus back from the dead. But today Jesus goes back to Heaven and so the disciples couldn't see Him anymore. So we put it out . . .

Ask a child to snuff the candle, using a snuffer if possible. Do it carefully – there's usually a lot of wax on large candles

	So the candle's out – but look at the smoke! Where's it going? (**Up**)
Watch it	It's going up – and disappearing – just like Jesus. Even so, though we can't see Jesus any more, He's still very close to us. Let's pray to Him now.

Ask the children to repeat the prayers after you

> **Lord Jesus,**
> **Today you ascended to Heaven.**
> **Be near us this morning as we pray.**
>
> **Lord Jesus,**
> **Friend and brother,**
> **May we see you more clearly**
> **Love you more dearly**
> **And follow you more nearly,**
> **Day by day, Amen**

BACK IN CHURCH

The children form up in a line down the front

Child 1	Today we learnt about 'ascension'.
Child 2	We tried it ourselves.
Child 3	Watch this, 1, 2, 3 . . .

All the children jump into the air

Child 4	We only managed to stay up for a second.
Child 5	But when Jesus ascended He stayed up and went back to . . .
All the Kids	Heaven!

Script 33   Traffic Lights

Easter 7

St John 17.11

THEME

This Sunday has an odd feel: the disciples are filling in time between the Ascension and the coming of the Holy Spirit at Pentecost. Not that they knew Pentecost was coming, of course; all they knew was that Jesus had told them to wait. So, while we're waiting, we think about the many ways in which God answers prayer.

SET UP

- The liturgical colour is White or Gold.
- Pictures from the CD-Rom.
- Prayers from the CD-Rom in a bag or a box, something handy.
- Black, red, orange and green marker pens.

WELCOME *the children and lead them in* **The Sign of the Cross** ✠ **(p. xxxvi).**

THE KYRIE   Lord Jesus, when you rose from the dead,
you defeated evil
Lord have mercy
Lord have mercy

Lord Jesus, when you rose from the dead,
you washed away our sins
Christ have mercy
Christ have mercy

Lord Jesus, when you rose from the dead,
you set us free
Lord have mercy
Lord have mercy

Ask the children to repeat **The Prayer for Forgiveness** *after you* **(p. xxxvi).**

THE EASTER GREETING

Run this three times, softly, louder, very loud indeed

Leader	Alleluia! Christ is risen!
Children	**He is risen indeed! Alleluia!**

BEFORE THE GOSPEL

Waiting

Leader Last Thursday was Ascension Day.
Anyone know anything about that? What happened? (**Jesus went up to Heaven**)
Exactly, Jesus went back to His home in Heaven.
But before He went home He told His friends to do something.
Pick up a Bible and read from Acts 1.4, emphasizing the word 'wait'

Optional Paraphrase

While Jesus was still with His disciples He said, 'Don't leave Jerusalem yet, wait for the Father to give you the Holy Spirit.'

I'm not sure the disciples understood the bit about the Holy Spirit, but they knew all about waiting: it's one of the most boring things you can do.

Any 'waiting' story would fit in nicely here. Here's the one I use

Gunnersbury Boating Pond

Leader When I was very little, my brother and I used to be taken by my Dad to the local boating pond. He used to row us about in a proper rowing boat, which was good fun, but I couldn't help noticing that the pond was full of other kids zipping around in paddle boats all by themselves.

CD33.1
So I went along to the jetty to see if they'd let me go out by myself,

CD33.2
and I saw this notice. *(It says, 'No child is allowed to take out a paddle boat until they are eight')*
Well, I was five. I could just about read, but I was terrible at arithmetic.
How long would I have to wait until I could take a boat out? (**Three years**)
You're quicker than me, it took me ages to do that sum.
'Three years!' I couldn't believe it. 'I can't possibly wait three years!'

So I went back to my Dad and got into the rowing boat with my brother.

I don't suppose the disciples liked waiting very much either. But even though Jesus had gone back to Heaven, they were very cheerful. Jesus still loved them, and the Church was getting bigger – there were 120 of them by now. So they sat together and prayed, and still the message came back, 'Wait'.

That's one of those things about prayer, God always answers you – but it's not always the answer you want. Which is just as well sometimes. Let's think about that.

Traffic Lights

Draw a blank traffic light

Leader   Right, this is a traffic light – can anyone help me fill it in?

The kids fill in the traffic light colours, run through what they mean, and write the commands up

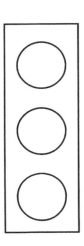

Red equals Stop

Amber equals Wait

Green equals Go

Now sometimes you're at a red light, and you're desperate for it to change – your Mum is late for something, and you're bored – and the red goes on being red.

So you think, 'Can't we just go anyway?'

Do you think it would be sensible to jump a red light? (**No**)

Why not? *(Brace yourself for tales of disaster)*

You are absolutely right. You just don't know what might suddenly crash into you.

Well prayer is like that.

You might want God to give you a green light and say, 'Go for it, I'll give you a hand'. But sometimes He doesn't, because He can see the articulated lorry thundering towards you, and you can't.

We have to learn to listen to God and see which light He's giving us.

I've got some prayers here **(CD33.3a–33.3e)** let's see if we can guess which colour God might put on them.

ACTIVITY

Run this as a group exercise. Read each prayer, discuss what colour you think God would give it, and ask a kid to colour it in with the appropriate traffic light. Keep it light, some of the prayers are quite fun. Stick them up as you go.

Leader	When Jesus was on Earth, He prayed to His Father many times, let's hear one of those prayers now.

THE GOSPEL PROCESSION

THE GOSPEL *St John 17.11*

Optional Paraphrase

Jesus raised His eyes to Heaven and said, 'Holy Father, I am no longer in the world, but my followers are in the world. Keep those you have given me true to your Name, so they may be one like us.'

AFTER THE GOSPEL

Leader	So Jesus asked God to help us be true to His Name, keep the faith, and hang in together.
	What colour do you think Jesus got for that prayer? (**Green**)
CD33.4	*Put up picture of green traffic signal*
	Do you think Jesus always got a go-ahead from God when He prayed?

Take any answer

	Actually He didn't. Let's look at the last prayer in my prayer bag: Jesus prayed this just before He was arrested.

Read out Jesus' prayer in Gethsemane

	'Father, if it is possible, let this Cup pass from me.'
	The Cup means all the suffering that Jesus knew was waiting for Him.
	Did God remove the Cup from Him? (**No**)
	No, He didn't.
CD33.5	*Put up picture of red traffic signal*
	Jesus ended that prayer, 'But nevertheless, not my will, but yours be done.' All Jesus really wanted was to do what His Father wanted so, if He got a red, He was prepared to accept that.

REHEARSAL

Practise your presentation for when you go back into church (see below).

FINAL	When we pray, we might get a green or a red, or an amber.
PRAYER	At the moment we're with the disciples, waiting for the Holy Spirit to come at Pentecost.
CD33.6	*Put up picture of amber traffic signal*
	That won't be until next week. Let's fill in the time, as they did, by saying the prayer Jesus taught us:

Our Father . . . (p. xxxvi).

BACK IN CHURCH

Go in with pictures **CD33.4**, **CD33.5** *and* **CD33.6**

Child 1	Today we thought about prayer and traffic lights.
Child 2	We thought that sometimes God gives us a green signal for our prayers.

Another child holds up picture **CD33.4**

Child 3	And sometimes we get a red.

Another child holds up picture **CD33.5**

Child 4	And sometimes we get an amber.

Another child holds up picture **CD33.6**

Leader	At the moment we think we're on an amber light because we're all waiting for the Holy Spirit to come at Pentecost.

(CD33.1)

Specimen cartoons for this script   (CD33.2)

Script 34   Blowing Things

Pentecost

St John 15.26; 20.22

THEME

This is the day that God the Holy Spirit burst in upon the disciples. 'Spirit' is the way we translate the Greek 'pneuma' which also means 'air'. (Pneumatic tyres are the sort you blow up.) Anything that uses air is suitable for the liturgy today – see what you can lay your hands on, hair dryers, fans, balloons . . .

SET UP

- The liturgical colour is Red.
- Charcoal – either the sort used for the thurible, or some from a barbecue kit.
- A thurible or a foil container for the charcoal to burn in. (Light it at least ten minutes before the session, so it has already turned white by the time the children arrive.)
- Some grains of incense if your church uses it.
- Balloons, not blown up – but inflate them a couple of times beforehand, so they're easy to inflate in performance.
- Drinking straws.
- Dried peas, or any small globular object – beads for example.
- Anything that uses moving air – like a hair dryer.
- A hand-held fan. Make one by pleating a sheet of paper if you can't find one.
- Warn your priest about the presentation (see p. 187).

WELCOME *the children and lead them in* **The Sign of the Cross** ✠ (**p. xxxvi**).

THE KYRIE   God our Father, your Spirit fills the whole world,
Lord have mercy
Lord have mercy

Lord Jesus, your Spirit fills our hearts,
Christ have mercy
Christ have mercy

Holy Spirit, fill us with the love of God,
Lord have mercy
Lord have mercy

Ask the children to repeat **The Prayer for Forgiveness** *after you* (**p. xxxvi**).

BEFORE THE OPENING PRAYER

Leader   Today is Pentecost.
                    It is the day when the Holy Spirit arrived as a mighty rushing wind.
                    'Spirit' can mean 'air' and air is an amazing thing.
                    It's all round us, it keeps us alive – but we can't see it.
                    Very like the Holy Spirit.
                    And it does something else – it feeds fire.
                    Watch . . .

Bring forward the charcoal – ask the children to gather round

                    I lit some charcoal this morning.
                    It's still alight, and very hot, but you can see it's gone white.
                    You can *feel* the heat

Put your hands over the charcoal as if you're warming them

                    But you can't see it.
                    But if I blow on it . . . *(Do so)*
                    There! The charcoal has begun to glow red.
                    If we put a bit of straw on that charcoal now it would burst into flame.
                    Christians think the Holy Spirit is rather like that, He blows on our hearts and makes them glow with love for God. Let's think about that as we pray.

OPENING   Almighty God
PRAYER   Today you sent your Spirit on the Church.
                    May the Holy Spirit breathe on our hearts
                    And make them glow with love for you
                    And your Son Jesus Christ. **Amen**

Put the charcoal carefully to one side

Blowing Things

Leader	So, air makes things glow. It also makes things move.

Demonstrate this with the ever popular inflated balloon trick: inflate a balloon, and let it go – the children love it

Did you get that?

Do it again

Let's see if *you* can make things move, just by blowing them.

The Pea Race

Run a Pea Race. Each child is given a straw and dried pea (or similar). The idea is that they blow the pea across the floor. Don't give them too huge a distance – and scoop up the toddlers, otherwise they'll try to eat the peas. Depending on your numbers and the size of the room, run this as a relay race, or let the whole lot go at once. Make sure you have a definite finishing line. Congratulate anyone who finishes the course, it's not as easy as you'd think.

The Holy Spirit

Leader	Well, we can manage peas. How would we be at blowing grown-ups? Let's try.

Stand another Leader in front of the kids and get them to blow the Leader

Useless! He/she hasn't moved an inch.
I think God the Holy Spirit could teach us a thing or two about blowing. Let's hear about Him in the Bible.

Sit down in story-telling mode to read the following from the Acts of the Apostles, 2.1–4

First Reading

When the day of Pentecost came round, the disciples were altogether in one room, when suddenly they heard the sound of a mighty rushing wind. The noise of it filled the house. Then they saw what looked like flames of fire, flickering over their heads – and everyone began speaking in foreign languages.

Close the Bible

Leader	Well, the disciples tumbled out of the house – I can't help thinking the Spirit blew them out – and they began to tell everyone about Jesus and how super it was to be a Christian.
	So you see God the Holy Spirit can be big and powerful – whooshing through houses and making a lot of noise, or He can be quiet – just tongues of fire, flickering over a disciple's head.
	Jesus talks about Him in the Gospel today. Listen and see if you can tell me if the Spirit turns up loudly or softly.

THE GOSPEL PROCESSION

THE GOSPEL *St John 15.26; 20.22*

Optional Paraphrase

Jesus said to His friends,
'I will send you the Spirit who comes from God, He will show you what is true.
Then you will be able to tell others about me, because you have been with me from the beginning.'
After He had risen from the dead, Jesus appeared to His disciples, and breathed on them, and said, 'Receive the Holy Spirit.'

AFTER THE GOSPEL

Leader	How did the Holy Spirit come that time? (**Softly**)
	Very quietly – just the sound of Jesus breathing on them.

REHEARSAL

Practise your presentation for when you go back into church (see below).

BEFORE THE FINAL PRAYER

Ask the children to stand in a circle

Leader	Sometimes the Holy Spirit comes as a mighty wind . . .
	That really blows your hair about.

Start up the hair dryer to max and blow a couple of willing victims

And sometimes He comes quietly, like a breath of air.

Ask the children to shut their eyes and go round, fanning their faces with a fan.

Tell me if you can feel the air
It's nice isn't it?
OK, open your eyes
It doesn't matter whether the Spirit comes loudly or softly, He always comes bearing gifts. He makes people wise, and brave and full of wonder.
We're going to pray to Him now.

Optional Incense

If you use incense – and if your smoke alarms will put up with it – bring the thurible forward

Leader   We'll just get the charcoal going again
I'll swing it, so the air round it begins to move
And put a few grains of incense on
Do all this   Incense is like the Spirit . . .
It's quiet, and lovely, and fills the whole room.

FINAL   The response is 'Bless us and keep us'
PRAYER   Can you say that?
Bless us and keep us

God the Father
Bless us and keep us

God the Son
Bless us and keep us

God the Holy Spirit
Bless us and keep us

Holy Trinity One God
Bless us and keep us

God the Holy Spirit,
You blew through the house where the disciples were today.
Blow through our lives
Blow us out on to the street
Filled with your joy
To tell people the Good News about Jesus Christ, **Amen**

BACK IN CHURCH

Take the balloons back into church
Blow them up before you get in and have a couple of responsible children hold them
so they don't go off prematurely
(This is one of those presentations when you warn the priest beforehand!)

Child 1	Today we heard about the Holy Spirit.
Child 2	He came zooming through the room where Jesus' friends were sitting, like a mighty rushing wind.
Child 3	Rather like this . . .

The kids holding the balloons let go . . .

Leader	We thought that was a brilliant example for us – that's how we should zoom off and tell people the Good News about Jesus.

Script 35 Trinity Sunday

St Matthew 28.16–20 or St John 3.5–7, 16

THEME

There are two possible Gospels today, both recalling Jesus' teaching about the Holy Trinity. Check with your priest which one you should use.

The doctrine of the Holy Trinity is notoriously difficult to teach. This session takes a line through experience. We can make sense of the world around us, in spite of the bewildering variety of things we see, hear, taste and so on. So, for example, we can feel cold metal, hear a fanfare and see a beautiful shiny object, put it all together, and we come up with the word 'trumpet'.

Similarly, the early disciples experienced God in three ways: they prayed to God the Father, they met God the Son, and they felt the power of God the Spirit at Pentecost. Yet God was not three different gods, but the One True God. These experiences were encapsulated (eventually) in the doctrine of the Holy Trinity.

Any session on the Holy Trinity will fall short of the Mystery, so try to use phrases like 'this reminds us of the Holy Trinity', 'this is a bit like the Trinity' – to warn the children that we haven't exactly wrapped it up.

SET UP

- The liturgical colour is White or Gold.
- Any plastic toy that looks like an alien: a spaceman, a Smurf or, if desperate, a plastic toy with some fuse wire antennae attached to its head.
- A jar of water and bowl – prime Leader 2 to come forward at the right moment.
- A bell, its clanger stuck to the side (so it doesn't give the game away), in a 'feelie' bag. (The session works even better if you have a member of the team who has a robust musical instrument, like a horn, that you could use instead.)

fuse wire

WELCOME *the children and lead them in* **The Sign of the Cross** ✠ (**p. xxxvi**).

THE HOLY TRINITY

Leader   We make the Sign of the Cross every Sunday.
It's a prayer we use a lot and in it we call God three things – can you
remember what they are? *(Start* 'In the Name of . . .' *if they hesitate)*
(Father, Son, Holy Spirit)

We remember the Father – the Creator of the Universe;
The Son, Jesus – who came down to our world;
And the Spirit – who lives in our hearts.
The Sign of the Cross helps us remember who's who.
Let's do it slowly

Start the Sign, touch your head . . .

The Father is at the top – in Heaven

Continue, bring your hand down to tummy level . . .

The Son, Jesus, came down to Earth

Go on, bring your hand over to your left . . .

The Spirit lives in our hearts

Finish over on the right-hand side . . .

And we finish by saying 'Amen'.
There is only one God, but we know Him as three People, Father,
Son and Spirit – we call that The Holy Trinity.
Today is Trinity Sunday, let's pray to the Trinity now in the Kyrie.

THE KYRIE   God our Father, you forgive everybody who says they are sorry,
Lord have mercy
Lord have mercy

Lord Jesus, you came down to tell us how much God loves us,
Christ have mercy
Christ have mercy

Holy Spirit, you fill our hearts with the love of God,
Lord have mercy
Lord have mercy

Ask the children to repeat **The Prayer for Forgiveness** *after you* (**p. xxxvi**).

OPENING PRAYER	God our Father,
	You sent your Son to live among us
	And your Spirit to make us holy.
	Through them help us
	As we try this morning
	To understand the Holy Trinity,
	Father, Son and Holy Spirit. **Amen**

Go straight into the Gospel Procession

THE GOSPEL PROCESSION

THE GOSPEL

Either: ***St Matthew 28.16–20***

Set up the Gospel before you read it

Leader   The Trinity was one of the last things Jesus taught His disciples. You'll hear Him speak about it in the Gospel today. Listen out, and put your hand up when you hear Jesus talking about the Trinity.

Optional Paraphrase

After Jesus had come back from the dead, the eleven disciples travelled to Galilee to a mountain where Jesus had said He would meet them.

And when they got there they saw Him, and they knelt down to worship Him (though some hesitated). Jesus came to them and said, 'God has made me King of Heaven and Earth, I want you to go all over the world, and make friends for me, baptizing them in the Name of the Father and of the Son and of the Holy Spirit. And remember, I am with you always, even to the end of the world.'

Or: ***St John 3.5–7, 16***

Set up the Gospel before you read it

Leader   Today we're going to hear something Jesus said to His friend Nicodemus. He was trying to explain to Nicodemus how people got to Heaven – by being baptized with water and receiving the Holy Spirit.
Then He said something about His Father and Himself.
Listen carefully and you should hear Jesus mention all three people in the Trinity.

Optional Paraphrase

Jesus said to Nicodemus: 'I tell you solemnly that you cannot get into God's Kingdom unless you are born of water and the Spirit. Human parents give their children life, but only the Spirit can change you into a Child of God.'

   God loved the people of this world so much that He gave them His only Son, so that anyone who believed in Him would never die.

AFTER THE GOSPEL

Leader   We've just heard Jesus talk about God as three People – who are they?
                (Father, Son, Holy Spirit)
                Three people – so how many Gods are there? Three or one?

Take all answers, but home in on '**One God**'

                That's really difficult – there's One God but He's Three people.
                How can we ever understand that?

Teaching Aliens

Leader   Well, this week I met someone who couldn't understand something that I found really simple. I found a way to help him out – I think it might help us.
                Here he is.

Produce the toy Alien: talk to it as though it's alive – nod it, shake it, talk to it

                His name's Sandy and he comes from outer space.
                Sandy told me that he comes from a very dry planet –
                Isn't that right mate?

The Alien nods vigorously

                It's so dry that they haven't got any water.
                So when Sandy wants a drink, he has a nice big mug of sand.
                What do you bathe in Sandy?

Sandy whispers in your ear

                Oh, mixed gravel.
                And what's your favourite food?

Another whisper

                Oh yes, I should have guessed, rock cakes.
                Anyway, I tried to explain to Sandy how nice water is –
                You hadn't hear of water, had you?

Shake the toy so it appears to say 'no'

> It was very difficult to get him to understand.
> I wonder if you guys could help me?
> What colour is water?

Some children may say blue. Establish that water, when you see it close to – like out of the tap – is transparent

> Sandy, water hasn't got a colour.
> What shape is water?

Some bright kids may already know that water is a 'fluid': establish that, when left to itself, water doesn't have a shape

> Sandy, water doesn't have a shape.
> What does water feel like?

That will probably do everyone's head in – but eventually someone will say it feels wet

> Er, Sandy, water feels wet.

Major tantrum from toy – make it look as if he's trying to escape from you. He eventually thumps his head on a table or wall

> Sandy is pretty upset . . .
> What's the matter?

Sandy goes straight to your ear – react

> OK, you needn't shout.

Listen again   Yup, I see.
To children   Sandy says I can't describe water to him by using another word he
> doesn't understand either.
> He's never heard of 'wet'.
> What shall we do?

Leader 2 comes forward with the jug and the bowl

> Brilliant – let's show Sandy what water is.
> Will someone pour this water into the bowl for me?

Invest a kid with the jug and bowl

> OK, pour – quite slowly –

Sandy takes a keen interest in everything as the kid pours the water

> Look, Sandy
> Water hasn't got a colour
> And it fills up the shape of anything it's poured into – it hasn't got
> its own shape.
> And this is what wet is . . .

Throw the toy in

> I hope he can swim

Pull the toy out. Sandy makes a determined effort to get back in again

> I think Sandy likes water
> So do you understand water now Sandy?

Big affirmative from Sandy
Put Sandy and the bowl etc. aside

> So you see we helped Sandy to understand water by showing him some.
> Sometimes you can't explain something – but you can feel, *experience*, it.
> And it's a bit like that with God.
> We can't always explain Him,
> But we can experience Him.
> Except of course, God is three things and one thing.
> How can we experience that?
> Well, actually we do that all the time – we just don't notice.
> When we experience things we use our senses.
> What are they? We can see things *(point to your eyes)*
> And what else?

Go through the other senses with the children

> (**Touch, taste, feel, smell**)
> Normally, we do all that at the same time, but if we separate our senses out, you'll see how one thing can be all sorts of things at the same time.

The Trinity Bell

Produce the 'feelie' bag

> Inside here I've got an object which I'd like you to feel.
> Don't tell me what it is, just think about how it feels.

Pass the bag round

> What does it seem to be made of? (**Metal**)
> Quite right, it feels cold and smooth like metal.
> Now shut your eyes – everyone – tight shut.

Unstick the clapper

> Listen carefully – what's this sound?

Ding the bell

(**A bell**)
OK, now you can look.

Produce the bell

And what can you see? (**A bell**)
Let's think about the bell.
It feels hard
It has a ringing sound
It looks shiny

Write up' hard', 'ring', ' shiny'

We experience the bell in three ways.
But it's just one bell.

Join the words up with straight lines to form a triangle

That's a bit like the Holy Trinity.

FINAL PRAYER

Gather the kids round a prayer candle, pick up a Bible, marked at Matthew 28.19

Just before He went back to Heaven, Jesus said to His friends, 'I want you to go all over the world, and make friends for me, baptizing them in the Name of the Father and of the Son and of the Holy Spirit.'
The disciples probably didn't understand that very well. You can imagine them thinking, 'Who are the Father, the Son and the Holy Spirit? I thought there was just One God?'
But when they thought about it, they realized that they had *experienced* God in three ways:
– They prayed to God the Father.
– They'd seen Jesus, who was God the Son
– And, a few days later, they'd felt the Holy Spirit, blowing through the house.
So, though they knew God was One, they experienced Him as Three People.
Only Christians know this – and it's one of the most important things we do know about God.

MUSIC

Either 'I believe in God the Father' *or, if there's time,* 'Father, in my life I see . . .' *or the traditional hymn* 'Holy, Holy, Holy, Lord God Almighty' *(the first and last verses are particularly good).*

Leader   Let's finish as we began, with **The Sign of the Cross** ✠ **(p. xxxvi).**

REHEARSAL

Practise your presentation for when you go back into church (see below).

BACK IN CHURCH

Line the kids up down the front

Leader   Today is Trinity Sunday.
          And we thought making the Sign of the Cross was a really helpful
          way to think about the Holy Trinity: we're going to make the Sign
          slowly.

Child 1   The Father is at the top – in Heaven.

The children start the Sign by touching their heads

Child 2   The Son, Jesus, came down to Earth.

The kids bring their hands down to tummy level

Child 3   The Spirit lives in our hearts.

They bring their hands over to their left

Child 4   **Amen**

Finish over on the right-hand side

Leader   There is only one God, but we know Him as three People, Father,
          Son and Holy Spirit – the Holy Trinity.

Script 36   Corpus Christi

(Roman Catholic)

St Mark 14.22–26

The Feast of Corpus Christi is celebrated on the Sunday after Trinity Sunday by Roman Catholics in some countries. Check with your priest – if you are celebrating Corpus Christi, this is your script (otherwise use *Script 37* **Practising**).

THEME

Today we thank God for giving us the Eucharist. Many churches will have a procession of the Blessed Sacrament today. This session focuses on the Host itself. Can God really be that small?

SET UP

- The Liturgical colour is White or Gold.
- At least ten balls of varying sizes. You are about to represent the Solar system so try to get a large ball for the Sun, two footballs for Jupiter and Saturn, two tennis balls for Uranus and Neptune, three ping pong balls for Venus, Earth and Mars, and a really tiny ball for Mercury.* (If you're stuck, round balloons will do instead.)
- A hazelnut.
- An unconsecrated wafer.
- A piece of pitta bread.

OPTIONAL

- You can add extra balls for various galaxies.

WELCOME *the children and lead them in* **The Sign of the Cross** ✠ **(p. xxxvi).**

---

* Some of you might be expecting Pluto in this list, but it lost its planetary status in August 2006. Nowadays it is just a 'dwarf planet', of which there are at least forty, and probably many more to be discovered.

THE KYRIE   Jesus, we are sorry for the time we have forgotten you,
Lord have mercy
Lord have mercy

Jesus, we are sorry for the times when we have been unloving,
Christ have mercy
Christ have mercy

Jesus, thank you for always being ready to hear us and forgive,
Lord have mercy
Lord have mercy

Ask the children to repeat **The Prayer for Forgiveness** *after you* (**p. xxxvi**).

OPENING   Lord Jesus Christ,
PRAYER   You are the Bread of Life.
Thank you for being with us today,
In the Gospel
In our hearts
And in the Holy Sacrament of the Altar. **Amen**

Leader   Today is the Feast of Corpus Christi. *(Write it up – look at it)*
Hmm, that looks like Latin to me.
Does anyone know what Corpus Christi means? (**The Body of Christ**)
OK, the feast of Jesus' Body – where *is* Jesus' Body?

(Take what comes, but establish that Jesus went up to Heaven in His Body)

Yup, Jesus' Body is in Heaven – we can't see it.
But Jesus knew how important it was for us to see and touch Him,
so He allows something here on Earth to be His Body for us.
Does anyone know what it is? *(Hold up the unconsecrated wafer)*
(**The Bread/Host at Mass**)
This is just bread. Jesus only enters it when the priest prays over it at Mass.
It hasn't happened to this bit of bread yet.
Even so, it's still very odd.
Jesus is God – how can God fit into a tiny bit of bread?
Let's think about that.

The Size of God

Gather the children into a circle

Leader   To get an idea of the size of God, we need to think about some of the things He's made. Let's start with the Sun.

Produce the largest ball you've got

Who wants to be the Sun?

Give them the ball and ask them to stand in the middle of the circle

Well the Sun is circled by planets. The first is a little one.

Show a tiny ball

Mercury.
Anyone want to be Mercury?

Give the child the ball and position him/her near the Sun
Then go through the entire solar system, each kid getting further away – if you have more than nine children, add asteroids and dwarf planets. Give the extra kids small balls and add them to the edge. (Don't add moons to the planets, it muddles things up)
The planets orbit in this order: Mercury, Venus, Earth, Mars, Jupiter, Saturn, Uranus, Neptune
If the children happen to know the order of the planets, encourage them to prompt you

Right so we've got the Sun and all the planets in the Solar system (plus some of the other things that orbit our Sun). Let's see them in action.

To the Sun   Hold your ball up, you stay still.
Mercury, start going round the Sun.
Now Venus . . .
Now Earth . . . *(and so on)*

Once the whole room has orbited a couple of times, call a halt

Now, supposing that, one day, God decided to move our Solar System and put it somewhere else. He'd have to pick up these planets and asteroids – let's try . . .
I'll pretend to be God for a minute, hand the Solar System over to me.

Ask the children to come forward, one by one, and give you their balls to hold. It doesn't matter if you drop a few – ad lib remarks like 'Ooops, there goes Mars . . .' Add in the asteroids, if you can, and the moment you find you're dropping everything call out

Stop!
I can't hold all this stuff. Let's roll it down the other end of the room.

Get rid of the balls

OK, sit down.

Settle the children

I can't even hold our weedy football solar system – but God could hold the real thing, no problem. That makes Him pretty big . . .

Mother Julian

Leader   Actually He's even bigger than we realize.
Let me tell you about Mother Julian.
She was a hermit who had a vision of the universe.
What do you think she saw? (**Stars, planets, black holes**) *(Anything the kids know about)*
Nope – she saw this . . .

Hold up the hazelnut

She saw something as small as a hazelnut, and she said to God – 'What's that?'
And He replied (in her vision): 'It is all that is made.'
And Mother Julian looked at the little hazelnut and got frightened.
'But God,' she said, 'it's so small. It'll get lost – who looks after it?'
'I do,' said God, 'I love it.'

And He held it in the palm of His hand.
So, from God's point of view, the universe is as small as this nut.
He doesn't hold the universe like this . . .

Mime holding a huge bundle

He can place it in the palm of His hand.

Put the nut in the palm of your hand

That makes Him even bigger than we thought.

Optional Philosophic Moment

Leader   Are we getting this right? Is God really big?
Throw me a ball someone . . .

Hold up the ball

Look, I'm bigger than this ball.
You can see that at once – because here's the ball . . .

And here's me.
We're both *things*.
But God isn't a thing at all.
He isn't part of the universe so, though He looks after it, being big or small – or yellow – or made of rubber *(bounce the ball)* isn't something we can say about God.
If God wants to have a shape or a size, He can have any shape or size He likes.*

Back to Main Script

Leader   So, God isn't bothered about size.
But one day, as He looked through His universe *(rotate the nut gently with your forefinger)*, He saw a planet that needed help.
So he became as small as this nut.
And then smaller.
And smaller still.
Until He was small enough to enter His own universe. And He looked round, and saw a tiny blue planet.
And landed on it as a little child.
What was the child's name? (**Jesus**)
So God became this size . . . *(indicate the size of an average baby)*
And before he left us, Jesus showed how, in future, He wouldn't mind going even smaller. Let's hear about it in the Gospel.

THE GOSPEL PROCESSION

THE GOSPEL *Mark 14.22–26*

AFTER THE GOSPEL

Leader   Jesus took a piece of flat bread *(hold up the pitta)*
And broke it *(tear it into pieces)*
And told His disciples that the bread was His Body.
It still is.
At every Mass Jesus is present in the Bread at the Altar.

REHEARSAL

Practise your presentation for when you go back into church (see below).

---

* The Swiss theologian Karl Barth said that 'for God it is just as natural to be lowly as it is to be high, to be near as it is to be far, to be little as it is to be great, to be abroad as to be at home'.

FINAL **DEVOTION**	Lord Jesus Thank you for finding us Thank you for saving us And thank you for still being with us In the Bread of the Altar, **Amen**

BACK IN CHURCH

Line up the children

Leader Today we thought about God's universe and how big it was.

The children stand with their legs apart and stretch their arms above their heads

Then we though about God coming down into His universe and getting smaller and smaller . . .

The children make themselves as small as possible

Until He was as small as a child.

The children jump up

Child 1 Today God is even smaller.
Child 2 He is here in a piece of bread.
Child 3 We think God doesn't mind how big or small He is.
Child 4 As long as He is with His people.

Script 37   Practising

Ordinary Time 8 (Roman Catholic)
(Sunday between 24 and 28 May
if after Trinity Sunday)

This may be replaced with Script 36 Corpus Christi

St Mark 2.18–20

THEME

Sometimes we set ourselves to do uncomfortable things, like tidying up the house, or going to the gym, or fasting in Lent. Normally we only do these things with a goal in view, like being ready for guests or preparing for Easter, but it's odd how often human beings get so absorbed in the means that they forget the ends.

In the Gospel today Jesus comments that His countrymen are so busy getting ready for the Messiah, they haven't noticed He's arrived.

SET UP

- The liturgical colour is Green.
- Alert any musicians you have among you that you are going to sing 'Allelu, Allelu, Allelu, Alleluia' at the end. (If you can't cope with singing rounds, don't worry, the song – plus actions – works perfectly well if you get the kids to chant it in unison.) The music can be downloaded from the Internet.
- Tell your priest that the kids are going to sing or chant a short song as part of their presentation.

WELCOME *the children and lead them in* **The Sign of the Cross** ✠ (p. xxxvi).

THE KYRIE   Lord Jesus you came to tell us the Good News,
                  Lord have mercy
                  Lord have mercy

                  Lord Jesus you came to forgive us our sins,
                  Christ have mercy
                  Christ have mercy

Lord Jesus you came to set us free,
Lord have mercy
Lord have mercy.

Ask the children to repeat **The Prayer for Forgiveness** *after you* (**p. xxxvi**).

OPENING
PRAYER
Lord Jesus, Saviour of the World,
When you came to live among us,
Your friends found that,
just by being near you, they were filled with joy.
Help us to feel their joy this morning
As we welcome you into our midst,
For your Name's sake. **Amen**

Getting Fit

Leader 1
Today I'm going to tell you something that will totally amaze you.
Name (indicate Leader 2 or a suitably primed teenager) was chosen
to run the 100 metres in the Olympics.
Of course he/she had to get fit.
Let's go through some of the exercises he/she had to do.

Run some very easy exercises: crouching down and leaping up, hands out from
shoulders – flap them up and down: touch your toes: press-ups (the children can have
a go even if you don't feel like it). Leader 2 joins in

Then came the day of the race.
You are all so fit now I bet you can run it.

Run a '100-metre' dash down to the end of the room. If you are in a confined space,
ask the kids to run on the spot – looking at a watch to time them. At the end of a
minute they sit down.
And all the time Leader 2 just goes on exercising

Hey – why didn't you run the race?

Leader 2
Oh, I was too busy exercising . . .

Leader 1
(To the kids) Was that sensible? (**No!**)
Quite, it's a very good idea to practise for something – but it's daft
not to do the thing you're practising for.
Now when Jesus was alive, his fellow Jews were always practising.
They knew God was going to send His Messiah – His Saviour – and
they wanted to be prepared.
So really holy Jews, like Pharisees or the sort of people who listened
to John the Baptist, used to pray and fast and get ready for the day

the Messiah would come. It used to make them rather serious.

Jesus met some of them once; we're going to hear about that in today's Gospel.

THE GOSPEL PROCESSION

THE GOSPEL *St Mark 2.18–20*

Optional Paraphrase

One day the followers of John the Baptist, and some of the Jews, were fasting. And some people came to Jesus and asked Him: 'Why is it that the disciples of John the Baptist and the disciples of the Pharisees fast, but yours do not?'

Jesus answered, 'Do you expect the guests at a wedding party to fast? Of course not! As long as the bridegroom is with them, they will eat. But the day will come when the bridegroom will be taken away from them – then they will fast.'

AFTER THE GOSPEL

Leader   So there were the Jews fasting away *and* John the Baptist's disciples, fasting as well. All of them waiting for the Messiah and trying to be holy. But Jesus' friends weren't fasting at all. Can you guess why?

They may – but if they're baffled, read this bit of the Gospel again

Jesus said, 'Do you expect the guests at a wedding party to fast? Of course not! As long as the bridegroom is with them, they will eat . . .' Who's the bridegroom? (**Jesus**)

Jesus didn't call Himself the 'bridegroom' because He was getting married, 'bridegroom' is one of the ways the Jews described God's Messiah.

So, in a way, Jesus is saying, 'Guys, there you all are fasting and saving your appetites – and all the time the party is happening! The Messiah has come!'

ACTIVITY

Leader   Well, the 'bridegroom' left us eventually – Jesus went back to Heaven. So Christians do fast every now and then, but we're supposed to be quite cheerful about it. After all, Jesus is coming back, and He's still around in His Church.

So it's a good thing to learn when to practise, and when to stop.

If you are an actor, you know automatically: you rehearse a play among yourselves – that's the practice bit – and when the audience turns up, you do the show – that's when you stop practising. We're going to go back and tell the adults about this – and we'll do it by giving them a show.

MUSIC

Practise a song with the kids, the best sort is a simple round – with movements if you are up to it. 'Allelu, allelu, allelu, alleluia, praise ye the Lord' *works very well. You can download the music from the Internet but chanting it very fast is just as effective. If the kids aren't up to singing it as a round, practise it like this:*
One half of the room stands up as they sing 'Allelu(ia)' *and sits down. The other half stands up as they sing* 'Praise ye the Lord'. *All stand and sing the last line.*

1st half *(Standing)* Allelu, allelu, allelu, alleluia	*(Sit down)*
2nd half *(Standing)* Praise ye the Lord	*(Sit down)*
1st half *(Standing)* Allelu, allelu, allelu, alleluia	*(Sit down)*
2nd half *(Standing)* Praise ye the Lord	*(Sit down)*
2nd half *(Jumping up again)* Praise ye the Lord	*(Sit down)*
1st half *(Standing)* Alleluia!	*(Sit down)*
2nd half *(Standing)* Praise ye the Lord	*(Sit down)*
1st half *(Standing)* Alleluia!	*(Sit down)*
2nd half *(Standing)* Praise ye the Lord	*(Sit down)*
1st half *(Standing)* Alleluia!	*(Sit down)*
Everybody *(Jumping up)* Praise ye the Lord!	

If you split the room to sing it as a round, each half sings all the lines and jumps up at the single 'alleluias', *like this*

Allelu, allelu, allelu, alleluia
Praise ye the Lord
Allelu, allelu, allelu, alleluia
Praise ye the Lord
Praise ye the Lord, *(Stand)* alleluia *(Sit)*
Praise ye the Lord, *(Stand)* alleluia *(Sit)*
Praise ye the Lord, *(Stand)* alleluia *(Sit)*
(Jump up again) Praise ye the Lord!

FINAL PRAYER

Finish your rehearsal with a short prayer

Glory be . . . (see p. xxxvii).

BACK IN CHURCH

Leader	Today we heard how some people were fasting and praying as they waited for the Messiah to come, while Jesus' friends were happy because the Messiah *had* come, and weren't fasting at all. We thought that showed us how important it was to know when to practise, and when to know the show has started.
	So we've been practising – and now we're going to give you a show. It's about how happy we feel that Jesus the Messiah has come into the world.

Cue song

Script 38   The Sabbath

Proper 4, Ordinary Time 9
(Sunday between 29 May and 4 June
if after Trinity Sunday)

This may be replaced with Script 36 Corpus Christi

St Mark 2.23–27

THEME

The Sabbath – that great Jewish contribution to human happiness – is a day off
once a week. It is important to be positive about the Sabbath, the Jews got it so
right. It is the day of the week on which we honour God by giving it back to Him,
clean and unused, and not doing a stroke of work.

But of course there were the rules. Human beings can't resist making rules, and
the Sabbath rules were so elaborate that the Sabbath had become the one day of
the week when you couldn't act normally – or even kindly. In the Gospel today,
Jesus reminds His fellow Jews why God gave them the Sabbath in the first place.

SET UP

- The liturgical colour is Green.
- Pictures from the CD-Rom.
- A small table.
- 24 pieces of pitta bread.
- Make some sticky labels to hand out for the procession (see below).
- An alarm clock with a bell.

WELCOME *the children and lead them in* **The Sign of the Cross** ✠ **(p. xxxvi).**

BEFORE THE KYRIE

Leader   Hi, I want to start by thinking about the week that's passed.
             How many days are there in a week? (**Seven**)
             Brilliant, and for most of those days we go to school or work –
             which ones are they?

*Encourage the children to chant '**Monday, Tuesday** . . .' etc. as you mark them off with your fingers*

> OK, that's five days, then there's Saturday, what do you do on Saturdays?

Take what comes

> Then there's Sunday, the day we go to church.
> It's a very good day to think back over the week.
> How did it go?
> I hope there were some nice things in it?
> But perhaps there were some moments that weren't so good.
> Let's put those right now.

THE KYRIE

> Lord Jesus, you came to free us from our sins,
> Lord have mercy
> **Lord have mercy**
>
> Lord Jesus, you told us that God would always forgive us,
> Christ have mercy
> **Christ have mercy**
>
> Lord Jesus, help us not to sin again,
> Lord have mercy
> **Lord have mercy**

OPENING PRAYER

> Eternal Father,
> We thank you for the past week.
> For the times we were happy
> For the times we got things right
> For the people who loved us.
> Thank you for giving us all the days of the week,
> Especially this day, Sunday,
> Help us to give it back to you
> Full of our love and praise. **Amen**

THE SABBATH

Leader

> So which day of the week do we go to church? (**Sunday**)
> Can we go any other day? (**Yes**)
> Of course we can, but Sunday is the day the whole parish tries to turn up to worship God together.
> Why did we choose Sunday? (**It's the day Jesus rose from the dead**)

Excellent, but long before there were any Christians or any churches, another set of people chose a day of the week to worship God on. Can you guess who they were? *(It doesn't matter if they don't know)* They were the Jews, the people that Jesus belonged to. For the Jews the week runs like this:

Cut out the days of the week from **CD38.1** *and get the children to stick them up in order for you. Pause to consider the result*

The Jewish week looks different from our one – can you see why? **(Sunday is at the beginning, Saturday at the end)***
Saturday is the last day of the week, it's the one on which Jews worship God and have a rest.
Why did they choose Saturday?

The kids might know – **(it was the day on which God rested)**

In the Creation story, God made the Heavens and the Earth in the first six days of the week – and on the seventh, He rested.
So the Jews rest too. They call the seventh day . . .

Write it up   'The Sabbath'
The Sabbath is a lovely day. It's a day on which Jews wear their best clothes, and eat super Sabbath food and don't do a thing.
Jewish priests always ate 'shewbread' on the Sabbath. Have you ever come across 'shewbread'? It looks like this. *(Produce 12 pittas)*

Shewbread

Leader   The Jews made 12 flat loaves of bread of the best flour they had and put them on a table in their Temple.

Pull out a table, stack the pitta in two piles of six

The bread was called the Bread of Presence, because it was placed next to the holiest part of the Temple, very near the presence of God. Of course, the bread couldn't stay there too long, it would get stale, so every Sabbath the Jewish priests ate it up and replaced it with another 12 loaves.
The catch was, the table always had to have 12 loaves on it – so as they took one off, they replaced it with another very carefully.
Can anyone guess how they did that?

---

* Actually, as far as the early Christians were concerned, Sunday *was* the first day of the week, but centuries of church-going on Sunday has made us all feel that it's at the end.

Produce the other 12 pittas and ask the kids to try: it's like Holy Spillikins, nobody really knows how the Jewish priests managed it

> Well that's all good fun, it's nice to have ceremonies. But it was only a ceremony, and sometimes you can skip ceremonies, especially in an emergency.

David and the Shewbread

Have the pictures ready

Leader	One day, long ago, the great Jewish hero David thundered into the
CD38.2	temple.
CD38.3	He was on the run, with his men.
	They were starving – so what do you think the priests did?
CD38.4	Yup, they gave them the shewbread
CD38.5	David and his mates probably ate up the fresh ones too.

The priests didn't mind. It was against the rules, but starving men are more important than a pile of loaves, however holy.

Jesus loved that story – and He remembered it when He and His friends were told off for not keeping the Sabbath. We'll hear it now.

THE GOSPEL PROCESSION

THE GOSPEL *St Mark 2.23–27*

AFTER THE GOSPEL

Leader	What were Jesus and His friends doing on the Sabbath that annoyed people? (**They were picking off bits of corn and nibbling it**)

Yup, as far as some people were concerned, that was work – and you weren't supposed to work on the Sabbath.

Jesus said, 'You're worried about my friends nibbling corn – what about David eating all those loaves?'

ACTIVITY

Set up a church procession. Do it very seriously, following your church's format.

A possible procession

Thurifer, boat boy, crucifer, two servers with candles, choir, more servers, MC, assisting priests, sub-deacon, deacon, celebrating priest.

Adapt your procession as you see fit, and dish out labels to all the kids – 'chorister', 'priest' and so on. Line them up, process round the hall, then get them to sit down randomly.

Leader   OK, that was a very good procession – but now it's the end of the service: we need to get back into that procession again.

See if the kids can do it. Show them how servers assemble by walking very purposefully – not running – and getting into line. Once the procession is in the right order, congratulate them and ask them to sit down

But supposing the service ends in quite a different way?
Supposing the service ends with one of the servers managing to set off the fire alarm? What do we do then?
I tell you what we do, we get out by walking sensibly, but very fast. Let's see you do it. when you hear the alarm, move to the edge of the room, anyone who touches a wall is safe.
Are you ready?

Set off the alarm bell on your clock
The kids scatter

Brilliant.
Forget about that procession!
You see, processions were made for people, not people for processions.

BEFORE THE FINAL PRAYER

Gather the children round the Shewbread table

Leader   Jesus loved the Jewish faith,
He loved the Temple,
He loved the Sabbath.
But He loved people and God His Father even more.
So, if the Sabbath got in the way of being kind to people, or worshipping God, He put the Sabbath gently to one side.
Jesus said, 'The Sabbath was made for man, not man for the Sabbath.'

FINAL PRAYER	God our Father, Thank you for giving us holy days. Thank you for giving the Jews the Sabbath And for giving Sunday to your Church. Help us in the coming week to love you and our neighbours And bring us back again next Sunday To worship you. **Amen**

BACK IN CHURCH

The children march in, in their procession

Leader	Today Jesus said, 'The Sabbath was made for man, not man for the Sabbath.' So we started thinking about holy rules and ceremonies and we set up a procession. At the front we had . . .

Go through the procession, finish with

Until we got to the very end with the most important person of all, *Name* here is the Priest!

We think processions are great – but there are moments when you have to do without them. In an emergency, for example. Watch this:

Either set off the alarm clock or shout 'Alarm!'
The children run back to their pews and/or parents

You see, processions were made for people, not people for processions.

(CD38.2)   (CD38.3)

Specimen cartoons for this script

Script 39   St Francis and the Pike

Proper 5, Ordinary Time 10
(Sunday between 5 and 11 June
if after Trinity Sunday)

This may be replaced with Script 36 Corpus Christi

St Mark 3.20–21, 31–35

THEME

In the Gospel today we hear of Jesus' family coming to take Him home. They may have thought Him mad (St Mark 3.21) but, given verse 20, they may have just thought He needed a rest. Family is big in the Middle East, you can't ignore them. However, Jesus sidestepped His relatives by looking round the crowd and extending His family. Anyone who does the will of God, He said, could be called His Mother, or Brother, or Sister.

Christians have been extending the family ever since, particularly St Francis. We'll hear today how Francis added the Sun, the Moon and a huge great pike to his family.

SET UP

- The liturgical colour is Green.
- Pictures from the CD-Rom.
- Enough A5 sheets of black paper for all the children – or one large sheet of black paper for the group.
- Pike bones from the CD-Rom. Print up several sets if you are going to get the kids to make pike. Make one large set for yourself, and have them ready when you tell the story.
- Stick(s) of glue.
- Halo from the CD-Rom, plus some 'Blu-Tack', so you can take it on and off the picture.

WELCOME *the children and lead them in* **The Sign of the Cross** ✠ **(p. xxxvi).**

Introduce the Kyrie

Leader	Look back over the week – was there anything we wish we hadn't done? Or things we forgot to do?
	Let's get rid of it now by telling God we're sorry.

THE KYRIE	Lord Jesus, you came to bring us back to God,
	Lord have mercy
	Lord have mercy
	Lord Jesus, you came to heal us from our sins,
	Christ have mercy
	Christ have mercy
	Lord Jesus, you came to tell us how much God loves us,
	Lord have mercy
	Lord have mercy

Ask the children to repeat **The Prayer for Forgiveness** *after you* (**p. xxxvi**).

OPENING PRAYER	Lord Jesus,
	You said: 'Anyone who loves me will keep my word
	And my Father will love them.'
	Help us to love you,
	To hear your word this morning
	And keep it
	Now and for ever. **Amen**

BEFORE THE GOSPEL

Leader	Before we hear the Gospel this morning, I'd like you to look at this picture.
CD39.1	*Put up the picture of St Francis*
	Can anyone tell me what sort of man this is?

They'll probably say 'monk' rather than 'friar' – let it go

	A monk – actually he's a friar, but it's much the same.
	This one's name is Francis.
	But if you met him you wouldn't say 'Hello Mr Francis', you'd say 'Hello *Brother* Francis'.
	And if you met this lady –

CD39.2   *Put up a picture of a nun*

Her name is Theresa.
Can you guess how you'd address her? (**Sister or Mother Theresa**)

CD39.3   *Put up a picture of a modern priest*

What would you call him? (**Father**)
The Church is full of mothers and fathers and brothers and sisters.
How did we get so many relations?
We'll find out in the Gospel.

GOSPEL PROCESSION

THE GOSPEL *St Mark 3.20–21, 31–35*

AFTER THE GOSPEL

Leader   That's a very interesting Gospel. Jesus had a family just like us.
In fact Jesus' family were so ordinary that, though they loved Him very much, they didn't always understand Him.
What did His family want to do? (**Take Him home**)
Why?

The children will probably have picked up that they thought Jesus was mad, direct their attention to verse 20. Jesus didn't have time to eat: perhaps they thought He needed a rest

In Palestine, where Jesus lived, you were supposed to listen to your family and obey them even if you were grown-up. (You still are actually.)
A whole load of brothers turning up to take you home was pretty serious, especially if your mother came too.
But Jesus looked round at His family, His friends, and the crowd, and He said, 'You are all my family. Anyone who does God's work is family to me.'
And Jesus meant it. He wasn't getting out of going home, He was thinking, 'Yes, family is great – but I've got a bigger family than my Mother and my brothers realize.'
And that's us.
Christians have been calling each other 'brother' and 'sister' ever since.
In fact there's one Christian who decided the whole universe was his family. His name was Francis. Brother Francis.

Indicate the Francis picture – and get rid of the others

Francis and the Pike – Part 1

Leader   Francis lived in Italy, hundreds of years ago, in the Middle Ages. He loved God so much that he gave all his money away and became a poor friar. He shaved his head, and put on rough clothing – rather like a sack – and kept it together with some rope round his waist.

Point out the sack and patches on the picture

Now even in the Middle Ages you couldn't walk round in a sack without people thinking you were a nut but, though people started off by laughing at Francis, they'd stop to listen to him as well.

Francis knew the Gospels off by heart – and he loved the bit we've just heard. He felt that everything in the world was his family, not just people, but birds, foxes – and socking great dangerous animals

CD39.4   like – this pike.

Francis went all round Italy teaching people about God and, one day, he sailed across a huge lake, to talk to the poor fishermen who lived on the island in the middle.

CD39.5   *St Francis preaching – ad lib*

There he is talking to the fishermen: they thought he was wonderful – and they gave him a present. The biggest fish they could catch.

CD39.6   *Pike in a bucket*

'That will do nicely for your supper!' they said, 'Have it with chips.' St Francis thanked the fishermen and got back in his boat.

CD39.7   He and the pike looked at each other and, when he was well out of sight of land, splosh! Francis threw the pike back into the water.

But the pike wouldn't leave him, it swum round the boat, so Francis

CD39.8   lifted up his hands and said, 'Brother Pike, may God bless you, be a good fish and love God.' Then he rowed away.

And ever afterwards the pike was noted for his piety and wonderful behaviour.

CD39.9   And when he died, the villagers gathered up his bones . . .

Look at your pile of pictures, search through them . . .

Blimey! (*Or whatever you say in your part of the world*)
Where are the pike's bones?

Leader 2 comes forward with the pile of bones – pick them up in dismay

They're in a bit of a mess.
Can anyone help me to put them in order?

ACTIVITY

Either dish out a complete pike skeleton to every kid, plus a sheet of black paper and some glue – or make a huge pike skeleton together on a large sheet of black paper. Make the pike by getting the kids to stick the bones on to the black paper.
When it's finished, admire the result and either go on with the big picture, or pick one of the kids' pictures to finish the story.

Francis and the Pike – Part 2

Leader	Brilliant – a very nice skeleton of a very holy fish.
	Just a minute, how did the fishermen know that this was the very pike that had followed St Francis?
CD39.10	*Leader 2 sticks on the halo*
	Oh, of course. So the fisherman gathered up the bones and buried the pike in a chapel on their island – and its tomb is there to this very day.
CD39.11	*(Picca is Italian for pike)*

BEFORE THE FINAL PRAYER

Leader   Do you think that story is true?

Run a non-heavy session on this. It doesn't matter whether they believe it or not.*
Establish that this is the sort of story people tell about St Francis. There are loads of them: he obviously did have some sort of influence on animals.

The fishermen thought it was true, and the story reminds us how much Francis loved animals, and thought they were children of God, just like us.

Francis is one of the great saints of the Church. Let's finish with one of his prayers.

FINAL PRAYER	Almighty God,
	We thank you for all the creatures you have made:
	For brother Sun and sister Moon,
	For brother wolf and sister bear,
	For brother pike and sister seal,
	And for our own brothers and sisters as well. **Amen**

---

* The Chapel of the Pike on the island in Lake Trasimeno really does exist. It contains the tomb dedicated to a pike with some very ancient pike bones in it.

MUSIC

Any hymn based on the Canticle of St Francis would be a good way to finish; the traditional one is 'All creatures of our God and King'.

BACK IN CHURCH

The children come in with the pictures below

Leader   Today we heard how St Francis . . .

Child 1 *holds up the Francis picture*

Leader   Loved the Gospel we heard this morning so much
That he called everything in the world his brother and sister.
Even big dangerous animals like . . .

Child 2 *holds up pike picture*

This pike.
In fact, we heard that this pike was such a good friend of St Francis
that, when it died, some fishermen gathered up its bones . . .

Child 3 *holds up skeleton picture minus halo*

And buried them properly in church.
We weren't too sure how the fishermen knew the bones were the
right one – then we realized that the bones must have had . . .

Child 4 *puts halo on*

A halo!
We don't know if the story is true, but it reminded us that everything
in the world is Family for a Christian.

(CD39.5)

(CD39.8)

Specimen cartoons for this script

Script 40 Bread

Proper 6, Ordinary Time 11
(Sunday between 12 and 18 June
if after Trinity Sunday)

This may be replaced with Script 36 Corpus Christi

Mark 4.26–29

THEME

Many of the Gospels in Year B talk about bread: ordinary bread, Living Bread, and the grains of wheat that are scattered on the earth that will make bread. This session starts the ball rolling. The children are encouraged to think about bread, and what a mysterious food it is.

SET UP

- Bread roll.
- Pictures from the CD-Rom.
- Wheat grain, or anything that looks like grain – puffed wheat or pumpkin seeds for example.
- A prayer candle (see p. xxiii).

WELCOME *the children and lead them in* **The Sign of the Cross** ✠ **(p. xxxvi).**

THE KYRIE   Lord Jesus, forgive us for the times we have forgotten you,
Lord have mercy
Lord have mercy

Lord Jesus, forgive us for the times we have been unkind,
Christ have mercy
Christ have mercy

Lord Jesus, you told us that God will always forgive those who are sorry for their sins,
Lord have mercy
Lord have mercy

Ask the children to repeat **The Prayer for Forgiveness** *after you* (**p. xxxvi**).

OPENING PRAYER	Lord God, Maker of Heaven and Earth: You have given us Sun and soil And grains of wheat, to make into bread. Help us to eat our daily bread With thankfulness, Knowing that it comes from you. **Amen**

Bread

Leader	Today we're going to think about bread.
CD40.1	*Put up picture of Roman* Way back in Roman times, rich Romans used to stop the poor Romans complaining by giving them . . . *(Write this in the balloon)* 'Bread and circuses'.
CD40.2	And if they threw you into gaol they gave you *(Write this on the 'Gaol Menu')* 'Bread and water'. Everyone needs bread. The Bible is full of people eating bread, and growing bread, and asking for bread. Some people seem to eat nothing but bread – this chap for example

Put up picture of Elijah (**CD40.3**)

I'm going to tell you a story about him.

Feeding Elijah

Elijah was a prophet, and he lived in Israel a very long time ago. One year there was a drought and God told Elijah to go to a village called Zarphath, where a widow would look after him. So off Elijah went and, lo and behold, the first person he met was a widow (you can tell a widow by her dark clothes) gathering sticks for a fire (**CD40.4**). 'Could you get me some water?' asked Elijah and, as she turned to go, 'and some bread too?'

'I can't give you any bread,' she said, 'all I've got is a handful of flour and a drop of oil. I've come out to gather sticks for a fire, so I can cook all I've got in my larder for me and my little boy. It will probably be our last meal on earth.'

'Don't worry,' said Elijah, 'Go home and make your fire. Make a roll of bread for me, and another for you and your son, and I promise you the flour in the bowl and the oil in the jar will not run out until the Lord God sends us rain again.'

So the widow did as Elijah said, and she, and the prophet, and her son, had enough bread to eat **(CD40.5)** as long as the drought lasted. And the flour in the bowl, and the oil in the jar, never ran out.

Leader   The bread that Elijah ate was quite ordinary – like this . . .

Pick up the roll

But it was mysterious too.

Refer back to the pictures

It came from the bowl of flour that God kept filled up.
Jesus knew that story. He probably thought Elijah's bread was mysterious as well – actually, Jesus thought all bread was mysterious. He looked at wheat grains, like this . . .

Sift the 'wheat grains' in your hands

and thought, how do they turn into bread?
Actually, how *do* they turn into bread? How do we make bread?

Take all answers
Establish that we sow seed, and it rains, and the seed grows and eventually we've got wheat that we can harvest. Ask the children to help you draw the process. If you use the template provided (CD40.6), you'll see that it follows the sequence described by Jesus in the Gospel below
Look at the picture

So there's the seed, and we know it does turn into corn; in fact, you could pull out the seeds and look at them under a microscope to see what happens – but it's still very mysterious.
Why do all those things happen to the seed?
And isn't it odd to think that, when you stand on a bit of muddy field, all these things are happening beneath your feet?
Jesus thought so. Let's hear Him talk about bread in the Gospel.

THE GOSPEL PROCESSION

THE GOSPEL *St Mark 4.26–29*

AFTER THE GOSPEL

Leader   Jesus described our picture – look, there's the man sowing seed – and there are the shoots and the full-grown corn.
Jesus said the Kingdom of God was like that.

Go through the picture again, to illustrate how the Kingdom grows

> God sows the seed – that's all the things we know about God, deep in our hearts. And God sends the sun and the rain – that's all the things He sends to help us, like the Bible or the Church, and, all over the world, very quietly, people learn to love God. Then one day, it's harvest time, and we're ready to go to Heaven.

REHEARSAL

Practise your presentation for when you go back into church (see below).

FINAL PRAYER

Gather the children in a circle, place the roll in the middle, beside the prayer candle

> Let's think about bread for a moment.
> As long as you've got bread you are OK. It's very precious stuff.
> Jesus thought we were as precious and as mysterious as bread.
> I'm going to pass our seeds round.
> Each one of them is precious – just like us – let's see if we can pass them round without spilling one of them.

Take a view as to what is practical and pass round a handful of seeds

> We're going to end with an 'Our Father', the prayer in which Jesus taught us to ask God for our daily bread.

Finish with an **Our Father . . . (p. xxxvi)**.

MUSIC

Two traditional harvest hymns fit in well: 'Come ye thankful people come' *(verses 1 and 2) and* 'We plough the fields and scatter' *(verse 1, do a repeat).*

BACK IN CHURCH

The Leader comes in with a very small quantity of seeds: six kids line up at the front – the last one has the bread roll. Other children read the script

Child 1	Today we heard Jesus talking about bread.
Child 2	He described how seeds grew silently in the earth until it was ready for the harvest.
Child 3	Jesus said God's Kingdom was like this seed . . .

The Leader very obviously sifts the seed in his/her hands

Child 4	It is planted in our hearts.

The Leader passes some seed to a child in the line – and the kids carefully pass it on, one to another

Child 5

Watching the others, so the last line times in with the last kid in the line

> And it grows . . .
> And grows . . .
> Until . . .

The last kid holds up the roll

> It's time for Harvest!

(CD40.1)

*Specimen cartoons
for this script*

(CD40.5)

Script 41   The Stilling of the Storm

Proper 7, Ordinary Time 12
(Sunday between 19 and 25 June
if after Trinity Sunday)

This may be replaced with Script 36 Corpus Christi

St Mark 4.35–41

THEME

Today's Gospel tells one of the classic miracle stories – Jesus' stilling of the storm on the Sea of Galilee. The children will enjoy acting this out, but don't let them get bogged down by the weather – the disciples' varying emotions are just as interesting, particularly the awe-stricken reaction at the end.

SET UP

- The liturgical colour is Green.
- Cast a grown-up or an older child as Jesus. He or she should look at the script beforehand – their part is very easy.
- Disciples' lines printed out from the CD-Rom.
- Some waves on sticks, template on the CD-Rom.
- Have a chair and cushion (for Jesus to fall asleep on) ready for the Gospel.
- Apostle faces from the CD-Rom.

Blue Card

Sellotape

cane

Back of wave card

Front of wave card

WELCOME *the children and lead them in* **The Sign of the Cross** ✠ *(p. xxxvi).*

THE KYRIE   Lord Jesus, you came to bring us back to God,
Lord have mercy
Lord have mercy

Lord Jesus, you came to heal us from our sins
Christ have mercy
Christ have mercy

Lord Jesus, you came to tell us how much God loves us
Lord have mercy
Lord have mercy

Ask the children to repeat **The Prayer for Forgiveness** *after you* (**p. xxxvi**).

Leader	Today's Gospel is about Jesus and His friends, in a boat, sailing across the Sea of Galilee, so it's a good Sunday for thinking about people who are at sea right now. Let's ask God to look after them.
OPENING PRAYER	Eternal Father, Lord of Sea and Sky, Bless and protect all sailors and fishermen As they go about their daily work on the sea. Be with them in storms and tempests And bring them safely back to harbour, we ask this through Jesus, your Son. **Amen**

REHEARSAL

Leader	Today we're going to act out the Gospel. I need some disciples *(choose some of the older children, you don't necessarily need 12)* And the Sea *(everyone else)* Right, the disciples make quite a lot of noise in this Gospel, let's run through their lines.

Stick up the disciples' remarks from the CD-Rom (**CD41.1**) *and cue them in, one by one*

And the Sea has a lot to do as well.

Dish out the 'Wave sticks': keep an eye on the very little ones; they may need some adult supervision. Hold a Wave yourself, to show the kids the movements

Hold your Waves just near your chest.
Now rock them a bit . . .
Yup, excellent.
Now – watch me – when I give the cue, make the Waves really rock:

Give the cue   Brilliant.

Do the 'kill it' cue – finger across throat

And now, when I give the cue, make them rock above your head . . .

Cue . . . then kill it

Fantastic.

Now when Jesus – that's *Name* – stretches out His hands, go very still.

OK get those Waves rocking above your head again – and watch Jesus:

Jesus gives the cue

Excellent.
I think we're ready to go . . .

THE GOSPEL PROCESSION

THE GOSPEL *St Mark 4.35–41*

Narrator   One day Jesus and His friends decided to cross the Sea of Galilee on a boat.

Place the chair and cushion in the middle of the 'Sea', the disciples line up behind the chair, so it looks like the prow. Jesus goes to the top of the line

Jesus was very tired

Major acting from Jesus here

He sat down at the front of the boat, found a pillow, and went to sleep.

He does so   Off they went, the sea was very gentle

Waves held still at chest level

And the disciples began to enjoy themselves

Disciples   **Wheee!** (*Get them to wave*)

Narrator   But halfway across, the waves began to bob

Cue some gentle rocking

Then they bobbed some more.

Cue a bit more

The disciples got nervous

Disciples   **Ooo-er!**
I feel sick!

Narrator   And then the waves went mad, the sea got rough, the rain came down, and there was a horrible storm.

Cue violent rocking

And the disciples were terrified.

Disciples   **Help!**
Mum!

Narrator	'Where's Jesus??!' said somebody – they all looked round.

Everybody looks round

And there He was, fast asleep at the front.
At this point the water rose so high it looked as if it was going to swamp the boat.

Cue the kids to hold their Waves above their heads

	And the disciples all yelled together:
Disciples	**WAKE UP JESUS!!**
Narrator	'Look at the sea,' said one of them, 'Don't you care that we are drowning?'
	Jesus stood up
	And He said to the Sea,
Jesus	'Be still!'
	He stretched out His hands

He does so

And the Sea went calm.

Which it does

Then He sat down again.
And the disciples went very quiet, and looked at each other, and said:

Disciples	**Who is this that even the wind and waves obey . . . ?**

Clap the kids – and encourage any spare adults to do the same

AFTER THE GOSPEL

Narrator	That was brilliant.
	You can see it was great being a friend of Jesus – but it was a bit nerve-wracking.

ACTIVITY

Leader	Let's go through all the things the disciples felt as they made that journey.

Stick up the (blank) Apostle faces **(CD41.2)**

At first they felt cheerful – can anyone draw in a happy face for me?

Get the kids to make three or four disciples look cheery

Then they got worried. How are we going to do worried?

The template **(CD41.2)** *will help – worry lines basically, and the eyes looking sideways at the other faces*

Then they were terrified!

The kids will know how to do this, but there is a template on **CD41.3** *if you want to do the classic 'Waah!' cartoon ('panic stricken' face)*

Then Jesus saved them – but they didn't switch back to happy smiles immediately.

Draw in the last face yourself, following the template

The disciples looked at Jesus and felt nervous.
'Who is this,' they said, 'who even the winds and waves obey?'
Well, they didn't answer their own question – but we can.
Who is the only Person in the Universe who can command the winds and the waves? (**God**)
Exactly, God.
Jesus could still the storm because He was God.

Practise your presentation for when you go back into church (see below).

FINAL PRAYER   We're going to say a very ancient poem together, about God, and sailors, and the sea. It's Psalm 107.
The response is:
God is strong to save

Some sailors went out on the sea in ships;
they were merchants on the mighty waters.
God is strong to save

They saw the works of the Lord,
And His wonderful deeds in the deep.
God is strong to save

God spoke, and a tempest arose,
The waves went up to the heavens, and back again to the deep.
God is strong to save

Then the sailors cried aloud to the Lord,
And He heard their prayer;
God is strong to save

He stilled the storm to a whisper,
And brought them safe to harbour.
God is strong to save.

Finish with a **Glory be** *. . .* (**p. xxxvii**).

BACK IN CHURCH

The children go in with the various Apostle faces, ready to hold them up on cue

Leader   Today we acted the story of Jesus stilling the storm – and we got very interested in the way the disciples coped with their boat trip. At the beginning of the story, they were happy.

Cue the children to hold up the happy faces

But, when the weather began to change, they got nervous.

Cue in anxious faces

And when the storm really got frightening, they were terrified.

Cue in the frightened faces

Jesus got up and stilled the storm – but the disciples didn't switch back to being happy immediately. Instead they looked at each other sideways.

Cue in last face

'Who is this,' they said, 'who even the winds and waves obey?' They didn't answer their own question – but we can –

To the children

Who *is* the only Person in the Universe who can command the winds and the waves?

Children   **God!**

Happy   Worried   More worried

Panic stricken   Astonished

(CD41.3)

Script 42 Jairus's Daughter

Proper 8, Ordinary Time 13
(Sunday between 26 June and 2 July)

St Mark 5.25–34

THEME

This is a gift of a Gospel to introduce the children to the idea of 'intercession' – the way Christians on Earth, and in Heaven, pray for each other.

SET UP

- The liturgical colour is Green.
- Pictures from the CD-Rom.
- A copy of *The Magician's Nephew* by C. S. Lewis.
- A sheet of paper and a ribbon to make a scroll (see below).

If possible, read the Gospel to yourself before the liturgy, and try to do as much as you can off the cuff. The pictures are numbered and you'll find the story flows quite easily. The salient points are:

1 Jairus running up to Jesus to tell Him his little daughter is ill.
2 Jesus hurries away with Jairus at once.
3 A woman touches Jesus as He goes through a crowd. She'd been ill for years and is healed.
4 Jesus knows somebody has touched Him and insists that whoever it is should come forward.
5 The crowd thinks He's being ridiculous.
6 The woman identifies herself, and Jesus confirms her cure.
7 On to Jairus' house, people rush out saying it isn't worth it, the child's dead.
8 'Do not be afraid,' says Jesus, 'only have faith. She is not dead but sleeping.'
9 He turfs out the mourners and says to the little girl, 'Talitha kum' ('Little girl, get up'). The child gets up at once.
10 The parents are overjoyed and Jesus tells them to give their daughter something to eat.

As the children must hear a real sentence from the Gospel, make sure you say Jesus' actual words in your re-telling

WELCOME *the children and lead them in* **The Sign of the Cross** ✠ (**p. xxxvi**).

THE KYRIE   God our Father, you know and love each of your children,
Lord have mercy
Lord have mercy

Lord Jesus Christ, you came to find us,
Christ have mercy
Christ have mercy

God the Holy Spirit, you live in our hearts,
Lord have mercy
Lord have mercy

Ask the children to repeat **The Prayer for Forgiveness** *after you* (**p. xxxvi**).

OPENING   God our Father,
PRAYER   As we come before you this morning,
We thank you for always being ready to hear
Our prayers,
The prayers of our friends,
And the prayers of the saints in Heaven. **Amen**

BEFORE THE GOSPEL

Pick up The Magician's Nephew *and a chair and sit among the children, as if you were going to tell them a story*

Leader   Today we are going to think about prayer, and we're going to do that by listening to a story from this book.

Hold up The Magician's Nephew. *See if anyone knows it, or the 'Narnia' books and films*

Can you tell me something about 'Narnia'?

Accept everything, but home in on the fact that in the 'Narnia' stories, animals can talk. Move on to the great Lion of Narnia

What's his name? (**Aslan**)

Ask the kids about Aslan – or tell them yourself if the 'Narnia' stories aren't being read at the moment

> Narnia is watched over by Aslan, the great Lion of Narnia. He is the Son of the Emperor over the Sea and, as we read the Narnia stories, we realize that the Emperor over the Sea must be God and Aslan (in Narnia) is an image of the Son of God, Jesus.
>
> Well, in one of the books, Aslan sends two children, Digory and Polly, off on an adventure. They ride away on Fledge, the flying horse, but it all takes longer than they expected, and on the second day the children realize they haven't got any food. (Fledge is all right, he can eat grass.)

Open the book – this bit is half way through chapter 12:

> 'Polly and Digory stared at each other in dismay.
> "Well, I *do* think somebody might have arranged about our meals," said Digory.
> "I'm sure Aslan would have, if you'd asked him," said Fledge.
> "Wouldn't he have known without being asked?" said Polly.
> "I've no doubt he would," said the Horse, "But I've a sort of idea he likes to be asked."'

Shut the book

Leader   Aslan is like God: he's always there, he can do anything – but he likes to be asked.
Let's think about that as we listen to the Gospel.

THE GOSPEL PROCESSION

THE GOSPEL *St Mark 5.25–34*

Run this freely, using the pictures

CD42.1–CD42.9

AFTER THE GOSPEL

Leader   That story was about two people who needed Jesus.
Who were they? (**The sick woman and Jairus's daughter**)
The sick woman crept up on Jesus, she had been suffering for years, and when she touched Him, she was begging for help. Of course she was cured, but Jesus still wanted her to talk to Him properly.
Prayer isn't magic; you don't just touch something and it happens.
In prayer you talk to God, and He talks to you.

Jairus's little girl was so ill she couldn't pray to Jesus – but her parents could. They *interceded* for her. That means they prayed *for* her.

God loves it when we pray for each other, so when the little girl's father came and interceded for her, Jesus ran back with him at once. Jesus is always ready to help – but He likes to be asked.

He doesn't just barge in, we have to invite Him.

We *pray* for ourselves, and we *intercede* for others.

And if there's one thing kids are good at it's praying. The Church really needs your help: let's think of some of the things we could pray for.

ACTIVITY

Make a list of intercessions. Start with the children. This Gospel normally happens in the summer term, so pray for a happy time in the holidays and for children who are going to a new school.

Move over to the Church, pray for anybody you like: priests, people on the sick list, anyone the kids come up with.

Only include the needs of the world if there's a major issue the children are concerned about: don't linger – the prayer shouldn't be too long.

Write your intercessions down, roll them up in a scroll and use the scroll as your Final Prayer.

FINAL	First let us pray for ourselves . . .
PRAYER	Now let us intercede for others . . .
	We make all these prayers through our Lord
	Jesus Christ. **Amen**

You could finish by asking Our Lady to intercede for us

Hail Mary . . . (see p. xxxvii).

Tie up the scroll with a ribbon and . . .

REHEARSAL

Practise your presentation for when you go back into church (see below).

BACK IN CHURCH

If the children return in time for the Offertory, ask the priest whether the children could offer their prayers, by placing the scroll on the altar

If the children arrive after Communion, offer the scroll to the priest as something that could be used in the week

In either case, make sure a child hands the scroll to the priest

Child 1	This Sunday we thought about prayer.
Child 2	We heard how Jairus interceded to Jesus for his little girl and we have thought of some intercessions we'd like the church to offer for other people.
Child 3	They're in this scroll and we'd like to give them to you now.

Hands the scroll to the priest

(CD42.3)

(CD42.2)

(CD42.8)

Specimen cartoons for this script

Script 43   Prophets

Proper 9, Ordinary Time 14
(Sunday between 3 and 9 July)

St Mark 6.1–6

THEME

Prophets have a tough time. This morning we take the children through some difficult moments in the lives of Amos, Elijah and Jeremiah to prepare them for the way Jesus was rejected by His own people in Nazareth.

SET UP

- The liturgical colour is Green.
- A sheet of A4 paper for each child – scrap is fine.
- Pictures and crowd captions from the CD-Rom.
- A notice with 'Desert' written on it, stuck to an exit door.
- A crown for Jezebel.
- Four people to play Amos, Elijah, Queen Jezebel and Jeremiah – they should be the sort of kids, or grown-ups, who don't mind being shouted at. They will need to read the scripts beforehand – all their parts are very short.
- If you've got any shepherd head-dresses from a nativity play (stripey towels are the classic) they would make your prophets look very authentic: but it's not essential.

WELCOME *the children and lead them in* **The Sign of the Cross** ✠ **(p. xxxvi).**

THE KYRIE   Lord Jesus, you came to bring us back to God,
Lord have mercy
Lord have mercy

Lord Jesus, you came to heal us from our sins,
Christ have mercy
Christ have mercy

Lord Jesus, you came to tell us how much God loves us,
Lord have mercy
Lord have mercy

Ask the children to repeat **The Prayer for Forgiveness** *after you* (**p. xxxvi**).

OPENING	God our Father,
PRAYER	You loved us so much that
	You sent your Son into the world.
	Help us to believe in Him,
	So that we may become your sons and daughters too. **Amen**

BEFORE THE GOSPEL

Put up the picture of Amos from the CD-Rom **(CD43.1)**

Leader   Today we are going to think about prophets – like this chap –
Does anyone know what a prophet is?

Take all answers. They will probably say he's somebody who can see into the future

Yup, that's what 'prophet' means nowadays – someone who can predict the future.
But there's different ways of predicting the future.
I could look into the future and say – wait a minute . . .

Hand to forehead, go into a trance

Yes, I see it clearly – next Saturday *Team* will beat *Team* – and the score will be . . .

Use whatever sporting event is attracting attention at the moment

That's quite an unusual way of being a prophet.
Most prophets predict the future like this . . .

Look round the room and do a bit of inspired common sense, e.g. if so and so keeps banging the floor like that she's going to get into deep trouble or, if we don't get a move on with this session, we'll be late for Mass

That's the sort of prophecy you get in the Bible.

Pick up a Bible, rifle through

There are loads of prophets in the Bible, all saying very sensible things about what will happen to God's people, the Jews, if they don't buck up. And, as the prophets were very close to God, they could often guess what God was likely to do in the future.
They didn't know exactly – but they were pretty close.
But the prophets only made it into the Bible once they were dead – when they were alive, they had a terrible time.
Let's see why:

PREPARATION

Leader	We're going to hear about three prophets, Amos – that's him . . . **CD43.1**
CD43.2	And Elijah and . . .
CD43.3	Jeremiah.
	We're going to tell their stories together, so we'll need a moment to practise.

Put up the crowd captions from the CD-Rom (**CD43.4–CD43.6**), *run through them with the children*

Dish out the A4 paper and ask the children to scrunch up their sheet into a paper ball

Prophets

Leader	Let's start with Amos . . .

Amos comes forward

Amos came from the South – that was the bit of Israel people always made fun of. Rather like *Name*.

Mention a rival town or village to yours, or whatever locality you all feel is particularly dimwitted

Anyway, Amos came to Jerusalem, and walked round all the fashionable bits, glaring at the cool people.

Amos wanders disapprovingly round the kids

He thought they looked fat and lazy.

Amos *(Ad lib)*	Look at you, you lazy lot, do you think God likes you loafing about? What about looking after the poor?
Leader	The cool guys hated that, they shouted at him . . .

Get the kids to yell out the captions one by one

Children	**Shut up Amos!**
	Go back to the South!
	Bog off!

Amos sits down looking very fed up

Leader	Then there was Elijah . . .

Elijah comes forward

He lived at the time of Queen Jezebel.

Jezebel comes forward. She needs a crown. Hand one over to Jezebel

Queen Jezebel wasn't a Jew – and she worshipped wicked gods.

Jezebel raises her hands in prayer

I'm afraid a lot of the Jews copied her.

The children copy her

	Elijah was furious and began to prophesy.
Elijah	*(Ad lib – or read from the script)*
	People of Israel, listen to me!
	There is only one God!
	You are not to worship foreign gods, they don't exist!
Leader	That made Queen Jezebel furious too, she called up a couple of her Heavies. Anyone want to be a Heavy?

Place the volunteers near to Jezebel

| | And she said: |
| **Jezebel** | OK men, get that prophet! |

The children chase Elijah round the room – he gets to the door labelled 'Desert'

| **Elijah** | Oh no, the desert, oh well, there's nothing for it . . . |

And slams through: the Heavies return empty-handed

Leader	Then there was Jeremiah.
	Now for this prophet, you need to have your balls of paper ready . . .
	In Jeremiah's time the people of Israel had got so bad, that God allowed the Babylonian army to invade Israel. The Babylonians had got as far as Jerusalem, and Jeremiah said:
Jeremiah	*(Ad lib or read from the script as follows)*
	People of Israel! You are being punished for your sins.
	The Babylonians are bound to win.
	Don't bother to fight.
	God will look after you if you turn back to Him.
Leader	And the people were so furious that they threw things at him.
	Let him have it, guys . . .

The kids throw their balls of paper at Jeremiah, he ducks behind a chair

So you see, it's tough being a prophet.
People don't always like you, or believe you.
Well, many people thought Jesus was a prophet.
Let's hear what happened to Him.

GOSPEL PROCESSION

THE GOSPEL *St Mark 6.1–6*

Optional Paraphrase

Jesus came to His home town, Nazareth and, on the Sabbath, He began to teach in the synagogue. The people who heard Him were astonished.

Some said, 'Where did this man get all this? He's just a carpenter isn't He?' And others said, 'Yes, He's Mary's son. Look, there are His brothers, James and Joses and Judas and Simon – and His sisters are over there.'

And they were furious with Him.

Jesus said to them, 'A prophet is honoured everywhere except in His own town, and among His own people.'

And Jesus was not able to perform any mighty deed in Nazareth, apart from curing a few sick people. He was amazed at their lack of faith, and He went on to some other villages, to teach there.

AFTER THE GOSPEL

Leader   So why didn't the people in Nazareth believe in Jesus?

Take all answers and establish that most of them thought He had a cheek in teaching them at all, he was only a local boy

> You see, it's all right reading about prophets in the Bible, but you don't expect to meet one. It's rather annoying.
> Suppose *Name* over there suddenly said he was a prophet. I must say I'd take a lot of convincing . . .
> And of course, prophets can be very irritating.
> Sometimes they tell us we've got it all wrong, or that we've got to buck up or sort our lives out. Nobody likes hearing that.
> One of the things Jesus said was that God was just as likely to love sinners as good people.
> Can you guess who would find that annoying?
> (**Yup, the good people**)
> Even nowadays, we find some of the things Jesus told us rather difficult.
> Can anyone think of some hard things Jesus told us to do?

This can go either way, stricken silence, or a whole list of uncomfortable sayings
Start the ball rolling with some of the following examples

Leader	Jesus said: Love your enemies; do good to those who hate you; take up your Cross and follow me; little children are nice (Some grown-ups find that very difficult) and forgive your brother. (That can be difficult too)

Sum Up

Leader	When someone says something you don't expect, you feel challenged. Jesus challenged people – and they didn't like it. He challenges us too: We don't always want to do what He says – but He is our Lord, and we should have a go.

REHEARSAL

Leader	We're going back into church to explain this Gospel to the grown-ups. I'll need two kids to play Jeremiah and Jesus and the rest of you, pick up those paper balls.

Practise your presentation for when you go back into church (see below). Limit the number of paper balls thrown at Jeremiah to six, designate someone to pick up the litter afterwards.

FINAL PRAYER	Jesus said, 'A prophet is honoured everywhere, Except in his own country.' Lord Jesus, help us to hear you Honour you, And keep your word. **Amen**

BACK IN CHURCH

The children go down the front, Jesus one side, Jeremiah the other
Six children have balls of paper ready . . .

Leader	Today we thought about the prophets, And we discovered they all had a tough time. Here's one, he's called Jeremiah.

Jeremiah stands forward

He had things thrown at him . . .

The kids chuck balls at Jeremiah

Then we read the Gospel
And we found that Jesus . . .

Jesus stands forward

Got into trouble too.
The people in His home town told Him to clear off . . .

All the children point emphatically at Jesus and then to the exit door

And He left.

Jesus retreats   But we don't want Jesus to leave

The children call Jesus back and he stands in the middle

Because Jesus' neighbours were wrong.
He was a true prophet and worth listening to.

(CD43.1)   (CD43.2)   (CD43.3)

Specimen cartoons for this script

Script 44   St John the Baptist

Proper 10 (Church of England)
(Sunday between 10 and 16 July)

St Mark 6.17–29

THEME

Today we hear the story of Salome and the death of John the Baptist. At first glance it seems to be deeply unsuitable for children, and some people might like to take up the Roman Catholic alternative for this Sunday and run a session based on St Mark 6.7–13 (Script 45). On the other hand, it is usually only adults who are nervous about John's martyrdom; children are normally unfazed. (They all know about Nearly Headless Nick from *Harry Potter*.) Consequently, this session offers you a couple of dramas about John – a long and a short. Choose the one you want to concentrate on during the session, remembering the short one is the easiest for a presentation back in church.

SET UP

- The liturgical colour is Green.
- Holy water stoup and hyssop – or a bowl with holy water in it and a DIY hyssop made with a bunch of leafy twigs (like rosemary).
- Picture of St John from the CD-Rom, or one from the Internet (keying in John the Baptist plus 'Memling' or 'Bouts' will bring up some nice simple images).
- Run through the script, check out the props, and make sure the Narrator has had a read-through before the session starts.
- Leader 2 should be ready to read Jesus' line at the end of the play.

Props for Play

- A stool.
- Seven scarves.
- A plastic sword/scimitar or axe.
- Crown.
- Plate with bunch of grapes or anything you feel looks like a feast.

- A wine bottle, and at least one wine cup for Herod to get drunk from.
- Rope/handcuffs, anything that makes it obvious that John is a prisoner.
- Large cardboard disc with a bite cut out for John the Baptist's head.

neck-size

Card disc

Optional Extra

- Portable music player. Some music for Salome's dance.

WELCOME *the children and lead them in* **The Sign of the Cross** ✠ **(p. xxxvi).**

BEFORE THE KYRIE

Leader   On this Sunday we remember St John the Baptist.
                What did St John do?

Take all answers, establish he baptized people

                Has anyone ever seen a baptism?
                What happens? *(Go with the flow)*
                Why does the priest pour water on the baby's head?

Take any answer

                There are lots of reasons – one is that water *washes* things.
                The water in Baptism is a sign that God will wash away anything
                that's wrong when He makes a person a new Christian.
                This is such a good idea that the Church often uses water to wash
                older Christians as well.

Pick up the stoup and hyssop

                So today we're going to use water to remind ourselves of our
                baptism, and how God can wash away our sins.
                We'll say a short Kyrie first.

THE KYRIE   Lord have mercy
              Lord have mercy

              Christ have mercy
              Christ have mercy

              Lord have mercy
              Lord have mercy

| Leader | We get sprinkled like this: |
| *To Leader 2* | May God forgive us our sins. |

Sprinkle the other person – who crosses him/herself and says

✠ Amen

Now sprinkle the children – and everyone else in the room

At the end say   I need to be sprinkled too – will somebody sprinkle me?

Hand the stoup over to a reasonably sensible child, when it's all over lead the children in . . .

| OPENING PRAYER | God our Father,
Your servant John lived and died doing your will.
Help us to hear his story today
And honour him in our hearts and prayers
For your Son's sake. **Amen** |

BEFORE THE GOSPEL

Show the children a picture of John the Baptist, talk through the wild country, John's clothes, the lamb (the saint holds a lamb because he hailed Jesus as 'The Lamb of God') and anything else shown in the painting
Establish that John lived rough, preached in the desert, baptized people and told everyone that Jesus was coming

| Leader | Well, Jesus did come – but John didn't just disappear. He went on preaching and he made some very dangerous enemies. We're going to hear about John the Baptist Part Two right now. |

THE GOSPEL PROCESSION

THE GOSPEL *St Mark 6.17–29*

St Mark tells the first part of the story backwards. The children will understand it better if you begin like this

King Herod* had got rid of his real wife and married his brother's wife, Herodias. When John the Baptist heard about this, he denounced the King and told him plainly that he had done wrong. Herodias was furious and told her husband to arrest John.

---

* Actually this Herod, the son of Herod the Great, was not a king but a 'tetrarch' (the governor of a fourth of a kingdom). Even so his people obviously called him a king and the story in St Mark reads so like the rumours that were going round the local bazaars, that keeping in its colloquialisms seems appropriate. Herod had abandoned his first wife and married Herodias, his niece, and wife of his half-brother (another Herod).

So Herod had John chained up and thrown into prison.

Continue from verse 19

AFTER THE GOSPEL

Leader	And that was how St John died. It's a very famous story. People have made films about it, and written plays and operas about it – and it's very difficult to do. You need a really good Salome, and you've got to work out how you're going to pretend to chop off St John's head. I wonder if we could have a go? Let's try.

Production Meeting

- *Choose an adult for the Narrator and cast John, Herod, Herodias, Salome, soldiers, Israelites.*
- *Take a view on Salome: some kids already know about the Dance of the Seven Veils, and like to have scarves about their person which they fling into the air. However, if you feel this is very inappropriate indeed, you could take the line of most mediaeval illustrators and make Salome a gifted acrobat. Any girl who can do a cartwheel gets the part . . .*
- *Discuss how to do John's beheading – and produce the cut-away 'plate': however you manage his execution, his head has to turn up on a plate.*
- *The story is narrated, the actions mimed.*

John the Baptist – the long version

Narrator (CD44.1)	The story of John the Baptist. John the Baptist was sent by God to prepare people for the appearance of God's Son, Jesus. So John went to the River Jordan, and loads of people turned up to listen to him.

John gets up on to the stool, the other kids gather round

John's message was very simple.
'Repent and be saved,' he said, 'for the Kingdom of Heaven is at hand.'

John can actually say this, if he's up to it, otherwise he just waves his hands about

Many people who heard him, believed him, and repented of their sins.

Most kids kneel down, keep a few back

And they were baptized by John in the River Jordan.
But some people didn't like John . . .

The other kids shake their heads and fists and heckle John – 'what a load of rubbish' etc.

And they refused to listen to him, and stomped off back to town, very cross.

All the kids sit down
John stays on his stool, arms folded. Clear a space round him

There was one person in Jerusalem who didn't like him at all.

Enter Herod – with crown on

Herod the King.
Herod had married his brother's wife and John told him how wrong that was.

John points his finger very emphatically at Herod

Herod was very annoyed

Indignation from Herod

And so was his wife . . .

Enter Herodias – also with crown (if you happen to have two)

Queen Herodias.
Eventually they became so cross they had John put in prison.

Herod orders the soldiers to tie John up and throw him into prison – the corner of the room

One day Herod gave a party – he invited his wife and her daughter Salome . . .

Enter Salome   And lots of guests.

Enter the rest of the kids, keep a couple of soldiers back

Everybody danced.

Cue party music if you've got it, otherwise just get the kids to stand up and show you how to dance. Faking bewilderment at how modern people dance usually does the trick. Cue 'kill it' fairly quickly

There was masses of wine and Herod drank far too much.

Herod keeps filling his cup from the (empty) wine bottle

Either   And, during the party, Salome danced the Dance of the Seven Veils. It was an amazing performance . . .

Salome dances: the other children do a count down on the veils: Seven! Six! Five! . . . and so on

Or And during the party Salome amazed everyone with her brilliant acrobatics.

Salome cartwheels across the front

Herod thought she was wonderful, and promised to give her anything she asked for.

Quick as lightning, Herodias whispered to Salome . . .

She does

And Salome answered, 'I want the head of John the Baptist on a plate!'

Herod was horrified, but he had promised in front of all his guests, so he told the soldiers to execute John, and off they went . . .

The soldiers march off to John's prison (with the sword and cut-away plate)

They cut off John's head

They surround him – swipe from sword

And brought it back on a plate . . .

Re-enter soldiers and John with his neck neatly fitting into the slice cut away from the rim

The guests were horrified.

All the lads, except Herod, sit down

Herodias was delighted, but Herod thought it was the stupidest thing he'd ever done.

Herod buries his head in his hands

John's friends took his body and buried it, and Jesus, when He heard the news, said:

Leader 2   'There has never been a greater prophet than John the Baptist!'

Encourage parents and spare grown-ups to clap the children

Leader   That was brilliant.
Now we need to do a cut-down version for the grown-ups back in church.

Practise the script below

John the Baptist – the short version

Line up the kids – John one end of the line, Herod, Herodias and Salome in the middle, and a grown-up who says Jesus' final line at the other end
Cast a few soldiers and give them the sword and the plate
The other kids fill up the gaps, and watch the action, turning their heads together – like the spectators at a tennis match

Leader   Today we heard about John the Baptist.

Usher John forward

He annoyed King Herod . . .

Herod (with crown) steps forward

And his wife, Herodias.

She steps forward

So Herod got his soldiers to arrest John . . .

The soldiers march over to John

And throw him in gaol.

John sits down abruptly

Meanwhile Herod gave a party, and Herodias' daughter, Salome, did such a brilliant dance . . .

Salome does one cartwheel

That Herod said she could have anything she wanted.
Her mother whispered in Salome's ear . . .

Herodias does so

And Salome asked for the head of St John on a plate.
So Herod ordered the soldiers to cut off his head, and bring it to him.

One soldier makes a fake swipe at John and they march him over to Herod, with his head in the plate

Leader 1   When Jesus heard the news, He said,

Leader 2   'There has never been a greater prophet than John the Baptist!'

Cue in a bow from all the children

FINAL   John was a great prophet. He told people that Jesus was coming; he
PRAYER   baptized Him, and called Jesus, the Lamb of God.

We remember John every time we pray to the Lamb of God in church. We'll finish with that prayer.

The Agnus Dei *Ask the children to repeat this prayer after you*

**O Lamb of God, who takes away the sins of the world,
Have mercy upon us**

**O Lamb of God, who takes away the sins of the world,
Have mercy upon us**

**O Lamb of God, who takes away the sins of the world,
Grant us peace**

BACK IN CHURCH

Run the short version of the play (see above)

(CD44.1)

Script 45   Travelling Light

Ordinary Time 15 (Roman Catholic

St Mark 6.7–13

THEME

Jesus sends His disciples out on their first missionary journey. Alarmingly, He tells them to travel light: they are to be totally dependent on the friends and hospitality God will send them.

SET UP

- The liturgical colour is Green.
- Pictures from the CD-Rom.
- A large rucksack.
- A pile of cushions, socks, a teddy – any daft thing a twit might take on a walking holiday (keep it bulky rather than heavy).
- Keep a second teddy in reserve for the obstacle course (see below).
- A watch with a second hand.
- Two pairs of Wellington boots, the sort a child of eight could get on: it's fine if they're too big.
- Label some chairs for an obstacle course – two have 'Over' on them, two have 'Under'.
- Pack another rucksack for after the Gospel with: a wallet/purse, spare jumper, and packet of biscuits.
- Have a walking stick and a pair of sandals to hand (not packed).
- A prayer candle (see p. xxiii).

WELCOME *the children and lead them in* **The Sign of the Cross ✠ (p. xxxvi).**

THE KYRIE   God our Father, we thank you for always being ready to forgive us,
Lord have mercy
Lord have mercy

Lord Jesus, we thank for telling us about the Father's love,
Christ have mercy
Christ have mercy

Holy Spirit, we thank you for helping us to say sorry,
Lord have mercy
Lord have mercy

Ask the children to repeat **The Prayer for Forgiveness** *after you* (**p. xxxvi**).

OPENING **PRAYER**	Lord Jesus, You call us to follow you, Help us to trust you To drop everything And run to do your will. **Amen**

BEFORE THE GOSPEL

Leader   *(With large rucksack)* OK, today we're going to think about travelling.

I'm going on a walking holiday, I've piled up some stuff to take with me.

I thought, well, I'll need some socks *(pack them)*

And perhaps I won't find somewhere comfortable to sit, so I'll get a cushion *(pack them)*

Actually two cushions would be more sensible *(pack them)*

Oh, and I'll need someone to talk to, so I'll pack my teddy.

Place a teddy on top of the rucksack and ad lib about any other stuff you've brought

And of course, I might be going through rough terrain, so I've got my wellies. *(Hold them up)*

So I'm all ready.

What do you think?

Take on board anything the kids may say. Make sure that Leader 2 joins in and sums up the feeling of the room

Leader 2   I've never seen such a useless bit of packing in my life.

You wouldn't even get to the end of this room.

Look, let me show you.

Trekking

Leader 2   This is a bit of rough mountain.

Set up your labelled chairs for an obstacle course

You have to get *over* these chairs – and *under* these.

Ask for volunteers to put on the wellies, put on the rucksack and hold the teddy in their arms, and then ask them to tackle the course. Place a grown-up by every chair to help the kids

> OK, off you go – we'll time you.

Run this a couple of times, and write up the times

> Now, supposing you don't have all this stuff, let's see what happens.

Get some kids to run the course without the kit or the boots, and time them

> What do you think, kids?

Hopefully they'll think it's a lot quicker and easier

Leader 1   OK, so what *should* I pack?
Leader 2   Let's think about that.

CD45.1 *Put up the picture of an empty rucksack from the CD-Rom and ask the kids to fill its compartments with kit. They can either draw it in, or use the separate pictures provided* **(CD45.2–CD45.5)**. *Keep it sensible: socks, toothbrush, tent, dried food, sleeping bag*

Leader 2   That's what I call a really sensible rucksack.
    Jesus talks about packing in the Gospel today, let's hear what He'd think of my rucksack.

THE GOSPEL PROCESSION

THE GOSPEL *St Mark 6.7–13*

AFTER THE GOSPEL

Leader 2   Right, so Jesus sent His friends off on their first preaching job.
    They were going to be away for a bit, so they'd obviously need to pack: here's another rucksack . . .

Pull out the other rucksack

    I've filled it with the sort of things that they'd need.
Leader 1   *(With Bible)* OK, I'll just check. Jesus said – oh, listen to this:
    'Don't take any money', *(peer in rucksack)* we'd better take that out.

Ask a child to remove the wallet

    'And no food' *(same business)*
    'No spare clothes' *(same business)*
    And actually no rucksack *(that goes too)*

Leader 2	Blimey, what *could* they take??
Leader 1	*(Checks out the Bible)* Just some sandals and a walking stick!

Hold up the walking stick and some sandals

| Leader 2 | Right, so there's my sensible rucksack *(indicate the picture)*
And here's what Jesus told people to pack, just a stick and some sandals.
Why did He do that? |

Probably rhetorical, see if the kids come up with anything

| Leader 1 | Well, obviously the disciples would move faster without luggage, but I think Jesus was thinking of something else.
He wanted His friends to trust God.
If you haven't got luggage, you have to rely on God to send you food, and friends.
He likes His friends to travel light. |

REHEARSAL

Practise your presentation for when you go back into church (see below).

BEFORE THE FINAL PRAYER

Gather the children round a prayer candle

| Leader | Look at the flame for a moment –
It's all by itself.
Jesus travelled light,
He had no home
And not many clothes.
And He wants us to travel light.
Not just socks and things
But things that distract us.
Think about the week ahead . . .
Is anything worrying you?
Ask Jesus to take it off your shoulders
Just ask Him once – and let it go!
He's there to help. |

MUSIC

The hymn 'Do not be afraid' works well here.

FINAL PRAYER	Jesus said: 'Come to me, all you who carry heavy loads And I will refresh you. Take my pack on your shoulders, you will find it's light and easy to carry.' Help us to follow you Lord, With light packs and trusting hearts. **Amen**

BACK IN CHURCH

Fill the rucksack again and take it back to church, plus the staff and sandals. Place the rucksack down the front (on a chair if possible)

Child 1	Today Jesus sent His friends out on their first preaching job
Child 2	He told them how to pack
Child 3	He said they weren't to take any money

Pulls out wallet and hands it over to a Leader

Child 4	Or food *(Same business with the biscuits)*
Child 5	Or spare clothes *(Same business with the jumper)*
Child 6	Or a rucksack! *(Ditch the rucksack)*
Leader	In fact all that Jesus' friends could take were *(hold them up)* a staff and some sandals! We think He told His friends this because He wanted them to . . .

All the Children Travel light!

(CD45.2)

(CD45.3)

Specimen cartoons for this script

Script 46   Sheep Without Shepherds

Proper 11, Ordinary Time 16
(Sunday between 17 and 23 July)

St Mark 6.30–34

THEME

Today's Gospel is another that draws on Palestinian shepherds and their sheep. It introduces the children to the word 'compassion': the way in which somebody can share, imaginatively, with someone else's distress. St Mark says that Jesus looked at the crowds dogging His footsteps and 'had compassion on them'. They were incredibly demanding, He and His disciples were tired to death – but Jesus recognized them as sheep without a shepherd.

SET UP

- The liturgical colour is Green.
- Sheep cut-outs from the CD-Rom, one in the Leader's pocket.
- Leader 2 ready to star as the Shepherd: he/she will need to read the script beforehand.
- Enough chairs to pen the children in.
- Cast a child to play the Lost Sheep.
- Marker pen.
- Pictures from the CD-Rom, stick the sunglasses on Jesus.
- The picture or icon you used of Jesus the Good Shepherd for Script 29.

detachable Shades

WELCOME *the children and lead them in* **The Sign of the Cross** ✠ (p. xxxvi).

THE KYRIE   Heavenly Father,
you saw that we were lost and sent your Son to find us,
Lord have mercy
Lord have mercy

Lord Jesus, you came to save us,
Christ have mercy
Christ have mercy

Holy Spirit, you help us to turn back to the Father,
Lord have mercy
Lord have mercy

Sheep

Leader   Today we are going to think about sheep.
We had a session on them not so long ago.
Do you remember one of the irritating things about sheep?
(**They wander off**)

Stick up five sheep cut-outs from the CD-Rom (**CD46.1**)

Yes, they will wander so you have to keep them fenced in. *(Draw a fence round them)*
How many sheep have I got? (**Five!**)
Really? There's supposed to be six!

Make a fuss about the missing one (he turns up in your pocket) as an accomplice surreptitiously moves a sheep out of the pen. Turn with pantomime horror to the flock

Hey! Now there're only four . . . Where did that sheep go?

As you retrieve number 5, another sheep wanders off: run this a couple of times

I bet you remember something else about sheep now – they're stupid.
They need looking after: sheep need shepherds.
Jesus once told us a story about a shepherd and his flock and we're going to tell it now.
We've got a shepherd.

Leader 2 steps forward

We just need his/her flock.

Auditions

Set up a sheep audition

Leader 1   Who wants to be a sheep?

Look at the forest of hands – make sure the adults join in

Hmm, lots of talent here. I think I'd better hear you.

Turn to a grown-up

What noise does a sheep make?

She moos

Leader 1   Useless!
What about you?

Another adult meows

Pathetic!
Does anyone know what a sheep sounds like?

The kids will probably all 'baa' together

Brilliant – you all get the part!
Let's practise those 'baas'.

Practise cueing in, and killing, the 'baas'

Right, now we need to get you fenced in.

You and the other Leaders surround the kids with chairs, they sit down within the compound

OK, we're ready to go.

The Lost Sheep

Leader 1   Once upon a time there was a shepherd, who had lots of sheep.
How many sheep *have* you got, shepherd?

Leader 2   Loads – wait a minute . . .

He/she counts the kids rapidly 1, 2, 3 . . . the counting gets faster and deeply improbable, ending with . . . 98, 99, 100!

Leader 1   Yup, that's a lot of sheep.
Well, every night the shepherd counted his sheep before he went to bed. And, when he was sure he had the full 100, he fell asleep.

The shepherd counts the sheep again, even faster, and falls asleep

But, while he was sleeping, one of the sheep sneaked out of the pen . . .

Cue a child to escape and help her to hide

He does so   And the next morning, when the shepherd woke up and went to look at his sheep, he realized immediately that something was wrong.

Leader 2   *(Ad lib all this, you should find it easy)*

Hello! I seem to have fewer sheep, wait a minute: 1, 2, 3 . . .

He starts counting again

. . . 97, 98, 99!
Ninety-nine sheep
Let's work this out

He takes a pen and goes over to the flip chart

Right, I had a 100 sheep. *(Writes up 100)*
Now I've got 99. *(Write it up as a subtraction sum)*
Er, 99 from 100 *(do the sum laboriously)*
That's – one!
Good heavens, I've lost a sheep!

The shepherd goes off to look for his sheep (ad lib this – he/she should be really bothered)

Hey, Sheepie!
Come on, Lambkin! Where are you?

He/she looks everywhere: the kids help by calling out **'warm, cold, colder'** *and so on. Eventually he finds the lost sheep, picks it up, and returns it to the pen*

Leader 2   Thank goodness, she's safe!
OK, where am I?

Over to the flip chart to do another sum

I had 99 sheep, I've found one, that's . . . um
Can anybody help me?

The children are usually beside themselves to give the answer

One hundred! You're right! I've got all my sheep back!
Cool! I think I'll go and have my breakfast.

Leader 1   So the shepherd went off to have his breakfast, very pleased that the lost sheep had been found.
That shepherd loved his sheep. And Jesus felt the same about the people who followed Him round Galilee. Let's hear about them in today's Gospel.

THE GOSPEL PROCESSION

THE GOSPEL *St Mark 6.30–34*

AFTER THE GOSPEL

Leader So Jesus' friends had been going round preaching, and they got back, and it had all been a great success – when suddenly it all got rather difficult.
It was like being a celebrity.

Put up picture of Jesus and co as celebs **(CD46.2–CD46.4)**

People were coming and going and following them around – and they had no time to themselves.
But Jesus wasn't a celebrity,
He didn't look at the world through sunglasses.

Take the sunglasses off Jesus

Jesus saw with compassion.
Compassion means seeing with love, feeling what someone else is feeling.
Jesus looked at those crowds and knew they felt lost.
They were sheep without shepherds.
So He sat among them, and talked to them.
He became their shepherd.

BEFORE THE FINAL PRAYER

Gather the children round the picture of Jesus the Good Shepherd
Talk through the picture, the sheep on His shoulders, the Greek words (if any) will be 'O Poimeen Kalos', pronounced 'Ho Poimeen Kalos'. The literal meaning is The Shepherd, Good

Leader Jesus is our Shepherd too.
That lamb on His shoulders is each one of us.

MUSIC

The traditional hymns 'The Lord's my shepherd' (verses 1, 2, 3 and 5) or 'The King of Love my Shepherd is' (verses 1, 2, 3 and 6) or 'Faithful Shepherd, feed me' work well here.

FINAL PRAYER	Lord Jesus Great Shepherd of your sheep, Help us to love you And follow you. And, if we do wander off, We ask you to look for us And bring us safely back To your sheepfold the Church. **Amen**

BACK IN CHURCH

As you go into church leave a responsible child at the back, to play the Lost Sheep

Leader 1   Today we discovered that *Name* was a shepherd and had a flock of a 100 sheep. We've brought some of them back into church with us.

Cue in the kids to 'Baaa', then kill it

Unfortunately, while we were in the Hall, one of the sheep wandered off and . . .
What's the matter, *Name?*

Leader 2   *(Scanning the flock)*
It's happened again!
I've lost a sheep – excuse me a moment.

Leader 2 looks round for the sheep, the children telling him/her when they're warm or cold. Find the sheep fairly rapidly and return to the front with the Lost Sheep – to cheers, if the children are up for it

Leader 1   *Name* really loves his sheep – and we realized that that was how Jesus felt about us.

(CD46.1)   (CD46.4)

Specimen cartoons for this script

Script 47   Five Loaves and Two Fishes

Proper 12, Ordinary Time 17
(Sunday between 24 and 30 July)

St John 6.1–13

THEME

The Gospel this Sunday describes the 'Feeding of the Five Thousand'. There have been many attempts to explain away this story – the most persistent being the suggestion that lots of people in the crowd had brought picnics really, but it wasn't until the little boy produced his that they were shamed into sharing their food. However, as there's no trace of this ingenious idea in the Gospel, this session will go for a straight reading of the text: Jesus performed a miracle.

Children enjoy the story just as it is. As adults we may see hints of the Eucharist in the miracle, but most kids are content to know that everyone got their lunch.

SET UP

- The liturgical colour is Green.
- A bread stick.
- A few Smarties or chocolate buttons on a dish.
- A basket with a fake bottom.
- Five mini rolls, and some small bite-sized chunks of bread placed under the false basket bottom.

- Two very small fish – make them out of anything: fish-shaped biscuits (if you've got the time) or a couple of fish-shaped cut-outs from a slice of toast (if you haven't).
- Wrap the five rolls and two fish in a tea towel, place them on the top of the basket, and give them to a sensible child (to turn up with during the Gospel).
- Cast Jesus, Philip and Andrew for the Gospel, they'll need to look at the script beforehand.

WELCOME *the children and lead them in* **The Sign of the Cross** ✠ **(p. xxxvi).**

THE KYRIE   God our Father, you are always ready to forgive us,
Lord have mercy
Lord have mercy

Lord Jesus, you taught us to say sorry for our sins,
Christ have mercy
Christ have mercy

Holy Spirit, you help us to repent when we do wrong,
Lord have mercy
Lord have mercy

Ask the children to repeat **The Prayer for Forgiveness** *after you* (**p. xxxvi**).

OPENING   God our Father,
PRAYER   You created everything
The earth, the sea and the sky.
You created us and gave us this world to live in;
You give us our food and our families.
We thank you for all your gifts,
And especially for the gift of Jesus Christ,
Your Son, our Lord. **Amen**

BEFORE THE GOSPEL

Sharing

Leader   *(Plus breadstick)* Today we're going to think about food, especially about giving it to other people.
It's very good to give away food – but it does have its down side.
Watch this – here's a bread stick *(hold it up)*
I like bread sticks, but I know I ought to share my food, so I'll give some of it away *(break off a bit of the stick)*
Anyone want some?

Hand it out and go on doing so until you've got about an inch left

OK, now I can have some.

Look at what's left

Anyone notice anything . . . ?
There's hardly any left.
That's what happens when you share things: they get smaller and smaller.
Let's try it with Smarties.

Dish out the Smarties until you've only got one left, look sadly at it

> Yup, the same thing seems to have happened.
> But oddly enough, every now and then, sharing doesn't have this effect. Sometimes it goes the other way.
> We're going to hear about that in the Gospel.

GOSPEL PROCESSION

THE GOSPEL *St John 6.1–13*

Have the basket to hand, ask the children to stand

Narrator   Jesus went away to the other side of the Sea of Galilee, with a large crowd following Him. He went up the hillside, sat down there with His disciples, and looked at the crowd.

Jesus comes forward and looks round at the kids

Narrator   He turned to Philip and said,
Jesus   Where can we buy some bread so that these people can eat?
Philip   Two hundred pounds would not be enough to give them even a roll.

Andrew comes forward with the child and its picnic

Narrator   Then Andrew, Simon Peter's brother, said to Him,
Andrew   There's a boy here who's brought you his picnic – what have you got there?

The child puts the basket down and unwraps the food, Andrew inspects it

> He's got five barley loaves and two fish – thanks son – but it's not nearly enough . . .

Jesus takes the basket

Jesus   Ask everyone to sit down.

Andrew and Philip get the children to sit down

Narrator   There was plenty of grass there and five thousand people sat down. Then Jesus took the loaves *(he does)*, gave thanks *(he holds them up)*, and shared them out to the people near Him. Then He did the same with the fish. *(Same business)*

Make it perfectly obvious that the loaves and fish have run out, but go on dishing out bread to anyone who wants it – from the bottom of the basket, of course. Keep some bits of bread back for your presentation in church

Narrator	Jesus went on handing out bread and fish until everyone had had enough to eat.
	And, at the end of the meal, the disciples filled 12 baskets – like this one – with the scraps left over.

AFTER THE GOSPEL

Leader	How did we do that?

The children will probably know – show them the basket

Yes, you're quite right, it was a trick.

But how did Jesus do it? There He was, sharing and sharing, and the food got more, not less.

It was a miracle.

But you know, miracles aren't magic.

When Jesus did miracles He wasn't like Harry Potter and saying a spell.

He was doing something that was quite normal and ordinary – as long as you're God. We can't do them, but God can.

And one of the things that God is always doing is making small fish

CD47.1 from big fish.

CD47.2 And loads of bread, from tiny little bits of bread

God loves making things – and He loves making lots of them.

Think how many cherries there are on a tree, or how many tadpoles there are in the average frog family.

Jesus said, 'The Son watches what the Father does and copies Him.'

And that's what He was doing when He multiplied the loaves and fishes.

REHEARSAL

Practise your presentation for when you go back into church (see below).

BEFORE THE FINAL PRAYER

Leader	God makes fish and wheat and frogs, and us.
	The Gospel today is about Jesus making things too – food for God's people.
	We'll think about that as we say Psalm 145 together.

**FINAL
PRAYER**

(From Psalm 145)
The response to the Psalm is:
The Lord is good to all

The Lord is good to all;
He has compassion on all He has made.
The Lord is good to all

The eyes of all creatures look to Him,
and He gives them their food in due time.
The Lord is good to all

He opens wide His hand,
and grants the desires of every living thing.
The Lord is good to all

MUSIC

The song 'Abba, Abba, Father' *sums up the session nicely.*

BACK IN CHURCH

Take in the basket with a few bits of bread on top, and more underneath. Line the children up along the front

Leader   Today we heard how Jesus took five rolls of bread

Show the congregation the top of the basket

And shared them out among five thousand people.
The Children's Church are now going to do their most ambitious
presentation ever and be five thousand people.

Send the basket along the line. Each child takes some bread, holds it up, and passes the basket to the next one – then they run round and join the line again. Keep it snappy and stop sooner rather than later

The food didn't run out and all five thousand had enough to eat.
Of course we are using a trick basket – but Jesus did it for real.

Script 48   Elijah's Breakfast

Proper 13, Ordinary Time 18
(Sunday between 31 July and 6 August)

St John 6.24–27

THEME

This is the first of a series of 'Bread' Gospels (the children will begin to think that first-century Jews ate nothing else). The next three Sundays concentrate on chapter 6 of St John's Gospel, in which Jesus describes Himself as 'Living Bread'. This session introduces the idea that some food comes from Heaven, via the story of Elijah's breakfast.

SET UP

- The liturgical colour is Green.
- Pictures from the CD-Rom.
- A very large die, either made by you or bought on the Internet (see p. xxi).
- A 'Food in the Desert' game is provided either as a board game on the CD-Rom or as something you set up yourselves.
  Either print up the game
  Or mark up 30 double sheets of newspaper, with a marker pen. (They will be spread over the floor, in sequence, like stepping stones.)
- Write 'HOREB' very large on sheet 30.
- Two small cushions.
- Four little pitta breads.
- Two jugs of water.

WELCOME *the children and lead them in* **The Sign of the Cross** ✠ (p. xxxvi).

THE KYRIE	God our Father, you are always ready to forgive us, Lord have mercy **Lord have mercy**
	Lord Jesus, you taught us to say sorry for our sins, Christ have mercy **Christ have mercy**
	Holy Spirit, you help us to repent when we do wrong, Lord have mercy **Lord have mercy**

Ask the children to repeat **The Prayer for Forgiveness** *after you* (**p. xxxvi**).

OPENING PRAYER	God our Father, Giver of all good gifts, We thank you for bringing us together this morning, For our families, Our breakfast And our friends. **Amen**

Breakfast

Leader **CD48.2**	OK, we've just thanked God for our breakfasts. *(Put up* **CD48.1***)* Here's my breakfast plate And it had a boiled egg and toast on it. *(Draw them on)*
CD48.3	*(Put up empty plate picture)*
	Would anyone like to draw in their breakfast? *(Encourage someone to draw their breakfast)*
CD48.4	Brilliant! Now here's a French plate Does anyone know what French kids have for breakfast? (**Baguette and jam, croissant, hot chocolate** – *anything the children come up with)* How about Arab children?

Someone may venture a guess – move on to your Arab breakfast story . . .

A Desert Breakfast

Leader **CD48.5**	Well, a friend of mine once took some kids on a trip across the Sinai desert. They went on camels and slept under the stars. *(Put up picture)* It was fantastic, and the best moment of the day was breakfast. She

said you'd wake up to the smell of the Arabs cooking flat bread on a camp fire, brewing coffee, and getting out little pots of fig jam and honey.

Elijah's Breakfast

Leader The prophet Elijah had a breakfast like that once, it happened hundreds of years ago, but desert breakfasts don't change much.

CD48.6 Elijah was on the run. That's not surprising because people don't usually like prophets. Prophets say things like, 'You're behaving really badly' and it drives everyone mad.

Well, Elijah seems to have annoyed everyone in Israel so he escaped into the desert, and sat under a bush feeling very sorry for himself.

CD48.7 'Lord God,' he said, 'I'm useless – I might as well be dead . . .'

CD48.8 Then he went to sleep.

And very early the next morning he felt a hand touching his shoulder. 'Wake up!' said a voice, 'your breakfast is ready . . .'

CD48.9 Elijah looked up and there were two nice hot scones, freshly cooked on a hot stone, with a jug of water.

Ad lib: Coffee hadn't been invented yet

CD48.10 Elijah looked round to see who'd done this –

CD48.11 It was an angel.

Elijah ate up the scones, and went back under his bush for a lie-in. But the angel tapped him on the shoulder again.

'Eat some more Elijah,' he said. 'God wants you to go all the way to Mount Horeb.'

CD48.12 And there was another breakfast!

So Elijah ate two breakfasts – and went on his way, feeling a lot better.

Sum Up

Leader I like that story. It shows that God knows how important breakfast is, and that angels are good cooks.

But those scones God sent Elijah turned out to be very mysterious – they kept him going for 40 days. Elijah had eaten angel's food.

Jesus talks about mysterious food in the Gospel today.

THE GOSPEL PROCESSION

THE GOSPEL *St John 6.24–27*

Start the Gospel with an explanation

After Jesus had fed 5,000 people with five loaves and two fishes, He disappeared for a while. People were getting too excited about Him, so He and His disciples went to the other side of the lake.

AFTER THE GOSPEL

Leader	That's an odd story. Jesus tells the crowds not to follow Him about for ordinary food that won't last – but to try and get food that will last for ever.
	What do you think He meant? *(Probably a rhetorical question)*
	Well, Jesus might have meant angel's food, but I think He meant the food He gave to His Church.
	The food we have every Sunday in church.
	What's that? (**The Holy Sacrament, the Bread we eat at Mass**)
	God loves giving us food. He loves giving us ordinary food – and Heavenly food. We get ordinary food at home, and Heavenly food at church.
	We also play games in church, let's set one up . . .

GAME

Food in the Desert

Ask the children to help you cover the floor with the newspaper sheets. Place the cushions on sheets 7 and 18, 2 pittas on sheets 11 and 21, and the 2 jugs of water on sheets 12 and 22. **CD48.13** *is a template.*
Look at the arrangement for a moment.

Leader	What does this remind us of?
	Yup, Elijah's two breakfasts. Let's see if we can get two breakfasts as well.

The children roll the die and hop from sheet to sheet. When they get to a cushion, they have to sit there until the die lands them either on the pitta bread sheet or the jug of water sheet. Either constitutes breakfast and they can continue their journey. The first to get to Horeb wins (but actually the fun is the hopping).
Given the sliding nature of newspaper, you may have to limit this to a representative of a team hopping round.
A board game is provided for people with small rooms, or far too many kids.
Give the winner of the game some pitta bread to take back for the presentation in church.

REHEARSAL

Practise your presentation for when you go back into church (see below).

FINAL PRAYER	Lord, You gave Elijah bread from Heaven, A sweet-tasting bread that was good to eat. Thank you for the bread you give us At every Eucharist. **Amen**

Finish with a **Glory be . . . (p. xxxvii)**.

BACK IN CHURCH

Leader — Today we heard how God sent the prophet Elijah two breakfasts. And we've just hopped round the room trying to get two breakfasts ourselves. *Name* won.

The winner holds up some pitta bread

But then we heard the Gospel in which Jesus told us not to rush round after ordinary bread, but to try and get the bread that will last for ever.

Where's that bread kids?

Children — **In church!**

Leader — So we've come back to join you!

(CD48.7)

(CD48.10)

Specimen cartoons for this script

(CD48.8)

Script 49   Manna

Proper 14, Ordinary Time 19
(Sunday between 7 and 13 August)

St John 6.41–43, 48–51

THEME

In the second 'Bread' Gospel, Jesus makes His great pronouncement, 'I am the bread of life' and compares Himself to the manna God sent to the Jews when they were starving in the wilderness.

SET UP

- The liturgical colour is Green.
- An unconsecrated wafer.
- Cast someone to play Moses: they will need to look at the script beforehand.
- Pictures from the CD-Rom.
- A large piece of card with 'Splosh!' written on it.

WELCOME *the children and lead them in* **The Sign of the Cross** ✠ (**p. xxxvi**).

THE KYRIE   God our Father, you are always ready to forgive us,
Lord have mercy
Lord have mercy

Lord Jesus, you taught us to say sorry for our sins,
Christ have mercy
Christ have mercy

Holy Spirit, you help us to repent when we do wrong,
Lord have mercy
Lord have mercy

Ask the children to repeat **The Prayer for Forgiveness** *after you* (**p. xxxvi**).

OPENING
PRAYER
Lord Jesus,
You said that if anyone loved you
Your Father would love them
And that you would come to them.
Come to us this morning
In the Gospel,
In our hearts,
In the bread of the Eucharist. **Amen**

If you've got more or less the same children as last week, remind them of the story of Elijah and how God sent him his breakfast

Leader   We're thinking about food (again) this Sunday. Particularly bread.
            There are all sorts of bread – let's see how many we know . . .

ACTIVITY

CD49.1–CD49.10 *Work through the bread pictures on the CD-Rom together, matching up the pictures and captions ('gingerbread', 'raw bread', and so on). End with 'Bread of Angels' and put up a picture of manna falling from Heaven*

Leader   Has anyone heard of the Bread of Angels? *(Rhetorical question)*
            It looks a bit like this:

Show them a small unconsecrated wafer

            Now this is the bread we use in church – when this piece is blessed
            at the altar it will be eaten by people at Holy Communion.
            But it hasn't been blessed yet, so it's still ordinary bread.
            And it's stuff like this that fell out of the sky one day, a very long
            time ago.

Exodus

Leader   This story goes back thousands of years to a time when the Jews
            were living in Egypt. They were the slaves of the Egyptians and they
            hated it.
            So God sent them a leader . . .

Moses stands forward

            He was called Moses, and God told him to get the Jews out of Egypt.
            Now, to tell this story properly, we need some Jews – who's good at
            running?

Everyone probably

OK, you can all be Jews.
Now we need some Egyptians.

Scoop up any non-runners, teenagers, and all the adults for the Egyptians; you need enough to make a good stamping noise
Ask the children to stand, place the Egyptians behind them, and practise walking, running on the spot, stopping, stamping, and saying 'Splosh!' altogether when you hold up the Splosh card

Right, we're ready to begin:
Well, Moses led the Jews out of Egypt.

Moses stands in front of the children

There he is.
And he took them off across the desert.
To start with the Jews just walked.

Cue in the kids walking on the spot

Then Moses looked up

He does

Moses   Stop!

Kill the walking

Leader   He listened carefully – what was that noise?

Cue in the Egyptians for a mass stamp

It's the stamp of feet!
Moses   Pharaoh has sent his army after us! Start running!

Cue in running on the spot

Moses   Stop! *(Kill it)*
Leader   Everyone stopped – there right ahead of them was a wide sea.
The Jews were horrified.
'Oh no!' they said, 'It's the Red Sea! We're done for!
This is all Moses' fault!'
And they all shook their fists at Moses.

Cue in some fist shaking

Moses   Stop panicking, God will save us.
Watch this . . .

He stretches out his hands

Leader	And, as Moses stretched out his hands, the waters of the Red Sea parted, and the Israelites walked through the water on dry ground.

Cue in walking – and kill it

But something quite different happened to the Egyptians.
Up they came, and they saw the Red Sea, with a path in the middle, and the Israelites just getting out on the other side, and they thought 'Gotcha!'
So they all stomped in . . .

Cue stamp
Kill it
Hold up 'Splosh!' card

Everyone	**SPLOSH!**
Leader	And the waters came back with a roar, and all the Egyptians were drowned.

Fantastic. Sit down.
Poor Egyptians! But the Israelites were safe. Well, sort of safe.
There were no more Egyptians to chase them, but they were still in the desert – and very soon they began to get hungry. So they shook their fists at Moses again. You can do that sitting down . . .

The children shake their fists at Moses

And Moses went away to talk to God about it.
God said, 'Say this to my people: "In the morning you will have as much bread as you can eat, then you will know that I am the Lord your God."'
And the next morning, once the dew had dried,
the Jews found fine white bread all over the ground.
Rather like this. *(Show them a wafer)*
'This', said Moses, 'is the bread the Lord has sent you.'
So they ate it up (it tasted delicious) and called it 'manna'.

Jesus knew that story very well. Let's hear what He said about it in today's Gospel.

GOSPEL PROCESSION

THE GOSPEL *St John 6.41–43, 48–51*

AFTER THE GOSPEL

Leader	OK, I'm going to put up two pictures:
CD49.11	One of Moses holding up some manna
CD49.12	And one of a priest holding up the Host in the Eucharist

Make sure there's a gap between the two pictures

> They look the same don't they?
> But Jesus said they were quite different.
> This bread **(CD49.9)** is manna, the Angel's bread. It came down from Heaven, but it's quite ordinary really. The people who ate manna lived and died just like us.

Turn to **CD49.12**

> This is the bread that Jesus promised to give us.
> It looks ordinary but, once the priest has blessed it, it becomes for us the Body of Jesus.
> Let's just look at Jesus . . .

CD49.13 *Put it between pictures* **CD49.11** *and* **CD49.12**

> In today's Gospel He said, 'I am the bread of life.'
> This bread **(CD49.10)** looks like the other one, but actually it becomes Jesus, the Living Bread *(Draw an arrow linking pictures* **CD49.12** *and* **CD49.13***)*
> The people who eat that will live for ever.
> Who *does* eat this **(CD49.10)** bread? (**Christians, us, we do**)
> I think that's something we should thank Jesus for.

REHEARSAL

Practise your presentation for when you go back into church (see below).

FINAL PRAYER	You gave us bread from Heaven, Lord: a sweet-tasting bread that was very good to eat.
	Lord Jesus, You are the Living Bread, Thank you for giving yourself to us At Holy Communion. **Amen**

BACK IN CHURCH

Go in with the pictures of gingerbread, etc.
The children line up at the front, ready to hold up their bread picture on cue

Leader   Today we thought about all sorts of bread:
                  gingerbread **(CD49.4)**
                  French bread **(CD49.6)**
                  flat bread **(CD49.1)**
                  shortbread **(CD49.8)**
                  raw bread **(CD49.3)**
                  toasted bread **(CD49.2)**
                  bread sticks **(CD49.7)**
                  and Angel's Bread – the Jews call that manna **(CD49.9)**.
                  And all these breads taste good and are very ordinary.
                  But in the Gospel today we heard about –
                  Living Bread! **(CD49.10)**
                  Jesus said anyone who ate that would live for ever.

(CD49.11)

(CD49.12)

(CD49.13)

Specimen cartoons for this script

Script 50   The Last Supper

Proper 15, Ordinary Time 20
(Sunday between 14 and 20 August)

St John 6.51–55

THEME

The third and last 'Bread' Gospel: the moment in St John, chapter 6, where Jesus says, 'the bread that I give is my flesh'. Some people feel uncomfortable about this: *flesh* is a queasy word, and it's easy to pass embarrassment on to the children. Christianity is concerned with flesh however, so we have to get over it. One way to cope with Jesus' saying is to go back to the Last Supper and put it in its context as a Passover meal.

The set up gives you the materials for a Jewish Passover meal. Do what you can: some pitta bread, grape juice, parsley or lettuce, and a spoonful of cream of horseradish, will give children the idea. The Passover re-enaction in this script is highly abbreviated and concentrates on some of the food and a couple of the ceremonies.

SET UP

- The liturgical colour is Green.
- A Bible.
- Props and food for a Passover meal. The essential ones are:
  - three pieces of matzos crackers – or pitta,
  - a jug of 'wine' (grape juice),
  - a dollop of cream of horseradish in a little bowl (don't get neat horseradish, it's too strong),
  - some flat parsley,
  - two candles in candlesticks,
  - a large tea towel,
  - four wine glasses,
  - a small bowl of salty water,
  - jug of ordinary water,
  - a cushion,

- matches, and
- a toy lamb.
- If you have a large number of children, be ready to lay this out on a mat, with the children sitting round. A smaller number can be accommodated round a table.
- Work out the youngest (literate) child present and give them a slip of paper with their line on it.
- Extras:
  - lots of cushions.
  - a bowl of 'charoseth': this is a mixture of apple sauce, cinnamon and grated almonds (check out nut allergies before you add the almonds). You can make the mixture during the session, if you feel the kids would like a cookery session; the result should be stiff and look like mud.

WELCOME *the children and lead them in* **The Sign of the Cross** ✠ (**p. xxxvi**).

THE KYRIE   God our Father, you are always ready to forgive us,
Lord have mercy
Lord have mercy

Lord Jesus, you taught us to say sorry for our sins,
Christ have mercy
Christ have mercy

Holy Spirit, you help us to repent when we do wrong,
Lord have mercy
Lord have mercy

Ask the children to repeat **The Prayer for Forgiveness** *after you* (**p. xxxvi**).

OPENING   Lord Jesus,
PRAYER   You came down to live among us,
You ate and drank with us
And had a Last Supper with your friends
Before you died on the Cross.
Help us to understand you better,
As we think about your Last Supper this morning,
Amen

Leader   Today we are going to listen to the Gospel straight away.

THE GOSPEL PROCESSION

THE GOSPEL *St John 6.51–55*

AFTER THE GOSPEL

Leader   Jesus said, 'The bread I shall give you is my flesh.'
                    What is flesh?

Take all answers, establish that it's skin and muscle
Pinch a bit of your arm

It's this stuff.
Jesus didn't mean us to eat His arm, did He? (**No!**)
What did He mean? Let's find out.
Jesus gave us His Body at the very last meal He ate before He died on
the Cross. It's called the Last Supper, and it was a very strange meal.
Now we all have strange meals sometimes. There's one we have at
Christmas, what do we eat then? (**Turkey, brussel sprouts, Christmas
pudding,** *and so on*)
Well the Jews have odd meals too: one of them happens at Passover,
and it was a Passover meal that Jesus ate with His friends.
So let's set up for a Passover meal.

Set up the Passover meal, taking on board the numbers you've got, and the food and
props you've managed to acquire. The layout should look like this.
The leader must have a cushion to lean against.
Designate a girl to light the candles

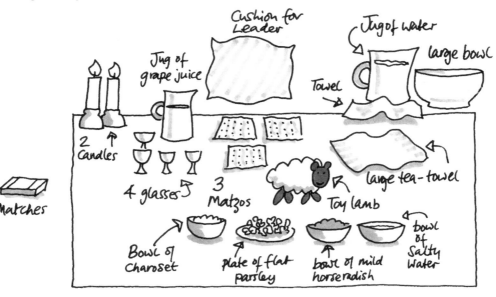

The Last Supper

It's just possible that some kids will remember last week's session. Go through it with them, and establish that:

Leader	The Jews were slaves in Egypt, they escaped, and the Egyptians chased them across the desert until they got to the Red Sea.

What happened then? (**Moses, with God's help, parted the waters, and the Jews got through on dry land**)

The Egyptians galloped in after them – what happened then? (**The waters came back and the Egyptians were drowned**)

So God saved the Jews.

They've never forgotten what God did for them that day and, ever since then, right up to now, the Jews have a Passover meal once a year so they can tell their kids the story of their escape from slavery.

At the beginning of the meal, a girl lights the candles; let's do that:

A girl lights the two candles

Now I want you all to spread out your right hands towards the candles as I say the Jewish blessing, the 'Kiddush'.

As the children stretch out their hands you say

Kiddush

Leader   'Blessed are you, O Lord our God, King of the Universe, who brings forth light out of darkness.'

So Jesus would have sat down with His friends, and a woman in the room – it was probably Jesus' mother, the Virgin Mary – would have lit the candles.

Optional Cushions

Leader   Everyone would have been sitting or lying on nice comfortable cushions. That was to show they were no longer slaves.

Then the youngest child present would say . . .

Youngest child   Why is this night different from all other nights?

Leader   And the grown-ups would tell all the children why this night was special.*

---

* If anyone is interested in who the 'child' was at the Last Supper, tell them there may have been kids present (it's not the sort of thing a Gospel writer would mention: women and children were 'invisible'), but if there weren't, the youngest person would have asked the question. In that case it was probably St John.

And as they told the story of the Jews' escape from Egypt, they ate special food.
In Jesus' time this included a lamb . . .

Put the toy lamb in the centre of the table

This was because the Jews sacrificed a lamb before they escaped. They smeared the blood of the lamb on their front doors and, when the Angel of Death went through the land of Egypt, he saw the houses with blood on and passed over them. That's why this feast is called the Passover.
Well we're not going to have roast lamb this morning, but we are going to have some of the other food, like this parsley.
The Jews call this karpas, and they dip the karpas in salt water – to remind them of the bitter tears they shed when they were slaves.
Would anyone like to try some?

Dip some small sprigs in the salt water and hand it to any child brave enough to try. Keep one sprig back for the presentation

Then the Leader of the Feast would take three pieces of flat bread –

Hold up the matzos or pitta

It had to be flat, because when the Jews escaped, they didn't have time to wait for their bread to rise.
And he'd break the middle one and wrap half of the broken piece in a napkin . . .

Do this
Then he'd ask a child to hide it. Who'd like to hide this?

Choose a small kid

Actually it's always hidden in the same place, behind my cushion . . .
Then he'd break up the rest of the bread and give everyone two bits.
Don't eat them yet!

Hand round pieces of matzos/pitta

Now, this is the odd bit. Everyone would make a sandwich by dipping the bread in some bitter herbs. That's this stuff.

Show the children the horseradish

It's hot, and if you eat a lot, like this . . .

Put a teaspoonful on one bit of matzo/pitta

It makes your eyes water.
That means you are a true Israelite – you are weeping, as you remember how awful it was to be a slave.

Of course you might not want to do that, so putting on a really tiny bit, one you can hardly taste, is fine

Smear a trace of horseradish on your other bit of matzos/pitta

Optional Charoseth

Then you dip the other bit of bread into this.

Show them the charoseth

This is yummy: it's just apple sauce with cinnamon (and almonds) added. It's supposed to look like mud, because when the Jews were slaves they had to make mud bricks.

Then you put your two bits of bread together – but you still don't eat them.

Pass round the bitter herbs (and charoseth). Half the kids won't want anything to do with them – that's absolutely fine – some will be very brave and scoop up a huge dollop of horseradish (have some water ready . . .)

Right, everyone got their sandwich ready? I'll say grace.

Grace

Leader   Blessed are you, O Lord our God, King of the Universe, who has commanded us to eat flat bread and bitter herbs.

Eat your sandwich. Congratulate any child who has had a go at the bitter herbs, and tell anyone with tears in their eyes they are a true Israelite. Clear the bread and bowls as you finish with them

And all the time, the leader would be praying, and pouring out glasses of wine, and handing them round.

Fill up the four glasses with grape juice

You get four glasses of wine at Passover, and you drink them the way we drink wine at Holy Communion – by sharing a glass together.

Pass round three of the wine glasses. Not all the children will want to drink, so ask the other adults to empty all three glasses before you go on

Then, at last, they'd eat the lamb *(remove the lamb)*
We'll have to imagine that, and, at the very end, a child had to find the hidden bread.
Where is it?

A child finds it   And everyone drank from the last glass of wine.

Place the piece of bread and the last wine glass before you

> And it was at this moment that Jesus did something odd.
> Let's hear what He did from the Bible.

Leader 2 *reads the following passage from St Luke 22.19–20 while* **Leader 1** *imitates the actions of Jesus as Leader 2 reads. Don't eat the bread*

Leader 2   Then Jesus took bread, and when He had given thanks, He broke it and gave it to them, saying: 'This is my body given for you: do this in remembrance of me.' He also did the same with the cup after supper, and said, 'This cup is my blood, poured out for you.'

Leader 1   What was Jesus doing?
Well, there are lots of answers, and one of them is He was giving us a *new* Passover.
Because God was about to save His people all over again, not from the Egyptians but from death. And it wasn't going to be a lamb that was going to die, but Jesus Himself. He wanted us to remember that. And we have – we've been doing the last bit of Passover ever since. We do what Jesus did, when we
Take bread
Bless it
Break it, and
Eat it.
And we remember how Jesus said it was His Body.
When do we do that? (**At Mass, at the Eucharist, at Holy Communion**)

REHEARSAL

Practise your presentation for when you go back into church (see below).

FINAL PRAYER

As the whole session has been a devotion, stay round the table and end by thanking God for Mass by saying

Leader   Lord, you gave us yourself as bread from Heaven:
a sweet-tasting bread that was very good to eat.

Finish with a **Glory be . . . (p. xxxvii).**

BACK IN CHURCH

Take the toy lamb, the parsley, the bitter herbs, and the last piece of matzos/pitta back into church

Leader   Today we remembered how Jesus had a Last Supper with His friends.
                        We heard about the lamb they ate . . .

A child holds up the lamb

                        And the parsley . . .

A child holds up the parsley

                        We ate some of that . . .
                        And the bitter herbs . . .

A child holds up the bitter herbs

                        We ate some of that too.
                        But when we got to the last piece of bread . . .

A child holds up the bread

                        We didn't eat it.
                        Instead we've come back to church so that we can remember together how Jesus 'took bread, blessed it and gave it to us saying, 'This is my Body'''.

Script 51   Staying the Course

Proper 16, Ordinary Time 21
(Sunday between 21 and 27 August)

St John 6.60–61a, 64b, 66–69

THEME

The Gospel today is about a crisis. Some of Jesus' disciples are disturbed by His teaching and decide to leave Him. Jesus turns to the Twelve to ask, 'What about you? Do you want to go away too?' St Peter's response is immediate and, in the circumstances, amazing, 'Where would we go? You have the message of eternal life.' The session is all about sifting, who can stay the course?

SET UP

- The liturgical colour is Green.
- Marker pen.
- Mats or sheets of newspaper, about 2 feet square.
- Apostle pictures from the CD-Rom.

WELCOME *the children and lead them in* **The Sign of the Cross** ✠ **(p. xxxvi).**

Introduce the Kyrie: look back over the week – was there anything we wish we hadn't done? Something we forgot to do?

Leader   Let's get rid of it now by telling God we're sorry.

THE KYRIE   Lord Jesus, you came to bring us back to God,
                       Lord have mercy
                       Lord have mercy

                       Lord Jesus, you came to heal us from our sins,
                       Christ have mercy
                       Christ have mercy

                       Lord Jesus, you came to tell us how much God loves us,
                       Lord have mercy
                       Lord have mercy

Ask the children to repeat **The Prayer for Forgiveness** *after you* (**p. xxxvi**).

OPENING **PRAYER**	God our Father, You sent your Son Jesus into the world To bring us back to you. Help us to stay faithful to Jesus, Today, and next week, And for the rest of our lives. **Amen**

Selection Panel

Leader   OK, I want to run some tests this morning.

Write up the headings 'Balance', 'Alertness' and 'Survival' on a flip chart or whiteboard

First, I want to find out who's really good at balancing.

Ask the children to stand on one leg, if they wobble too much, they have to sit down. Go round the room, tapping wobblers on the shoulder – they sit down at once. Get the grown-ups to join in, they'll be terrible . . .
At the end, write up the name of the winner

So *Name* is really good at balancing.

Now, how about alertness?

Split the room into 'Land' (one wall), 'Sea' (the middle) and 'Air' (the opposite wall) Line the children up in the middle. When you call Land!, *they rush to the 'Land' wall;* Air!, *to the opposite wall;* Sea! *back to the middle. Mix up the commands and take them unaware every now and then by calling out the same command twice. Be merciful to begin with, but gradually weed out the kids who jump the wrong way until you get a clear winner*

OK, *Name* is very alert indeed.

Now, how are you on survival?

Take a view on numbers and spread out the mats/newspapers round the room. Ask the children to stand on them – you can have two or more kids per sheet, but their feet mustn't be on the floor

OK, chaps, you are all polar bears, and you are in deep trouble because the ice you are standing on is melting. The mats are the ice, and the floor is the sea.

Now when I say SWIM! You jump off the ice and swim round the sea, and when I say ICE! you jump back on a mat – any mat. Anyone with a foot in the sea is out. SWIM!

And off they go. After a couple of runs, start taking mats away . . .

Anyone with even the tiniest bit of them in the sea is out
The last kids on the last mat are the winners

> So, *Name, Name* and *Name* are natural survivors.
> Well, if I ever need to start up a commando unit, I'll know who to come to.
> But supposing I'm not looking for commandos?
> Supposing I'm looking for disciples, for people I can trust? Running and jumping aren't really that important.
> Jesus knew what He was looking for in His disciples, let's hear about it in the Gospel.

THE GOSPEL PROCESSION

THE GOSPEL *St John 6.60–61a, 64b, 66–69*

Optional Paraphrase

After listening to Jesus' teaching, some of His disciples said, 'This is too hard for anyone to understand!' Jesus knew that people were grumbling about Him, and He also knew who would stick by Him.

Some disciples left Him and Jesus said to the Twelve, 'What about you? Will you go too?' Simon Peter answered, 'Lord, where would we go? You have the message of eternal life.'

AFTER THE GOSPEL

Leader   That's an interesting Gospel: it shows that to start with Jesus had loads of disciples, but some of them couldn't cope with Him and went home. How many did Jesus have left? (**12**)
And what do you think made them stay?

Take all answers, home in on Simon Peter's '**Lord, where would we go?**' *Peter and the others loved Jesus: they trusted Him*

> So when Jesus was getting His band of friends together He was looking for people who could love and trust Him.

ACTIVITY

Write up 'Trust'

Leader   So what names am I going to put up here?

CD51.1–CD51.2 *Put up the pictures of the Apostles as the kids remember them. With some judicious cheating they usually manage the lot*

	Brilliant, that's all 12.
	Did they all stay faithful to Jesus? (**No**)
	Who was the disciple who betrayed Him? (**Judas Iscariot**)
	Yes, Judas is one of the saddest people in the Gospels.
	Let's put him to one side.
Do so	Still, we've got 11 left.
	Anyone here want to be a disciple?

Allocate an Apostle to 11 of the children for the presentation (see below). If you haven't got 11 kids, allocate two or three each

REHEARSAL

Practise your presentation for when you go back into church (see below).

FINAL	Lord Jesus,
PRAYER	Thank you for St Peter
	And the other faithful disciples.
	Help us to follow their example,
	To love and trust you,
	And follow you, like them,
	All the way to Heaven. **Amen**

MUSIC

John Bunyan's hymn 'He who would valiant be' ends the session well.

BACK IN CHURCH

Line the children up down the front

Leader	We heard today that many of Jesus' disciples deserted Him.
	And we remembered how even one of His 12 friends betrayed Him.
	But still there were 11 left – they were:

The children reel off the Apostles' names one by one

We thanked God for the faithfulness of the Apostles, and we ended by saying,

All the Children Amen!

Script 52   Washing

Proper 17, Ordinary Time 22
(Sunday between 28 August and 3 September)

St Mark 7.1–4a, 5, 14–15

THEME

Is cleanliness next to Godliness? Jesus takes a relaxed view of the matter, though obviously (in today's Gospel) He is thinking of ritual washing. Very good in its way, but not an indicator that you are a spotless person inside.

SET UP

- The liturgical colour is Green.
- Pictures from the CD-Rom.
- Holy water stoup and aspergillum – or a bowl of holy water and a hyssop (for sprinkling) made by tying some leafy twigs together.
- A jug of water,
  a bowl and
  a hand towel.
- A Mary of Egypt comic strip is provided: it is in black and white in case they'd like to colour it in.

WELCOME *the children and lead them in* **The Sign of the Cross ✠ (p. xxxvi).**

BEFORE THE KYRIE

Leader	Anyone here ever jumped in a puddle?
React to the response	
	Golly, all of you?
	How about mud? Have you ever got mud all over your shoes?
Same business	So what happens when you get home?
	There you are, soaking wet, mud up to your knees. What do you do?

Take all answers, home in on, 'I take my shoes off, I have a bath'

Yup, you get clean again, and you leave your muddy shoes by the front door.
Well, coming to church is rather like that.
Any stupid or bad thing we've done is like mud. Some horrible bit of dirt that makes us look a mess. God likes us, even with mud on our faces, but He'd rather we were clean.
So let's leave our sins at the front door, and ask God to wash us from our sins.

THE KYRIE   Lord God, we are sorry for the times we have been unkind,
Lord have mercy
Lord have mercy

Lord God, we are sorry for the times we have forgotten you,
Christ have mercy
Christ have mercy

Lord God, we ask you to forgive us
Lord have mercy
Lord have mercy

Leader *(With the Holy Water stoup)*

Now I'm going to say a prayer from the Psalms,
and then I'm going to sprinkle you with Holy Water.
As you feel the splash, cross yourself and say **Amen**.

(From Psalm 51)

Have mercy on me, O God,
Wipe away the things I've done wrong,
And wash me from my sin. **Amen**

Sprinkle the children – and ask someone to sprinkle you

Ask the children to repeat **The Prayer for Forgiveness** *after you* (**p. xxxvi**).

OPENING   Almighty God,
PRAYER   You send us every good thing
Fill our hearts with love for you
This day, and always. **Amen**

Washing

Leader
Did everyone get wet?
That's good.
Now we can feel we're clean from our sins.
But supposing I missed someone?
Would that mean God hadn't forgiven them? (**No**)
The water is only a sign of God's forgiveness.
When He washes away your sin, it happens inside you; in your heart.
It doesn't really matter if you get wet or not.
But we like our signs to be good signs, so we try our best to splash you.

Holy Washing

Pull out a jug of water, a bowl and a towel

Leader
In Jesus' time, people were very keen on using water as a sign. They used it whenever they felt unclean.
We're not talking muddy knees, but the sort of uncleanness you feel when you've done something wrong.
In fact, some people washed themselves when they'd bumped into someone who didn't believe in God,
or had touched an animal they weren't allowed to eat.
They did it like this . . .

Someone stands poised to pour water from the jug into the bowl, they have a towel draped over their arm

First I pray:
Blessed be God who has commanded me to wash my hands.
Amen.
Then I wash.

Stand with your hands and arms over the bowl as water is poured on them
Wash your hands and forearms very thoroughly and dry them, using your helper as a towel rail. If any children want to try, give them a go*

Holy washing was so important in the Jewish faith that some Jews thought that if you didn't do it, it meant your inside self wasn't clean – you were a sinner.
Let's hear what Jesus thought about that.

---

* Some children may notice this is the same way the priest washes at the altar. Comment on it if they do, but don't insert the information. They have enough to be getting on with.

THE GOSPEL PROCESSION

THE GOSPEL *St Mark 7.1–4a, 5, 14–15*

Optional Paraphrase

Some Jews from Jerusalem noticed that Jesus' disciples ate their food without washing their hands and praying. No faithful Jew eats without obeying the rules and washing his arms to the elbow. So they said to Jesus, 'Why do your disciples not obey the law but eat with unclean hands?'

Jesus called a crowd round Him before He answered, then He said,

'Listen to me, all of you. Nothing on the *outside* of a person can make him unclean *inside*.'

AFTER THE GOSPEL

Leader	Well what do you think?
	Did Jesus think you should wash your hands before meals?

Take any answer that comes

It sounds as if He didn't think it was very important.

But Jesus isn't talking about ordinary washing.

What worried Him was that some people muddled up being clean outside with being clean inside.

It's not the same. You can be a really smelly person and yet be a great saint. I'm going to tell you about one.

St Mary of Egypt

CD52.1	Here she is.
	Mary lived ages ago, in the third century. She met up with a group of pilgrims who were going to Jerusalem and joined them for a laugh. Now, Mary was not the most well-behaved person in the world and, when she got to Jerusalem, she found an invisible force stopped her from going inside the church.
	She was horrified and looked round. A picture of the Virgin Mary caught her eye and she heard the Virgin say, 'Go into the desert, Mary, you will find peace there.'
	So she bought three loaves of bread, and off she went to the desert. And there in the desert she prayed, and asked God to forgive her sins – which He did at once.

And Mary liked being alone with God so much that she stayed in the desert. Her food ran out, so she ate any plants she could find, and her clothes rotted away, so she grew her hair.

CD52.2
CD52.3
CD52.4
CD52.5

And she never had a bath, and she didn't care what she looked like. But, when she died, a lion guarded her body until God had sent one of His monks, a chap called Zosimus, to bury her. Zosimus and the lion buried her together and as Zosimus prayed over her body he realized she was a great saint.

So that was an unwashed saint

CD52.6

Here is a very clean one:

It's a Scotsman called St Mungo, who used to say his prayers standing up to his neck in cold water every day, and died when he was 115, while he was having a bath.

Saints look different outside, but inside they are all holy.
God is more interested in us being clean inside than out.

ACTIVITY

CD52.7 *The children may like to fill in the Mary of Egypt comic strip together*

REHEARSAL

Practise your presentation for when you go back into church (see below).

FINAL
PRAYER

Lord Jesus,
Friend of Sinners
Fill our hearts with your love
So that we stay clean inside. **Amen**

BACK IN CHURCH

Take back the pictures of St Mary and St Mungo

Leader

Today we heard about two saints:
One was St Mary of Egypt

A child holds up her picture

She never took a bath, but lived in the desert – very close to God.
Another was St Mungo

A child holds up his picture

He said his prayers standing up to his neck in cold water
And died in his bath when he was 115.

But we realized God doesn't really mind how clean you are outside,
as long as you are clean . . .

All the Children Inside!

(CD 52.1)

(CD 52.3)

(CD 52.4)

(CD 52.6)

Specimen cartoons for this script

Script 53   Jesus Heals a Deaf and Dumb Man

Proper 18, Ordinary Time 23
(Sunday between 4 and 10 September)

St Mark 7.31–37

THEME

One of Jesus' classic miracles – and a very physical one. Jesus uses His fingers, spit and breath to heal the deaf man. A couple of games, in which the children listen, speak and run around, reinforces how wonderful our bodies are, and how God loves them being in working order.

SET UP

- The liturgical colour is Green.
- Two toy cars.
- A few plastic cups.
- Practise the Pro-Active Our Father (see below) so you can do it in front of the children.

WELCOME *the children and lead them in* **The Sign of the Cross** ✠ (**p. xxxvi**).

THE KYRIE   Lord God, we are sorry for the times we have been unkind,
Lord have mercy
Lord have mercy

Lord God, we are sorry for the times we have forgotten you,
Christ have mercy
Christ have mercy

Lord God, we ask you to forgive us,
Lord have mercy
Lord have mercy

Ask the children to repeat **The Prayer for Forgiveness** *after you* (**p. xxxvi**).

OPENING
PRAYER

The opening prayer is taken from Psalm 146
The response to the Psalm is:
Praise the Lord!
Praise the Lord!

My soul give praise to the Lord!
It is He that gives bread to the hungry
Praise the Lord!

It is the Lord who loves the just
And protects the stranger
Praise the Lord!

It is the Lord who gives sight to the blind
And sets the prisoners free
Praise the Lord!

Reversing the Car

Ask the children to stand in a circle

Leader

OK, we're going to play a really simple game.
We're going to pass this car (*hold it up*) round the circle.
It's going to go round clockwise.

Start it going

Excellent, now when I say 'REVERSE!' go the other way!

Run this for a minute or two, then stop. Pick up the second car

OK, that was obviously too easy. So now this car (the first) goes
round clockwise, and this car (the second) goes round anticlockwise,
and when I say 'REVERSE!' they both change direction.

*Chaos normally ensues: keep it going and, as the children get proficient, add a further
refinement. Any child actually holding a car can call out 'REVERSE!'*
At the end, ask the children to sit down, facing the front

BEFORE THE GOSPEL

Leader

I think you did that brilliantly.
Did you notice how many senses you used for that game?
You had to *watch* the car. What else? (**Listening, touching**)
And other bits of your body had to be working properly – you had
to use your hands to pass the car, and some of you shouted out
'REVERSE!'

It's fantastic when your body is working properly. Jesus hated it when people had something wrong with them.
He always wanted to heal them.
Let's hear about one man He met in the Gospel today.

THE GOSPEL PROCESSION

THE GOSPEL *St Mark 7.31–37*

AFTER THE GOSPEL

Leader   So what was wrong with the man? (**He was deaf and dumb**)
And what did Jesus do? (**He healed him**)
How? *(Get all the details – refer back to the Gospel)* (**Jesus put His fingers in the man's ears, He spat, He touched the man's tongue, He sighed, He spoke**)
Jesus used His whole body to put that man right.
Why do you think He did that? *(A rhetorical question probably)*
I think it was because the deaf and dumb man couldn't hear Jesus, so he needed to watch Him. He could see Jesus *doing* things, so he knew Jesus was helping him.

Well, if Jesus liked using His body, so should we.

GAME

Running Around

Split the children into teams and run a relay race in which they have to hop, crawl, cartwheel, walk backwards – anything really – between two points. If you want a quiet moment, make one lap dependent on carrying a full plastic cup of water to the finishing line
One drop spilt and they're out

REHEARSAL

Practise your presentation for when you go back into church (see below).

BEFORE THE FINAL PRAYER

Ask the children to stand for the final prayer

Leader   Well, we've been using our bodies a lot this morning
So we'll carry on doing so as we pray.

Show the children how to do the Pro-Active Our Father (below). Run it at least once before you pray it

FINAL **PRAYER**	Our Father who art in Heaven – *look up* Hallowed be your name *(arms up in prayer gesture)*

Your kingdom come *(arms still up, rotate on the spot)*
Your will be done on Earth *(point down)*
As it is in Heaven *(point up)*
Give us this day our daily bread *(hands together in prayer)*
And forgive us our trespasses *(knock chest three times)*
As we forgive those who trespass against us *(shake hands with the people round you)*
And lead us not into temptation *(fold arms)*
But deliver us from evil *(shake your heads (no way!))*
For thine is the kingdom, the power and the glory *(arms up in prayer)*
For ever and ever *(hands together in prayer)*
Amen! *(punch the air with your fist)*

BACK IN CHURCH

Children lined up at the front, with a couple of leaders facing them to cue in the Our Father actions

Leader	Today we heard how Jesus healed a man who was deaf and dumb. Obviously God loves it when our bodies are working well, so we've learnt to pray to Him, using our bodies.

Then run the Our Father

Script 54   The Messiah

Proper 19, Ordinary Time 24
(Sunday between 11 and 17 September)

St Mark 8.27–30

THEME

Jesus asks the disciples who they think He is and Simon Peter says, 'You are the Christ'. 'Christ' is Greek for 'Messiah'. Peter's insight is astonishing but he still seems to have thought of the Messiah in the traditional way, as the God-sent hero who would free Israel. Not surprisingly, he objects when Jesus tells him that the Messiah's destiny is to suffer and die for His people.

SET UP

- The liturgical colour is Green.
- Line up a row of chairs to make a rudimentary bus.
- Download some pictures of Batman, Superman and Spiderman from the Internet.
- Pictures from the CD-Rom.
- Bible marked up at Zechariah 9.9.
- Crucifix.
- Prayer candle.

WELCOME *the children and lead them in* **The Sign of the Cross** ✠ **(p. xxxvi)**.

THE KYRIE   Lord God, we are sorry for the times we have been unkind,
Lord have mercy
Lord have mercy

Lord God, we are sorry for the times we have forgotten you,
Christ have mercy
Christ have mercy

Lord God, we ask you to forgive us,
Lord have mercy
Lord have mercy

Ask the children to repeat **The Prayer for Forgiveness** *after you* (**p. xxxvi**).

OPENING
PRAYER   God our Father,
You saw that the human race had wandered away from you,
So you sent your Son Jesus Christ
To find us and bring us back.
Help us to listen to your Son in the Gospel this morning. **Amen**

A Bus Ride

Leader   Right, today we thought we'd take you on a bus ride.

Set up the chairs

Name (Leader 2) is going to drive, I'll be just behind him/her, and the rest of you can have the other seats – hop on board!

Everyone gets on the bus, Leader 2 mimes taking off the hand brake, 'Vroom vroom', and off you go

OK, do everything I do:
We're going through some very mountainous country,
here comes a bend

Bend slightly over to your left

And another

Bend slightly to your right

The road's getting bumpy

Jump up and down in your seat

Here's a massive bump

Leap up and sit down

Oh no! That bump knocked out the brakes!
We're going too fast! Here's a bend!

Bend right over to the right

And another

Bend right over to the left

And another

Over to the left again

OH NO! We're going over the edge! *Name* can't stop the coach!
HANG ON!

Clutch the seat in front

> Wow! Look up! Can you see anything? (**No!**)
> Well I can. Is it a bird? Is it a plane?
> No it's a man – red cloak, blue tights . . .
> Who can it be??? (**Superman**)

Wave

> Hi Superman! We're safe!
> Phew! *(Lean back in chair)*

Put the chairs back and get the children seated on the floor as normal

Superman

Leader Thank goodness Superman turned up – I'm sorry you didn't see him
> But I bet you all know what he looks like?

Put up pictures of Batman, Superman and Spiderman from the Internet

> Which one is he? *(They'll tell you at once)*
> And who are these other guys? *(They'll tell you that too)*
> These are really useful people to know if you're in trouble.
> Has anyone got their mobile number? (**No**)
> Rats! Or their email? (**No**)
> Why not? (**They don't exist**)
> I'm afraid you're right. They are just people in stories.

Take down the pictures

The Messiah

Leader Now hundreds of years ago, the Jews knew they were in trouble.
CD54.1 They had the Romans ruling them
> And they had to pay Roman taxes,
> And have the Roman army bullying them.
> And they longed for a hero to come and save them.
> The super thing was that, when they read their Bibles, they could see
> that God was going to send them a Hero one day – He was called the
> Messiah.
> Look, here's a bit about Him.

Pull out your Bible

> 'Rejoice, people of Zion!
> Shout for joy, Jerusalem!
> Look, your king is coming to you
> Triumphant and victorious!'

CD54.2   That sounds good. People couldn't wait for the Messiah to come.
Perhaps He'd look like this –
Well, one day, Jesus was walking with His disciples and He asked
them who they thought He was. Let's hear what they said.

THE GOSPEL PROCESSION

THE GOSPEL *St Mark 8.27–30*

Use the word 'Messiah' instead of 'Christ'

AFTER THE GOSPEL

CD54.3   *Put up the picture of Peter*

Leader   St Peter got it right. Who did he say Jesus was? (**The Messiah**)
Yup. The trouble is – what sort of Messiah was St Peter thinking of?
I think he hoped the Messiah would look like this . . .

CD54.4   *Stick **CD54.4** in the Peter thought bubble of **CD54.3***

But Jesus knew more about the Messiah than Peter – and He knew
His Bible better too. Let's just look at the Bible passage again . . .

Pull out the Bible

Peter read this bit:
'Shout for joy, Jerusalem!
Look, your king is coming to you
Triumphant and victorious!'
But he hadn't noticed that it went on like this:
'He comes *humbly*, riding on a donkey.'
CD54.5   Jesus knew that bit. He knew that the Messiah's job was not to lead
a huge army, but to be humble, to be a servant – and to die for His
people.
But Peter didn't want to hear.

REHEARSAL

Practise your presentation for when you go back into church (see below).

BEFORE THE FINAL PRAYER

Gather the children round a crucifix, put a lighted candle in front of it

Leader	This is an image of a real super hero: Jesus the Messiah, dying for us. Jesus said that the Messiah would suffer, and be put to death, and buried – and that He would rise again on the third day. St Peter wasn't listening very hard at that moment, but we are. Let's make the Sign of the Cross as we say:
FINAL PRAYER	We adore you O Christ **We adore you O Christ**
	And we bless you **And we bless you**
	✠ Because by your Holy Cross ✠ **Because by your Holy Cross**
	You have saved the world **You have saved the world. Amen**

BACK IN CHURCH

Take in the Messiah-as-super-hero – **(CD54.4)** *stuck in* **(CD54.3)** *– and the crucifix*

Leader	Today we heard how St Peter hailed Jesus as the Messiah. Unfortunately Peter and Jesus' friends hoped that the Messiah was going to look something like this . . .

A child holds up Super Messiah

But Jesus had to tell them that the real Messiah was going to save His people like this . . .

A child holds up the crucifix

Well we've got two heroes in front of us here:
which one is the real Messiah?

The children point to the crucifix

Yes, Jesus is the Christ, God's Messiah.

Script 55   Who's the Greatest?

Proper 20, Ordinary Time 25
(Sunday between 18 and 24 September)

St Mark 9.30–37

THEME

One of the most impressive things about St Mark's Gospel is that it doesn't edit the behaviour of the disciples, but tells it as it was. The Twelve can be dense, or frightened, or – as we discover in today's passage – pushy. Such writing encourages us to believe in their more attractive qualities: their love for Jesus, and their readiness to spread His word.

SET UP

- The liturgical colour is Green.
- Pictures from the CD-Rom.
- 12 sticky labels/name tags for each of the disciples.
- Cast someone as Jesus (see below).
- Identify the smallest child in the room (a baby is fine).

WELCOME *the children and lead them in* **The Sign of the Cross** ✠ (**p. xxxvi**).

THE KYRIE   Lord Jesus, you taught us to ask God our Father to forgive us,
Lord have mercy
Lord have mercy

Lord Jesus, you showed us how we should forgive others,
Christ have mercy
Christ have mercy

Lord Jesus, you told us how the Father would always forgive those who were truly sorry,
Lord have mercy
Lord have mercy

Ask the children to repeat **The Prayer for Forgiveness** *after you* (**p. xxxvi**).

OPENING **PRAYER**	Lord Jesus, Though you are the Son of God You came down to Earth And became the servant of all. Help us to follow your example And serve others. **Amen**

Processions

Leader   This morning I want us to think about important people.
Who do you think is the most important person in this country?
(It doesn't matter who they say – **the Queen, the Prime Minister, even a famous footballer***)*
And who's the most important person in this room?

Don't give them a chance to answer – tap your own chest

Me!

Put down any rebellion from the other Leaders

Who's at the front, dealing with this lot? Me.
And who's the most important person in this church?

There may be several candidates, establish that it's the vicar or the parish priest

That's very interesting, because you'd never guess it from the way we process into church.
Look, here are all the people who process into church at the beginning of the service.

If you have run Script 38 (page 207) recently, see if the children can remember who is in a church procession

CD55.1–16 *cover every sort of server, priest, choir member I can think of: pull out the ones suitable for your church and stick them randomly on your board*

Let's line them up properly.

See if the children can line them up in the right order. A possible order is given below – all you need worry about is getting the priest/celebrant at the end

> **A Grand Procession**
>
> Thurifer with boat boy or girl, crucifer, candle bearers, choir, spare servers, the master of ceremonies, reader, spare clergy, sub-deacon, deacon, celebrant.

Admire the result, and point out that the more important people are at the end: the priest is at the very end

Leader   Why do we put the priest at the back?
                    Well, it's because of today's Gospel – it's about a line-up as well.
                    I need 12 people to be Jesus' disciples . . .

Dish out the name tags and stick them on your volunteers. If you haven't got 12 children, press-gang the grown-ups, or give a kid two names. Put them in a line

Right, could you look at your name and remember who you are.
Name is going to be Jesus – and he's at the front, as he's the only one who knows where they're all going.
Well, Jesus and His friends went all round Palestine preaching the Good News. But of course there were no trains or cars, so they had to walk.
Jesus led the way, and everyone followed Him – off you go.

The line starts to walk round the room, not too fast

But every now and then they'd get fed up:
Sometimes Peter would be at the front

Peter goes to the front

Then it was John

John gets ahead of Peter

Then it was . . . *(Go through all the Apostles)*

The others are: Andrew, Big James, Bartholomew, Little James, Jude the Just, Judas Iscariot, Philip, Thomas, Matthew, Simon the Zealot

Then they started to push and argue.
Can you act a bit of arguing?

Get the kids to wag fingers and flap arms

Brilliant!
And eventually Jesus stopped.

He does   Everybody went quiet, and Jesus said . . .

Jesus   What are you arguing about?

| Leader | All the disciples hung their heads, they didn't want to say anything because they were ashamed. So what did Jesus do? |

Let's find out in the Gospel.

THE GOSPEL PROCESSION

THE GOSPEL *St Mark 9.30–37*

AFTER THE GOSPEL

| Leader | What did Jesus do? (**He took a little child and put it in front of them**) |

Get 'Jesus' to bring the smallest child to the front of the room – it might have to come with its Mum or Dad

Why did He do this? *(See what the children make of it)*
I think one of the main reasons is that Jesus wanted to surprise the disciples – a little kid was greater than any of them.
Why do you think Jesus liked children so much?

Children often don't have a view on this, make sure a grown-up is ready to say 'because children are nice'

Yup, children are nice.
And they're sensible: they know they're little, so they don't try to push grown-ups out of the way.
Jesus didn't want His friends to push or shove, He wanted them to be kind and sensible – like a child.
He said that anybody who behaves like that will be the greatest in the Kingdom of God.

| **FINAL PRAYER** | Let's say the Family Prayer of the Church together (**p. xxxvi**) **Our Father . . .** |

GOING BACK TO CHURCH

| Leader | Jesus also said, the first will be last, which is why in Christian processions the important person is always the last one – at the end. |

Let's form up to go back into church.
Who's going to be at the end?
Me? (**No**)
No, you're right, it's going to be little *Name*.

BACK IN CHURCH

Line up the children

Leader	Today we heard that Jesus' disciples had an argument about who was the greatest.
	It made us wonder who was the greatest person in the Children's Church. I thought it was me.
	But then we read the Gospel and discovered it was the smallest person in the room.
	Who was that guys?
Children	*Name!*

Somebody holds up the smallest child

Script 56   St Thomas in India

Proper 21, Ordinary Time 26
(Sunday between 25 September and 1 October)

St Mark 9.41

THEME

The Gospel is a mixed bag this morning: this session homes in on Jesus saying that even the smallest thing you do for Him will receive a reward. This is a nice corrective to that rather depressing dictum some of us were brought up with, that 'being good is its own reward'. Jesus is no puritan and is happy to reward His disciples.

SET UP

- The liturgical colour is Green.
- Pictures from the CD-Rom.
- Print up the template for a palace.
- Pieces of coloured paper about 3 inches square: the children are going to construct a palace out of these, so choose colours that look harmonious – gold and silver squares for the roof would look nice.
- A piece of A1 paper to stick the palace on.
- Glue.

WELCOME *the children and lead them in* **The Sign of the Cross** ✠ **(p. xxxvi).**

THE KYRIE   Lord Jesus, you came to call sinners,
Lord have mercy
Lord have mercy

Lord Jesus, you came to find the unhappy,
Christ have mercy
Christ have mercy

Lord Jesus, you came to tell us how much God loves us,
Lord have mercy
Lord have mercy

Ask the children to repeat **The Prayer for Forgiveness** *after you* (**p. xxxvi**).

OPENING PRAYER	Lord God King of Heaven, Help us to do your will here on Earth, As we hurry towards the joys you have promised us, In your Kingdom, Where we shall live with you for ever and ever. **Amen**

BEFORE THE GOSPEL

Rewards

Bring a chair forward and sit down

Leader	I'm going to tell you a story. About 150 years ago a young man met a tramp in Piccadilly. The young man's name was Harry, but he was no ordinary chap, he was a lord. And the tramp was his uncle. Let's look at them

Hold up pictures **CD56.1** *and* **CD56.2** *from the CD-Rom*

Here's Harry – he was a Viscount.
And here's the tramp – he was a Marquess.*
So both of them had titles, and they should have been pretty rich.
But something had happened to the Marquess.
He dressed like a tramp, and people said he rooted round dustbins for his lunch. And he didn't want anyone's help.
Well, Harry recognized his uncle and thought it only polite to sit down and talk to him. So they sat on a doorstep together, and chatted for half an hour – and then Harry went off to a restaurant for his lunch, and the Marquess disappeared off to a nearby dustbin.
And, astonishingly, two weeks later, Harry discovered his uncle had died and left him his vast fortune. So that tiny good deed received a huge reward.
Jesus talks about good deeds in the Gospel this morning. We'll hear it now.

THE GOSPEL PROCESSION

---

* They were the Viscount Lascelles and the Marquess of Clanricarde if anyone is interested. A Marquess is much grander than a Viscount.

THE GOSPEL *St Mark 9.41*

AFTER THE GOSPEL

Leader
That was short wasn't it?

Jesus said that anyone who does a really small good deed, like giving someone a cup of water, would be rewarded.

What sort of reward? Do you think if I sat down and talked to tramps like Harry I'd get a fortune? (**No**)

No, I think you're right.

How do we get rewarded for our good deeds?

See what comes up, the conversation normally gets on to Heaven on its own account

Well, apart from the fact that we feel happier when we're being nice to people, and we certainly make the world a happier place, the rewards that Jesus is thinking about are dished out in Heaven.

Not everyone realizes that. This bloke for example . . .

CD56.3
This is a picture of King Gundaphorus, who lived in India 2,000 years ago. I'm going to tell you another story . . .

St Thomas in India

Leader
This is about Gundaphorus and Jesus' friend, St Thomas.

Now listen guys, this is only a story. It's not in the Bible. It seems that St Thomas went to India (actually that bit is probably true) and became an architect for Gundaphorus.

CD56.4
There's St Thomas with his architect's T Square – he'll need that for drawing building plans.

Well Gundaphorus gave Thomas loads of money to build a magnificent palace for him, and then went off on his elephant somewhere and left Tom to get on with the job.

And Tom spent the money on the poor and the homeless, and every time Gundaphorus wrote to him to say, 'How's the palace coming on?' Tom would write back and say, 'Fantastic! It's got turrets and towers, and I just need some more money to give it a roof of silver and gold.'

So Gundaphorus gave him more money – and Tom spent it on the sick.

You can imagine what happened when Gundaphorus got back. He rushed round to Tom's office. 'Where's my palace?' he shouted. And Tom said, 'Ah, well. I should have told you about that – the palace I am making for you is being built in Heaven.'

CD56.5	'Oh really?' said Gundaphorus, 'Throw that man in gaol!'
	Then something odd happened. Gundaphorus' brother, Gad, died and went to Heaven.
CD56.6	There he goes.
	And when he got there, he saw the most amazing palace – towers, turrets, marvellous roof – what do you think that was made of? (**Silver and gold**)
	Yup, you're right.
	And he asked if he could stay there.
	'No,' said the angels, 'that's been built for somebody else. King Gundaphorus.'
	'That's my brother!' said Gad, 'Let me talk to him, I'm sure he'll let me stay.'
	Well, it was against the rules, but Gad was allowed to visit Gundaphorus for an afternoon. And he rushed in to tell him about
CD56.7	the wonderful palace he had in Heaven.
	'By the way,' said Gad, 'where's that nice architect you had?'
	'Just a minute,' said Gundaphorus – and quickly got Thomas out of gaol.
CD56.8	*Add picture 8 to picture 7*
	So they all had tea together, and St Thomas explained that every good deed that he'd done with Gundaphorus' money had become a brick in Heaven.
	And that's how the wonderful palace had been built.

Palace Building

Leader	It's a good story isn't it?
	But you'll notice we haven't got a picture of the palace – however,
CD56.9	we *have* got a plan and some bricks.
	So let's make one.

Get out your 'bricks' and, depending on numbers, either gather round a table, or stick the A1 sheet up and make the palace as a group activity, with kids coming out to place a brick or a turret. You don't have to follow the template, the kids will probably come up with something much better

BEFORE THE FINAL PRAYER

Admire the palace

Leader

I like that story, it shows how the smallest things we do on Earth turn into bricks in Heaven and build something wonderful.
God notices the smallest things – cups of water, being polite – and rewards them.

FINAL PRAYER

God our Father,
Accept all the things we do for you,
And turn them into blessings,
We ask this through Jesus your Son. **Amen**

Finish with a **Glory be . . .** (**p. xxxvii**).

BACK IN CHURCH

Bring in the picture

Leader

Today we heard how St Thomas built a wonderful palace for an Indian king.

Hold up the picture

The palace was built in Heaven and every brick was a good deed performed by St Thomas on behalf of the king.
We're hoping to start on our own pile of bricks in Heaven this week.

(CD56.1)   (CD56.6)   (CD56.7)

Specimen cartoons for this script

Script 57   Jesus Blesses Children

Proper 22, Ordinary Time 27
(Sunday between 2 and 8 October)

St Mark 10.13–16

THEME

The Gospel today contains the famous line 'Suffer the little children to come unto me and forbid them not'. Children were naturally loved in the Holy Land, but childhood as such was not rated. Jesus startled His followers by admiring children just for being kids. Their particular qualities, of innocence and trust, made them uniquely fitted to enter God's Kingdom. Ever since then, the Church has taken children seriously, and some saints are particularly associated with them: particularly St Nicholas *aka* Santa Claus.

SET UP

- The liturgical colour is Green.
- Gold coins (either chocolate coins or 'pirate' money from a party shop), gift wrapped.
- Three pairs of long socks.
- A paper mitre, template on the CD-Rom.
- Somebody prepared to play St Nicholas.
- Three chairs set down the front.
- One kid's shoe.
- A marker pen.

WELCOME *the children and lead them in* **The Sign of the Cross** ✠ **(p. xxxvi).**

THE KYRIE   Lord Jesus, you came to call sinners,
Lord have mercy
Lord have mercy

Lord Jesus, you came to find the unhappy,
Christ have mercy
Christ have mercy

Lord Jesus, you came to tell us how much God loves us,
Lord have mercy
Lord have mercy

Ask the children to repeat **The Prayer for Forgiveness** *after you* (**p. xxxvi**).

OPENING   Lord Jesus,
PRAYER   Friend of children,
                Be with us this morning,
                And bless our time together. **Amen**

BEFORE THE GOSPEL

Leader 1   *(Looking rather business-like)* Good morning, everyone.
                   Before we start, I'd like to check up on the age range in here.
                   Anyone over 21? *(That accounts for the grown-ups)*
                   Anyone here under 21?

React to the hands that go up and, taking your cue from the age of the oldest kid present, do a count down

                   OK, so who's 12? 11? 10? 9? 8?
                   Surely there's nobody here who's 7 . . . ?

And so on – when you get to '3', the smallest children will probably need their Mums to prompt them.

                   Good heavens – stand up a moment, will you?

Go among them comparing their sizes with your own

                   Yes, I thought so.

To the other grown-ups

                   Chaps, we're surrounded by kids!
                   Look, nothing but kids – everywhere!
                   How did that happen?
Leader 2   I expect the answer is in the Gospel.
Leader 1   I certainly hope so . . .

THE GOSPEL PROCESSION

THE GOSPEL *St Mark 10.13–16*

Use the line 'Suffer the little children to come unto me . . .' as you tell the story. It's one of those phrases from the King James Bible that has got into the language – and you'll be using it again if you do a presentation back in church.

AFTER THE GOSPEL

Leader 1	So, why are there so many children in church? (**Because Jesus liked them**)
	Why?
Leader 2	I think it's because children are nice, and they get on with God.
Leader 1	Well, ever since Jesus took children in His arms and blessed them, the Church has always taken kids seriously.

St Nicholas

Leader 1	I'm going to tell you about a bishop who was very good with children.
	He lived a long time ago, and his name was Nicholas.
	Here he is . . .

Enter St Nicholas, with mitre on (**CD57.1**)

Now I'm going to need three girls to help me.

Ask the girls to get a chair each, and sit on them

Thanks!

Right, these three girls were sisters, and very poor.

So poor that they knew that when they grew up they wouldn't be able to get married.

In those days nobody got married without a 'dowry' – that's some money to help set up house. Without a dowry, most girls would end up as servants – or worse, as slaves.

It made the girls very unhappy. They sat at home, with their chins on their hands.

They do so

And they never went out to play.

Well Bishop Nicholas got to hear about this. So one night he stood outside their house, and he saw the eldest girl washing her socks and hanging them up to dry.

Give the first girl a pair of socks, she wrings them out and hangs them on the back of her chair

Then all the sisters went to sleep.

The girls sit on the floor, with their heads pillowed on their arms on the seat of their chairs

Nicholas crept in, and put a present in her sock.

Nicholas creeps in, very anxious not to wake them: he slides the first packet of coins in her sock and exits

> And the next morning, the girl found the present.

She does so – encourage her to open it

> Wow! She's got some money – enough for a dowry.
> The next night, the second girl washed her socks and hung them up.

Same business – St Nicholas creeps in and leaves some coins which the girl finds

Same business The next, the third girl washed her socks and hung them up – but this time none of the girls went to sleep, they just pretended to.

The girls peek through their fingers

> Nicholas didn't dare go into the room – so he threw her a present down the chimney.

Nicholas throws the present so it lands by the third girl

> She opened it *(she does)* and she'd got a dowry too.
> So the three sisters put their money away . . .

They hand it to you for distribution afterwards (if it's chocolate)

> Cheered up and went out to play.

Exit girls And Nicholas went on doing good and was eventually made a saint.

Exit Nicholas He was made the saint of children and, in Holland, on St Nicholas's Eve – that's 5 December – Dutch children leave out their shoes on the window sill.

Hold up the kid's shoe

> And the next morning – 6 December – they find they've been filled with . . .

Pour in some of the coins you've been using

> Goodies!

Optional Moment with Santa Claus

Leader Does St Nicholas remind you of anyone? **(Father Christmas!** *Somebody may say* **Santa Claus,** *put that on hold)*
Yup, they're very similar.
Does anyone know a short way of saying Nicholas? **(Nick)**
Right. If somebody is called Nicholas we often give him a *nick*name and call him 'Nick'.
What happens if a girl is called Katherine? **(Kate, Katy, Cathy)**

Write the two names up

> In England we make a nickname by using the first bit of the name and shortening it.

Underline the first letters of Nicholas and Katherine

> But in Europe they use the last bit of the name.
> So in Germany, if you are called Johannes *(write it up)*,
> you're called 'Hans'. *(Underline the last few letters)*
> And if you're called Nicklaus (which is just Dutch for Nicholas),
> you're called . . . ? (**Klaus**)

Same business   And supposing you are a saint? St Klaus . . .

> Well, the word for saint in some countries is Santa, so St Nicholas becomes *(write in the Santa)* 'Santa Klaus'.
> That's why Father Christmas sometimes gets called 'Santa Claus'.
> He's not the same really – but he does the same sort of things as St Nicholas, leaving presents for kids, and coming down the chimney.

REHEARSAL

You will need to get the children to practise their line for when they go back into church (see below).

BEFORE THE FINAL PRAYER

Leader   What I like about St Nicholas and Father Christmas is that they both turn up when we are celebrating the birthday of Baby Jesus. It reminds us how important children are in our Faith.
Let's ask for St Nicholas's prayers to finish with.

FINAL PRAYER   The response is: **Pray for us**.
Holy Nicholas, present giver,
Pray for us
Holy Nicholas, friend of Jesus,
Pray for us
Holy Nicholas, protector of children,
Pray for us

Lord Jesus,
We thank you for your servant Nicholas.
Help us to be like him,
Kind and generous and filled with your love. **Amen**

BACK IN CHURCH

Go back in with Nicholas and the three girls – all reunited with their money

Leader   Today we heard how St Nicholas . . .

He stands forward

Discovered that three sisters . . .

They stand forward

Were very poor
So Nicholas left them some money in their socks.

The girls hold up their presents

Nicholas did this because he loved children –
And he loved children because Jesus loved them too.
Can you remember what Jesus said about children, kids?

All the Children 'Suffer the little children to come unto me.'

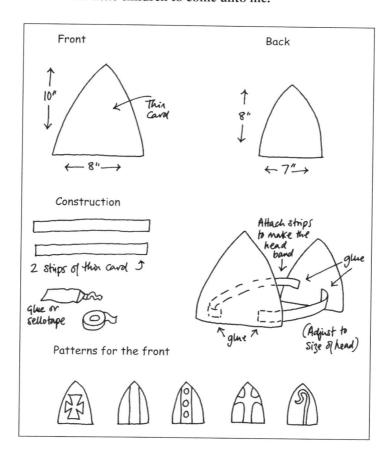

(CD57.1)
Bishop's mitre
template

Script 58 The Rich Young Man

Proper 23, Ordinary Time 28
(Sunday between 9 and 15 October)

St Mark 10.17–22

THEME

The Rich Young Man is a worry: do we have to give up all our money to follow Jesus? Probably not, but this session flags up the sort of things that might make it difficult for us to squeeze into Heaven.

SET UP

- The liturgical colour is Green.
- Ten Commandments on flash cards from the CD-Rom.
- Cast the Rich Kid (he'll need to see the script beforehand).
- Props for the Rich Kid:
  - some money,
  - sun specs,
  - a notebook and a pencil.
- Large rucksack full of stuff – footballs to bulk it out, plus a purse, some mobile phones, iPods, Gameboys, whatever the latest technological craze is, on top.
- Two chairs down the front.

WELCOME *the children and lead them in* **The Sign of the Cross** ✠ **(p. xxxvi).**

THE KYRIE   Lord Jesus, you came to call sinners,
Lord have mercy
Lord have mercy

Lord Jesus, you came to find the unhappy,
Christ have mercy
Christ have mercy

Lord Jesus, you came to tell us how much God loves us,
Lord have mercy
Lord have mercy

Ask the children to repeat **The Prayer for Forgiveness** *after you* (**p. xxxvi**).

OPENING
PRAYER

Lord God
King of the Universe,
Help us to keep your laws.
Help us especially to love you,
And our neighbour. **Amen**

BEFORE THE GOSPEL

The Rich Kid

Leader

We're going to start with a story.
Once there was a rich kid . . .

Enter the Rich Kid

He had loads of money . . .

The Kid flashes some money

Some cool shades . . .

He adjusts his sun specs

And was an unbelievably snappy dresser.

Ad lib on whatever the Kid is wearing

But this Kid wasn't just a cool dude, he was good.
Really good.
He knew all the Jewish laws and he obeyed every one of them.
Let's just run through them.
The Jews have Ten Commandments, here they are . . .

Put up the Ten Commandments (**CD58.1**) *Read them out as they go up*

1 Worship the one God
2 Don't pray to idols
3 Honour God's name
4 Keep the Sabbath
5 Honour your parents
6 Do not murder
7 Do not commit adultery
8 Do not steal
9 Do not perjure yourself
10 Do not covet.

The Rich Kid provides a running commentary and he ticks them off in his notebook.
Worship God – easy – Keep the Sabbath, done that . . . etc.
Move over to the Kid

Leader	What's the notebook for?
Kid	I keep a note of all the Rules I've obeyed.
Leader	How are you doing?
Kid	Really well. In fact I think I'm ready to have a talk to Jesus.
Leader	Good luck!
Kid	Thanks!
Leader	And the Rich Kid went off to find Jesus.
	We'll hear what happened in today's Gospel.

THE GOSPEL PROCESSION

THE GOSPEL *St Mark 10.17–22*

AFTER THE GOSPEL

Leader   Jesus liked that young man, he was a nice chap and obviously having a go. But I think He felt the young man hadn't got the point.
It's good to obey God's rules, but it's more important to love God.
So Jesus went through these Commandments *(reel off 5 to 10)* and then went back to the first one.
Was the young man really loving only God?
Were there some other things he loved just as much?
Like his money, or his shades, or his iPod?
So Jesus asked him to give away all his stuff, and come and follow Him.
How did the young man feel about that? (**He couldn't do it**)
I don't think I could either.
Jesus doesn't ask everyone to give away their stuff, but He might if He thinks your possessions matter too much to you.

Getting through the Gate

Leader   A little later Jesus said, 'It's as difficult for a rich person to get into the Kingdom of Heaven as it is for a camel to go through the eye of a needle.'
Have we got any millionaires here? (**No** – *presumably*)
Actually, we're richer than we think.
Let's make 'the eye of a needle' – or rather a very narrow gate.

Place two chairs back to back with a very small space between them

> OK, that's the Gate to Heaven
> Now, who thinks they can get through?

Choose a volunteer

> OK, but before you go, you'll have to take your possessions with you.

Put the rucksack on her/his back – and place two sturdy people on each of the chairs, so they don't move. Make sure the kid can't slip through

> What's getting in the way? (**The rucksack**)
> OK, what have we got in here?

Pull out the stuff on the top

> Money, yup, iPod, coo that's a nice mobile, a football, another football! *(Talk through whatever you've got)*
> You know, I think the sensible thing would be to ditch all these.

Put the rucksack to one side

> Now try

And the child gets through

> Well done!

BEFORE THE FINAL PRAYER

Leader   You see possessions can get in the way: it's like me mucking around with Facebook instead of saying my prayers. Or some kid going off to football instead of going to church.
That's something we need to think about.

MUSIC

The Irish hymn 'Be thou my vision, O Lord of my heart' *fits in well, particularly verse 4.*

FINAL   Lord Jesus
PRAYER   You loved the rich young man who came to you.
Help us to try as hard as he did to serve God.
And help us to have a go at anything you ask of us. **Amen**

BACK IN CHURCH

Bring back the re-packed rucksack, another volunteer, and set two chairs down the front of the church (with two solid people to keep them immobile)

Leader   Jesus said in the Gospel today that rich people would have a difficult time squeezing into Heaven.
So we tried it out.
This is the narrow gate to Heaven. *(Indicate the chairs)*
And *Name* here is going to try to get through – with all this stuff on his/her back.

The child doesn't manage it

So we thought if he/she ditched the rucksack, they'd have a better chance.

He/she does   Jesus was right, possessions can get in the way.

(CD58.1)

Script 59 Sitting beside Jesus

Proper 24, Ordinary Time 29
(Sunday between 16 and 22 October)

St Mark 10.35–45

THEME

The disciples are at it again. This time it is James and John trying to bag the best places in the Kingdom of Heaven. Jesus takes their request seriously but points out the seating arrangements in Heaven are more complicated than they think. He also indicates that James, John (and the rest) are asking for the wrong sort of things. Being a disciple of Jesus is not about being first in the line. That's something we explore in this session.

SET UP

- The liturgical colour is Green.
- 13 chairs down the front.
- Get a couple of leaders to sit at the back to start a disturbance (see below).
- Write out 13 cards with the names of Jesus and the twelve disciples on them.
- Music, and something to play it on, for 'musical chairs'.

WELCOME *the children and lead them in* **The Sign of the Cross** ✠ (**p. xxxvi**).

BEFORE THE KYRIE

Ask the children to think about last week

Leader   Did we do anything wrong?
              Did things get in a mess?
              Let's get rid of all that by saying the Kyrie.

THE KYRIE   Lord Jesus, you came to call sinners,
Lord have mercy
Lord have mercy

Lord Jesus, you came to find the unhappy,
Christ have mercy
Christ have mercy

Lord Jesus, you came to tell us how much God loves us,
Lord have mercy
Lord have mercy

Ask the children to repeat **The Prayer for Forgiveness** *after you* (**p. xxxvi**).

OPENING   God our Father
PRAYER   Help us to hear the Word of your Son this morning,
And put it into action in the week ahead. **Amen**

OPENING SESSION

The Leader apparently starts the session

Leader   Right, before we hear the Gospel this morning . . .

But is interrupted by a Disturbance

Disturbance

Some jostling starts on the back seats. A wants to sit next to B, C *has bagged a place for* D, *whatever . . .*
The Leader is shocked. Run it like school

Leader   What's this ghastly noise?
You want to do what?
Well, *Name* is sitting there.
No, I don't want to hear any tales.
You'd better all come forward and sit down here.

Bring them down the front

To the kids   Anything like this happen at school?

Cue for anecdotes

Yup, we like to sit next to our friends.
Jesus' friends felt like that as well.
We heard a story about them a couple of weeks ago, how they all jostled to be at the front of the line near Jesus.

Why do you suppose they did that?
(Because Jesus was nice/ because they wanted to be His best friend)

Take all answers and add

Because He was important.
And if it was great to be best friends with Jesus on Earth, just think how cool it would be to be best friends with Him in Heaven.
Let's see what the disciples were up to . . .

Musical Chairs

Set 13 chairs along the front

Leader   Right we need a Jesus.

Give somebody a Jesus card and sit him/her in the middle

And the disciples. How many were there? (**12**)
Great, let's sort out their names.

Hand out the cards as the children come up with their names

(*They are* Andrew *and his brother* Peter, Big James *and his brother* John, Bartholomew, Little James, Jude the Just, Judas Iscariot, Philip, Thomas, Matthew *and* Simon the Zealot.)

Once you've got all 12, ask them to sit down. Put Philip on Jesus' right hand and Simon on His left

OK, we're all seated.
Now, every now and then the disciples would try to sit right next to Jesus:
So Peter would swap with Philip. (*He does so*)
Or Thomas would get Simon to get up, and nick his place. (*He does this by running a 'look behind you' gag*)
It was rather like a game.

Run a musical chairs game. Play some music as the disciples pace round the line of chairs (Jesus stays quietly in the middle). When the music stops, there's a scramble to sit next to Jesus. Run this a couple of times so all the kids in the room have a go. At the end, wrap it up by saying

OK, so *Name* and *Name* got to sit next to Jesus.
But that's just what happened on Earth. Supposing you wanted to sit next to Him in Heaven? That's more serious.

Swap the person playing Jesus and play the game again, this time start taking chairs away. The game ends with three chairs – Jesus in the middle and the last two disciples sitting on each side

Who've we got?

Ah, it's *Name* and *Name*.

Now once, the brothers James and John managed to get on each side of Jesus.

Place the kids with the 'James' and 'John' cards beside Jesus (of course they may have won the game and be there already)

And James said . . .

Stand behind James and say his words for him

'Master, will you do something for us? Can John and I sit next to you when we go to Heaven?'

And Jesus said . . .

Put a hand on Jesus' shoulder before he/she says anything

Let's find out just what Jesus said in the Gospel.

THE GOSPEL PROCESSION

THE GOSPEL *St Mark 10.35–45*

Optional Paraphrase

James and John, the sons of Zebedee, said to Jesus,
'Teacher, we want you to do us a favour.'
And He replied, 'What is it?'
They answered, 'Allow us to sit on each side of you in Heaven.'
Jesus said to them, 'You don't know what you are asking. Can you go through what I'll have to go through before I return to Heaven?'
'Yes!' they said.
Jesus said, 'Then you will. But even so, it's not for me to decide who is to sit on my right hand or on my left. Those seats will go to those for whom they have been prepared.'
When the other disciples heard about this, they were indignant with James and John, but Jesus called them all together and said, 'You know that in this world important people boss other people around. That is not to happen with you. If any of you wants to be great, you must serve the others, and if anyone wants to be first, he must be the slave of all. I didn't come to be served, but to be a servant.'

AFTER THE GOSPEL

Leader   What did James and John ask?
          (**To sit next to Jesus in Heaven**)
          And what did Jesus say?

See what the children can remember, basically He said, 'Probably not'

          Was Jesus cross?

This is slightly dependent on how you read the passage
Establish that Jesus doesn't seem to have been cross

          Jesus knew that James and John liked being near Him, but they
          don't know what they're asking.
          The seating arrangements in Heaven aren't something that Jesus can
          just dish out: that's something that God the Father does.
          So Jesus reminded His disciples that Christians don't push and shove
          to be in the best place: they are called to serve other people and to let
          them go first.

REHEARSAL

Practise your presentation for when you go back into church (see below).
Line up the children

Leader   Today there was a bit of a scramble to get the best seats in
          Heaven. Everyone wanted to be first in the queue.

Choreograph a scramble, in which the kids in the middle and the back swap places
with the child at the front

          But Jesus told us in the Gospel that He expected His friends to serve
          other people and let them go first. So now everyone wanted to be
          last.

Choreograph another scramble in which the kids try to swap places with the child at
the end

          We're still working on it!

MUSIC

The obvious choice is the hymn 'Brother, sister, let me serve you'.

BEFORE THE FINAL PRAYER

Leader   All the great saints knew they were here to serve God and other
              people.
              Do you remember what the Virgin Mary said, when she agreed to
              become the mother of God's Son?
              She said, 'I am the servant of the Lord.'
              Let's ask for her prayers as we try to be God's servants too.

FINAL PRAYER

Finish with a **Hail Mary** . . . (**p. xxxvii**).

BACK IN CHURCH

See above

Script 60   Bartimeus

Proper 25, Ordinary Time 30
(Sunday between 23 and 29 October)

St Mark 10.46–52

THEME

Jesus heals blind Bartimeus. Bartimeus may have been blind but in some ways he could see better than the crowd around him.

SET UP

- The liturgical colour is Green.
- Prayer candle.
- Scarves for blindfolds.
- Props for the listening test (see below): anything you can find, like a box of matches, a mobile phone, bell, etc.
- Cast people to play Jesus and Bartimeus, they should look at the script beforehand.
- Sun specs.
- Speech captions from the CD-Rom **(CD60.1–CD60.14)**.

WELCOME *the children and lead them in* **The Sign of the Cross** ✠ **(p. xxxvi)**.

THE KYRIE   Lord God, we are sorry for the times we have been unkind,
Lord have mercy
Lord have mercy

Lord God, we are sorry for the times we have forgotten you,
Christ have mercy
Christ have mercy

Lord God, we ask you to forgive us,
Lord have mercy
Lord have mercy

Ask the children to repeat **The Prayer for Forgiveness** *after you* **(p. xxxvi)**.

BEFORE THE OPENING PRAYER

Light the prayer candle and comment on the light it throws: how beautiful the flame is

Leader	Today we are going to hear the story of a blind man.
	Shut your eyes for a minute, imagine what it's like to be blind.
	How could we describe the candle flame to somebody who couldn't see?

OPENING PRAYER	*(Ask the children to say the prayer after you)*
	God our Creator,
	You made the sun and the moon,
	You made light and flame.
	Thank you for giving us eyes to see them
	And bless all those who cannot see
	Through Jesus Christ our Lord. Amen

BEFORE THE GOSPEL

Listen Up

Leader	Well, blind people can't see things – but they are very good at listening.
	Let's see how good we are at listening.

Blindfold various kids and see if they can identify various noises, like dinging a bell, striking a match, a mobile phone ringtone, jingling keys, zipping an anorak, flicking the pages of a book – anything you can think of

A blind person would know all those sounds.
Being blind makes you listen very hard.

Bartimeus

Leader	The man in the Gospel today was called Bartimeus. He'd been blind all his life – but he was good at listening and touching and guessing. There won't be any pictures this morning, because Bartimeus only heard what was going on.
	We'll be like him and listen hard to the Gospel.

REHEARSAL

You will need a Narrator and people to play Jesus and Bartimeus (in sun specs). Jesus and Bartimeus read out their lines as the speech captions go up, and the children call out the crowd lines. Practise this and the 'stampede' effect they're asked to do before you read the Gospel.

THE GOSPEL PROCESSION

THE GOSPEL *St Mark 10.46–52*

Narrator	As Jesus drew near to Jericho, Bartimeus the blind man was sitting by the roadside begging.
CD60.1	*(Speech caption)* **'Spare a penny for the blind man!'** He heard a crowd going by.

Cue the children to get up fast, tramp on the spot, cut the FX with a 'kill it' cue, and sit down fast

	And he asked what was going on. They told him:
CD60.2	*(Speech caption)* 'Jesus of Nazareth is passing by.' Then Bartimeus cried,
CD60.3	*(Speech caption)* 'Jesus, Son of David, have mercy on me!' And the crowd tried to shut him up.

Cue this in caption by caption, then all shout the captions together

CD60.4	*(Speech caption)* **'Be quiet!'**
CD60.5	*(Speech caption)* **'Shut up!'**
CD60.6	*(Speech caption)* **'Get lost!'** But he shouted at the top of his voice,
CD60.7	*(Speech caption)* 'Jesus, Son of David, have mercy on me!' Jesus heard him and stopped. He said,
CD60.8	*(Speech caption)* 'Bring the blind man to me.' So they did .
CD60.9	*(Speech caption)* **'Oi you!'**
CD60.10	*(Speech caption)* **'Come over here!'** And, when Bartimeus came near, Jesus asked him,
CD60.11	*(Speech caption)* **'What do you want me to do for you?'** He replied,
CD60.11	*(Speech caption)* **'Lord, let me receive my sight.'** And Jesus said to him,
CD60.13	*(Speech caption)* **'Receive your sight; your faith has made you well.'** And immediately Bartimeus received his sight.

He takes off his sun specs

And followed Jesus, glorifying God; and all the people, when they saw it, called out with him,

CD60.14   *(Speech caption)* **'Praise be to God!'**

AFTER THE GOSPEL

Leader   Bartimeus couldn't *see* Jesus' face, but he knew a lot about Him. He knew Jesus loved him, he could feel Jesus' love in his heart. Bartimeus is a super person to know about, because we can't see Jesus either, but – like Bartimeus – we can listen to Him, and pray.

REHEARSAL

Practise your presentation for when you go back into church (see below).

BEFORE THE FINAL PRAYER

Ask the children to shut their eyes and press their hands on their chests

Leader   Can you feel your hands on your chest? They're very close to your heart. That's how close Jesus is to you. Let's talk to Him.

FINAL   Lord Jesus,
PRAYER   Thank you for healing Bartimeus. Thank you for being near to us.

Lord Jesus, Friend and Brother, May we know you more clearly, Love you more dearly, And follow you more nearly, Day by day. **Amen**

MUSIC

The hymn 'Lord the light of your love is shining' ('Shine, Jesus, Shine') finishes the session well – especially if you light a prayer candle as you sing it.

BACK IN CHURCH

Go back with Bartimeus wearing sun specs

Leader   Today we heard about blind Bartimeus . . .

Bring him/her forward

	He heard that Jesus was going by and called out . . .
Bartimeus	Jesus, have mercy on me!
Leader	But all he heard were angry voices
Children	**Shut up!**
Leader	But Bartimeus went on calling out, because he knew that Jesus loved him.
	And sure enough, Jesus restored his sight.

Bartimeus takes off the sun specs

In many ways, Bartimeus could see better than the people round him.

Script 61 The Great Commandment

4 before Advent, Ordinary Time 31

St Mark 12.28–32

THEME

Jesus tells a Jewish scholar (a 'scribe') that loving God and your neighbour sums up the whole of the Jewish Law. The scribe completely agrees with Him.

SET UP

- The liturgical colour is Green.
- Pictures from the CD-Rom.
- At least 21 sheets of blank paper for the children to roll up into scrolls.
- Enough brightly coloured ribbon for the children to tie up their scrolls.
- One scroll already made up.
- 2 Bibles.

labelled → AMOS ↖ *rolled up sheet of paper* ↙ *'tied with ribbon*

WELCOME *the children and lead them in* **The Sign of the Cross** ✠ (**p. xxxvi**).

THE KYRIE   Lord Jesus, you came to bring us back to God,
Lord have mercy
Lord have mercy

Lord Jesus, you came to heal us from our sins,
Christ have mercy
Christ have mercy

Lord Jesus, you came to tell us how much God loves us,
Lord have mercy
Lord have mercy

Ask the children to repeat **The Prayer for Forgiveness** *after you* (**p. xxxvi**).

OPENING **PRAYER**	*(From Psalm 18)* Say after me, the response to the psalm: I love you, Lord **I love you, Lord**

I love you Lord, for you are my strength,
I love you, Lord

I love you Lord, for you are my rock,
I love you, Lord

I love you Lord, for you are my Saviour,
I love you, Lord

Leader   Good morning kids
Right, I'm going to really depress you.
I'm going to talk about homework.

Depending on the time of year, ask them if anyone has still got some homework to do for Monday

Bad luck!
When I was a kid I sat at a table, and piled books round me and did my homework like that. How do you do it?

Take what comes: **exercise books, Internet, school books** etc.

Supposing you saw a grown-up with piles of books round him, reading, writing, polishing his glasses, reading some more – would he be doing homework? (**No**)
No, he'd probably be researching something – we call people like that 'scholars'.
Now in Jesus' time there were lots of scholars. The Jews called them 'scribes' – and I'm going to introduce you to one . . .

Simon the Scribe

CD61.1   He was called Simon the Scribe,
He read everything.
CD61.2   He read the Bible in Hebrew and Greek
CD61.3   He read all the books of the Law
CD61.4   He read all the books of the really important prophets
CD61.5   He read all the other prophets too
And he thought, and thought.
He'd read all this stuff,

He'd read that God wanted us to be kind to the poor,
And pray to Him,
And obey all the Jewish Law.
And Simon thought, there must be a way of summing it up. What does God really want me to do most of all? Then he heard Jesus was in town, so he went to ask Him. We'll hear what happened next in the Gospel.

THE GOSPEL PROCESSION

THE GOSPEL *St Mark 12.28–32*

Optional Paraphrase (*with an extra verse from St Matthew 22.40*)
One of the scribes had heard Jesus talking to the others and realized He gave very good answers. So he said to Jesus, 'What is the most important of the Command-ments?'
And Jesus answered, 'The first one is, "You must love the Lord your God with all your heart, and with all your soul and with all your mind." And there is a second commandment which is almost the same, "You must love your neighbour as your-self." These two commandments sum up all the Law, and all the prophets too.'
The scribe said, 'Well spoken Master! What you have said is true!'

AFTER THE GOSPEL

Leader   So Jesus told Simon that all the books he had read could be summed up in two commandments. Can you remember what they were?
              (**You should love God, and your neighbour**)
              Jesus said love was the most important commandment, it's called the Great Commandment.
              I think it would be good to tell the people back in church about this, and we're going to do it by showing them all the books Simon had read.
              We've got his two Bibles here.

Hold up the Bibles

              But what he probably read mostly were scrolls.

Hold up a ready-made scroll

              So I'm going to ask you to make some scrolls – we'll need:

Look at **CD61.3**

              Five scrolls for the Law.
              And how many scrolls for the important prophets?

Get them to count up the scrolls in **CD61.4**

How about all the others? **(CD61.5)**
Sixteen!

Dish out the paper and ribbon to the children and give them each an individual scroll to make. You could ask them to draw things on their scrolls first: a large 'RULES' for the books of the Law, or Moses writing down the Commandments, and the individual prophets with their names on the 'prophet scrolls'. Depending on numbers, you might add other books of the Old Testament, or give a child two or three scrolls to make

REHEARSAL

Practise your presentation for when you go back into church (see below).

BEFORE THE FINAL PRAYER

Ask the children to sit down, with their scrolls

Leader Simon the Scribe read all these scrolls.
And Christians read the Bible *(hold it up)*, which has got all Simon's scrolls in it. And all the scrolls, and the whole Bible, tell us the same thing – that we must love God and love our neighbour.

FINAL PRAYER Lord Jesus,
You told us that the Great Commandment was love.
Help us to remember that Commandment
And love God
And our neighbour
With your help,
Amen

MUSIC

The hymn 'We are one in the Spirit', *with the refrain* 'They'll know we are Christians by our love' *sums it up.*

Adventurous groups may like to try the Taizé chant, 'Ubi caritas et amor, Deus ibi est'. ('Wherever there is love and charity, God is there too.')

BACK IN CHURCH

The children line up down the front with their scrolls

Leader   In the Gospel today, we heard Jesus talk to a scribe.
The scribe had read everything:
He'd read five books of the Law

The children hold up the five Law scrolls

He'd read all the important prophets.

The children hold up those scrolls

He'd read all the other prophets.

The children hold them up

In fact, he'd read everything he could find in the Bible.

Hold up any extra scrolls

And he asked Jesus, 'What does God want me to do most of all?'
Jesus answered:
Child 1   Love God
Child 2   And love your neighbour.
Leader   That sums up all the books of the Bible.

(CD61.3)

(CD61.1)

(CD61.5)

Specimen cartoons for this script

Script 62   The Widow's Mite

Ordinary Time 32 (Roman Catholic)

St Mark 12.41–44

THEME

Everybody gets the point of the Widow's Mite, especially when it's played out with chocolate buttons. The word 'mite' is from the King James Bible. It was a tiny coin, worth half a farthing (an eighth of an old penny).

SET UP

- The liturgical colour is Green.
- A packet of chocolate buttons or some small innocuous sweeties.
- Cast two people to be the rich guy and the poor guy (see below).
- Give the poor guy two sweets, the rest go to the rich one.
- Marker pen.
- A blow-up die (see page xxi).
- Print up the Board Game on the CD-Rom **(CD62.1)**.
- A packet of plastic counters, or 'pirate' money (see page xxii).

WELCOME *the children and lead them in* **The Sign of the Cross** ✠ **(p. xxxvi)**.

THE KYRIE   Lord Jesus, you came to call sinners,
Lord have mercy
Lord have mercy

Lord Jesus, you came to find the unhappy,
Christ have mercy
Christ have mercy

Lord Jesus, you came to tell us how much God loves us,
Lord have mercy
Lord have mercy

Ask the children to repeat **The Prayer for Forgiveness** *after you* (**p. xxxvi**).

OPENING **PRAYER**	Lord God our Creator, You gave us the world And all the things in it. You gave us our families And our friends. Help us to be as generous as you. **Amen**

Sharing Things

Leader   This morning I'd like to introduce you to two people . . .
               A rich one . . .

The rich guy steps forward

               And a poor one . . .

The poor guy steps forward

               Both these guys liked to be generous and, when they had something
               nice to eat, they shared it out.
               So when *Name* (the rich one) had a packet of chocolate buttons, she
               put aside ten – and handed them out.

She does so Then she ate the rest herself.

She probably puts them in her pocket

               But when *Name* (the poor one) had two chocolate buttons, he gave
               both of them away.

Which he does I want to sort this out. *Name* gave away ten sweeties – *(write up ten)*
               And *Name* gave away two – *(write up two)*
               Who gave away the most?
               Take any answer, but don't comment
               Jesus once watched people putting money into the Poor Box in the
               Temple, and He saw some people rather like *Name* and *Name*. Let's
               hear what He thought about them.

THE GOSPEL PROCESSION

THE GOSPEL *St Mark 12.41–44*

Use the words 'Poor Box' instead of 'Treasury'.

AFTER THE GOSPEL

Leader

So what did Jesus think?
Who'd put the most into the Poor Box?

They may say the rich guy, in which case agree with them, but add

Jesus didn't think so, He thought the widow had.
Why was that? (**She'd put in everything she had**)

On the other hand, the children may get it immediately

Being generous is not about giving people your leftovers, it's about giving them a proper meal which costs you something.
God notices that.
Let's see how good we'd be at giving.

ACTIVITY

The 'Everything Has Got to Go' Game

Set up the board game (**CD62.1**) *on a table for a small group of kids – or stuck up on a wall for two teams to play. Try to make sure everybody has a chance of throwing the die.*
Both the characters in the game start off with a pile of money which they have to get rid of before they can land on the last square. The first to get there wins, the fun is finding reasons to shed your money.

REHEARSAL

Practise your presentation for when you go back into church (see below).

FINAL
PRAYER

Lord Jesus,
You saw the widow give all her money to the poor,
We thank you for her love and generosity
And ask you to help us copy her example. **Amen**

BACK IN CHURCH

Bring the rich guy and the poor guy down the front. Give the poor guy two chocolate buttons, and the rest to the rich one.

Child 1   Today we heard that *Name* was really rich.
Child 2   She had loads of chocolate buttons.
Child 3   And she gave ten away.

The rich guy counts out ten very carefully, and pockets the rest

Leader   Then we discovered that *Name* was very poor, he only had two chocolate buttons.

The poor guy holds them up pathetically; encourage the congregation to say 'Ah!'

Child 4   But he gave them both away!

And so he does

Leader   *(Touching each child as he names them)* Jesus would have said that *Name* had given away much more than *Name*.

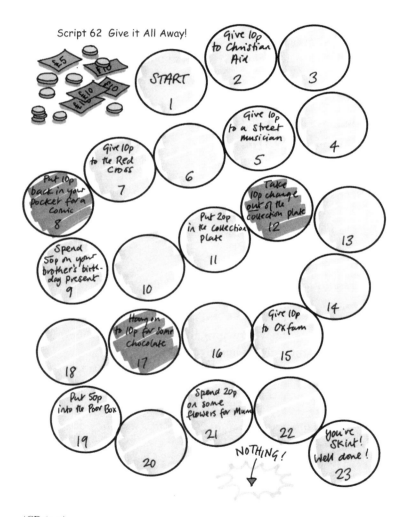

Script 62 Give it All Away!

(CD62.1)

Script 63   The Last Trumpet

2 before Advent, Ordinary Time 33

either St Mark 13.1–8 or St Mark 13.24–32

THEME

The Church of England and the Catholic Church use different Gospels today, but they are both about the End of the World, and can be combined in one session. Children are used to secular doomsday scenarios, so it's sensible to give them the Christian version, based on that very exciting idea – the sounding of the Last Trumpet.

If you have a bugler or trumpeter in your church, this is the moment to kidnap them! Otherwise you can download the trumpet calls mentioned in the text from YouTube (reference below).

SET UP

- The liturgical colour is Green.
- Pictures from the CD-Rom.
- A trumpeter/bugler or audio clips of trumpet calls.
- At the time of going to press, the site www.youtube.com/watch?v=czHqZFL7rKY had a nice clean clip of the 'Reveille', 'Assembly', 'to Arms' and 'Cavalry Charge'. In any case you should be able to find these at YouTube by typing in these names.
- You will also need a clip of a solo bugler playing the 'Last Post'.
- If you want an image of angels playing the trumpet, tap 'angel musicians Memling' into Google images and you'll get a good selection. Memling's line-up of angels has trumpeters on the right or, if you find his Last Judgement in the Web Gallery of Art (www.wga.hu/), you'll come across a couple of angels blowing the Last Trumpet from a tower. There is also a photo on the CD-Rom.

WELCOME *the children and lead them in* **The Sign of the Cross** ✠ **(p. xxxvi).**

THE KYRIE   Lord Jesus, you came to bring us back to God,
Lord have mercy
Lord have mercy

Lord Jesus, you came to heal us from our sins,
Christ have mercy
Christ have mercy

Lord Jesus, you came to tell us how much God loves us,
Lord have mercy
Lord have mercy

Ask the children to repeat **The Prayer for Forgiveness** *after you* (**p. xxxvi**).

OPENING   God our Father,
PRAYER   One day your Son will return to us on the clouds of Heaven,
Help us to look out for Him –
Ready to greet Him whenever He comes. **Amen**

BEFORE THE GOSPEL

With a Bible marked up at St Mark 13.1–4

Leader   I'm going to start this morning with a reading from Mark's Gospel.
It goes like this:

As Jesus was leaving the Temple, one of His friends said to Him,
'Master, look at the size of these stones! What a wonderful building.'
Jesus said, 'Yes, look at these great buildings! Yet one day not a
single stone will be left on another; everything will be pulled down.'
Jesus' disciples said, 'When is this going to happen?'

Look up from the Bible

I think we'd all like to know that.
Actually the Temple was pulled down in AD 70, but Jesus went on
to describe the End of the World – and that's what the disciples were
interested in.
How will we know the End of the World is coming?
Well, I'm going to tell you. We'll hear a trumpet.

Trumpets

Leader   I like trumpets. Let's look at the sort of people who play them . . .
CD63.1   What sort of musician is that? (**A soldier**)
Soldiers use trumpets a lot. They use them to give orders.

In the old days, trumpeters were used in battle, to tell the troops when to charge, or retreat – that was long before mobile phones. Even today we use trumpet calls, on the parade ground, or to wake people up.

Let's see how it works.

Trumpet Calls

Leader   OK, you are a bunch of soldiers
Stand up! Nice and straight
Now 'stand at ease'
OK, it's been the end of a long day, so you can go to sleep . . .
Lie down, and listen out for a trumpet call, it's called the 'Reveille'.
When you hear it, jump up . . .

Let the kids lie down, then play the 'Reveille'

OK, now the next trumpet call will ask you to 'assemble' – that means get into two rows – wait for it . . .

Play the 'Assembly'

Right, now the next call will be the 'Call to Arms' – that means you march down to the end of the room, and turn, ready for anything.

Play the 'Call to Arms'

And the next call is the Charge. When you hear that, you run down the room and stop when you get to me.

Play the 'Charge'

And the last one is the 'Last Post', that tells you the battle is over and it's time to sleep.

Play the 'Last Post' – as the kids lie down again

Brilliant, sit up.
Well, soldiers aren't the only people who play trumpets.

CD63.2   *(Or any image you've found of angels and trumpets)*

The angels play them too.
Some of them are due to play The Last Trumpet at the End of the World.
Which trumpet call do you think they will play?

The Charge? The Assembly? The Last Post?
Nope, none of these. It will be this one . . .

Play the Reveille again

The Reveille, the Wake Up call.
The people who are alive will hear it and look up, and the people who are dead will hear it and wake up, and it will all be very exciting – but what will they see?
Let's find out in the Gospel.

THE GOSPEL PROCESSION

THE GOSPEL *St Mark 13.24–27*

Optional Paraphrase

Jesus said to His disciples: 'One day the sun will be darkened, and the moon will lose its brightness, and the stars will come falling out of the sky. Then you will see the Son of Man coming on the clouds in great glory, and He will send His angels to gather His chosen from the four winds, from the ends of the Earth to the ends of the sky.'

AFTER THE GOSPEL

Leader   So, at the end of the world, God will dismantle all the things He's made – the sun and the moon and the stars – does that sound scary?

Take any reaction

It'll be OK actually. Because, if we happen to be around at the time, we'll look up and we won't just see stars and things, we'll see someone coming down to greet us. Who will that be? (**Jesus**)
He'll be sending His angels to gather us up to take us to Heaven.
That sounds OK too.
When do you suppose this is going to happen?

Take any answer, most children put it comfortably in the future

I expect you're right – not for hundreds of years – but Jesus told us to stay awake and listen out.

REHEARSAL

Practise your presentation for when you go back into church (see below).

BEFORE THE FINAL PRAYER

MUSIC

The Spiritual 'When the saints go marching in' *is a nice upbeat way to finish – especially the verse that begins* 'When the band begins to play'.

FINAL PRAYER   Heavenly Father,
You have promised that one day
You will bring us all safely home.
Hasten the coming of that day
When we will live for ever
With you, and Your Son, and the Holy Spirit. **Amen**

BACK IN CHURCH

Line the children up at the front of the church

Leader   Today we heard that one day Jesus would return on the clouds of Heaven.
We decided that, even if we were fast asleep when that happened . . .
The children sit down with their heads in their hands
We would hear the trumpet call . . .

The children look up and cup a hand to their ear
Cue trumpeter or bugler if you've got one, it doesn't matter if you haven't

And wake up!

The children spring to their feet

(CD63.1)

(CD63.2)

Script 64   Christ the King

Last Sunday before Advent, Ordinary Time 34

St John 18.33–37

THEME

The Christian year ends with the splendid feast of Christ the King. It's a time to celebrate the fact that, though the rulers of this world still think they call the shots, Jesus Christ rules securely in Heaven and will gently bring the whole world under His sway.

SET UP

- The liturgical colour is White or Gold.
- The stained-glass window grid and panes from the CD-Rom **(CD64.1)**.
  Cut it into its component parts, so that the children can colour in the panes and reassemble the whole thing on a sheet of A1.
  Take a view as to how many children you have in your group: you don't have to cut out each pane for small groups, give them whole sections.
- Colouring pens for the children.
- A1 sheet of paper.
- Glue.
- Warn the priest that you'll be bringing in a major work of art.

WELCOME *the children and lead them in* **The Sign of the Cross ✠ (p. xxxvi).**

THE KYRIE   King Jesus, you came to bring us back to God,
Lord have mercy
Lord have mercy

King Jesus, you came to heal us from our sins,
Christ have mercy
Christ have mercy

King Jesus, you came to tell us how much God loves us,
Lord have mercy
Lord have mercy

Ask the children to repeat **The Prayer for Forgiveness** *after you* (**p. xxxvi**).

OPENING PRAYER	*(From Psalm 93)* Say the response to the psalm after me

> The Lord is King
> **The Lord is King**
>
> The Lord is King
> He is robed in majesty
> **The Lord is King**
>
> He has made the world so firm
> It cannot be moved
> **The Lord is King**
>
> His throne has stood firm
> From all eternity
> **The Lord is King**

BEFORE THE GOSPEL

Kings and Queens

Leader	Let's talk kings and queens. Can you tell me the names of any? (**Queen Elizabeth**) Any others? *(Probably not, unless they come up with historical kings)* Well I'll tell you one, King Juan Carlos. He's the King of Spain. Keep him in your head for a minute while I ask you something else. What do kings and queens wear on their heads? (**Crowns**) Yup, has anyone seen a picture of the Queen in her crown? (**Yes**) Well, you'll never see a picture of King Juan in his crown. He's got one OK – but Spanish kings never dare put it on. They say there's only one King who can wear a crown – and it's not them. Let's find out who that is in the Gospel.

THE GOSPEL PROCESSION

THE GOSPEL *St John 18.33–37*

(Preface the Gospel with this)

Leader   The Gospel describes the moment when Jesus has been arrested and is brought before Pilate. Pilate is a Roman, and can't understand what all the fuss is about, so he talks to Jesus privately. This is what he said:

AFTER THE GOSPEL

Leader   Pilate wanted to know if Jesus was a king – what did Jesus say? (**Yes, He was**)
He was, but He said He wasn't a normal king, otherwise He'd have had an army to protect Him.
Jesus said, 'I haven't got that sort of kingdom.'
Well, Pilate thought that a king without an army wasn't dangerous, so he wasn't too worried about sending Him off to be crucified.
Pilate thought *he* was the king really.
But he was wrong. The Spanish kings know better.
They think that Jesus is their King, and leave the crown for Him to wear.
Our Queen thinks the same. She does wear her crown as it happens, but she also holds this – it's an orb.
Draw a picture of an orb.

Show the children that an orb is a symbol of the globe, the world – with a cross on it

The Queen holds that to remind herself that the world is ruled by Jesus.
All Christian kings and queens know who the real King of the World is. And so do we.
I think it would be nice for us to show the people back in church what King Jesus looks like. Let's make a picture of Him.

ACTIVITY

Ready Steady Colour!

Dish out the pieces of the stained-glass window (**CD64.1**) *and get the kids colouring and gluing the panes on to the grid.*
Don't worry about colour consistency – a certain variety looks nice – but try to get the big areas (like Jesus' face and robe) more or less one colour. Some side panes are

blank – the children can either colour them in with a light colour (like yellow) or add tiny angels or candles.

FINAL PRAYER

You will probably only have time for a **Glory be . . . (p. xxxvii)**.

BACK IN CHURCH

Take in the picture and encourage the priest to admire it and go through it with the children. He/she might notice Jesus' crown, His hand raised in blessing, the Alpha and Omega on each side of Him.

(CD64.1)

Script 65   Saint Spotting

Any Saint's Day

Revelation 7.9–12

THEME

This is an extra session, in case you find your church is celebrating a major saint and has, for once, ditched the Gospel of the Day.

As you'll see, the script accommodates any saint and – if your one isn't mentioned – just look him or her up and put them in. Wikipedia has a good section on saints under 'saint symbolism'. What you want to know is the attribute of the saint, the thing he/she holds in pictures. (St Peter, for example, always holds keys.) This session is about recognizing saints by their attributes (their props), most of which you'll find you can replicate. (Though you'll have trouble with St Agatha, her attribute is two breasts on a plate.)

However we're not just into Spot a Saint, we want the children to realize that there are millions of unknown saints and that they themselves are saints in training.

SET UP

- Pictures from the CD-Rom.
- There is a list of saints and their attributes at the end of the script, choose the ones you can do (adding to their number as you see fit).
- Stick the attributes in a large container, like a wastepaper basket.
- Create an 'L-plate', put it on some string so a child could wear it round its neck.

WELCOME *the children and lead them in* **The Sign of the Cross** ✠ (**p. xxxvi**).

Today is St *Name's* day, so we are going to think about all the saints in Heaven as we pray.

OPENING PRAYER	God our Father, Today we thank you for the holy men and women who are your saints.

May they pray for us as we try to follow their example,
We ask this through Jesus Our Lord. **Amen**
When the saints lived on earth they were just like us.
They behaved badly, just like us, and they asked God to forgive them.
Let's follow their example,

THE KYRIE	Lord Jesus, we are sorry for the things we have done wrong, Lord have mercy **Lord have mercy**

Lord Jesus, we are sorry for forgetting to listen to you,
Christ have mercy
Christ have mercy

Lord Jesus, thank you for your promise to love and forgive us,
Lord have mercy
Lord have mercy

Ask the children to repeat **The Prayer for Forgiveness** *after you* (**p. xxxvi**).

SAINTS AND THEIR PROPS

Prop Show

Pull out the prop basket, it should be bristling with interesting things like large rulers and plastic axes
Talk through how many saints there are, and how difficult it is to remember their names

Leader	It is even more difficult if you want to make pictures of them. How do you know if a painting is of St Peter? You could put his name underneath of course, but the painting would look like a cartoon. So painters have come up with a cunning wheeze – they give the saint a 'prop'. Something to do with the sort of person they were. So when you see the prop you know the Saint. Can anybody remember what St Peter's prop is? (**Keys**)

If the children can't remember, just put up the picture

CD65.1	What's Peter holding? (**Keys!**) Yes, Jesus gave him the Keys of Heaven.

CD65.2   OK, let's think of another saint. St Agnes.
                  'Agnes' means lamb – what do you think her prop is? (**Lamb**)

Put up the picture

                  Quite right.
                  Now, we've got a basket of props here, all belonging to various
                  saints.
                  Let's get the saint attached to his or her prop . . .

Start pulling out props, get kids down the front to hold them

                  Ah, this scythe is for St Isidore – *swish it* – he is the patron saint of
                  farm workers . . .

Put Isidore's name up on the whiteboard

                  This chalice is for St John.
                  Have we got a John or a Joanna here?
                  Great hold that – ugh, what's inside? *(A plastic snake)*
                  John always holds a chalice with a snake in it because somebody
                  once tried to poison him.

Write John's name up

                  And this Ruler *(or set-square)* is for St Thomas.
                  He holds that because he's supposed to have been an architect.

And so on, there is a list of saints and props at the end of this script.
At the end you should have an impressive line up of saints

Game

Put all the props back and invite the kids up to take a prop – they can only have it if
they can remember the saint to whom it belongs. (Give some outrageous hints.)

FINISH

Leader   How many Saints do you think there are?
                  Nobody knows, not even the Bible. There are *millions* of saints –
                  and there'll be even more when we get to Heaven.
                  Let's hear about them in the Bible:

BIBLE READING *Revelation 7.9–12*

AFTER THE READING

Leader   There's lots of odd things in that bit of the Bible – but you get the
                picture, there are loads of saints, round the throne of God.
                But if we were there we'd know who they were immediately.
                If we saw a saint with eyeballs, for example, we'd know it was?
                (**St Lucy** – *they always remember her*)
                Now here's a saint you probably haven't heard of.

Call a victim to the front

                This is Saint *Name*.
                Do you think this kid's a saint? (**No!**)
                Well, what does saint mean? (**Holy**)
                And what are Christians called?

(A rhetorical question)

                'The Holy People of God'.
                Well if Christians are holy, young *Name* here must be holy, and so
                has got to be a saint. What attribute do you think St *Name* should
                have?
                I know what I think . . . *(give them the L-plate)*
                A learner saint
                And so are we.

FINAL   Learners need lots of help so let's ask the saints to pray for us –
PRAYER

*Get a line of kids down the front, holding the saint props, and construct the litany
round their names*

Litany   **Holy Peter**
                Pray for us
                Holy Helena
                Pray for us

And so on. Finish with

                God our Father,
                We thank you for the saints
                May their prayers help us,
                And may we join them one day,
                to live with you for ever in Heaven.
                Amen

MUSIC

There's a fine crop of modern and traditional hymns for this day. 'For all the saints' *is the classic, but* 'Be thou my vision' *and* 'He who would valiant be' *are stirring calls to service. If you have focused on the children's capacity for sainthood,* 'I the Lord of sea and sky' *fits in well.*

BACK IN CHURCH

Line up the kids and props – as you point to them, each child calls out the name of his or her saint and attribute

'I'm St Isidore, and I've got a scythe.'

Even so you might have to go along the line and gently extract the information
End with the learner saint

Saints and their attributes

St Peter	Keys (of Heaven and Purgatory)
St John	Chalice (borrow a spare) with rubber snake: John was offered a poisoned chalice once, and survived
St Isidore	Plastic scythe (he is the patron saint of farm workers)
St Joseph	Toy hammer or saw
St Olaf	Toy axe (Olaf used an axe as a unique method of converting the heathen)
St Paul	Toy sword
St Gabriel	A lily (actually the lily belongs to our Lady, he must have plucked it in one crucial picture and has been stuck with it ever since)
St Lawrence	Gridiron, grill, grill tray from oven (he was grilled)
St Roche	Toy dog (who used to beg for him – St Roche had plague and couldn't approach people, so his dog got bread for him instead)
St James	A cockle shell: the badge of the pilgrims who go to St James's shrine in Spain
St Andrew	A (chocolate) fish: he was a fisherman
Sts Cosmas & Damian	Toy stethoscope: they were brothers and doctors
St Stephen	Stones (get some from the Lent desert): he was stoned to death
St Thomas	Long ruler or set-square, he was an architect
St Leonard	Chains, he is the patron of prisoners
St George	Toy dragon or an England flag, he's the patron saint of England

St Patrick	Shamrock or clover leaf – a large cardboard version – or a plastic snake (he ejected all the snakes from Ireland)
St David	A dove, rather a difficult prop to find, you might have to make do with a leek. Annoyingly neither prop has a satisfying explanation. He is however the patron saint of Wales
St Lucy	Eyeballs, you can actually find these among the children's section in various tourist shops, or joke shops. Making a couple out of a pair of ping pong balls is just as good. St Lucy was blinded
St Agnes	A woolly lamb (a pun on her name)
Our Lady	Baby Jesus, borrow the Infant Jesus from the Crib set
St Mary Magdalene	A jar of oil: make it see-through so the kids can see the oil; it's the oil she brought to the Tomb
St Clare	A lamp – another pun, she shines as clear (Clara) as light
St Helen	Either a wooden cross, or some nails: she found the True Cross
St Mary of Egypt	Plastic Skull: she meditated on skulls and things as a hermit in the desert
St Catherine	A wheel – they tried to kill her on a wheel, it didn't work, the wheel went out of control and killed 50 heathen philosophers. I suppose a Catherine wheel firework would just pass muster

You don't have to do all these saints, pace the session and do as many as keeps it zingy. Balance out the male and female saints – but don't be gender specific with the kids. If a boy wants to hold a lamb, fine.